LISTENING FOR DEMOCRACY

D1477358

OTHER BOOKS BY ANDREW DOBSON

An Introduction to the Politics and Philosophy of José Ortega y Gasset

Jean-Paul Sartre and the Politics of Reason: A Theory of History

Justice and the Environment: Conceptions of Environmental Sustainability and Dimensions of Social Justice

Citizenship and the Environment

Green Political Thought (4th edition)

The Green Reader (edited)

The Politics of Nature: Exploration in Green Political Theory (edited with Paul Lucardie)

Fairness and Futurity: Essays on Environmental Sustainability and Social Justice (edited)

Environmental Citizenship (edited with Derek Bell)

Citizenship, Environment, Economy (edited with Angel Valencia)

Political Theory and the Ecological Challenge (edited with Robyn Eckersley)

The Politics of Protection: Sites of Insecurity and Political Agency (edited with Jef Huysmans and Raia Prokhovnik)

Biosecurity: The Socio-Politics of Invasive Species and Infectious Diseases (edited with Kezia Barker and Sarah Taylor)

Listening for Democracy

Recognition, Representation, Reconciliation

ANDREW DOBSON

OXFORD
UNIVERSITY PRESS

OXFORD

UNIVERSITY PRESS

Great Clarendon Street, Oxford, OX2 6DP,
United Kingdom

Oxford University Press is a department of the University of Oxford.
It furthers the University's objective of excellence in research, scholarship,
and education by publishing worldwide. Oxford is a registered trade mark of
Oxford University Press in the UK and in certain other countries

First Edition published in 2014

Impression: 1

Published in the United States of America by Oxford University Press
198 Madison Avenue, New York, NY 10016, United States of America

British Library Cataloguing in Publication Data
Data available

Library of Congress Control Number: 2013950747

ISBN 978-0-19-968244-7 (Hbk.)
ISBN 978-0-19-968245-4 (Pbk.)

Printed and bound in Great Britain by
CPI Group (UK) Ltd, Croydon, CR0 4YY

Acknowledgements

I am indebted to colleagues and friends who have invited me to give papers on themes in this book and responded generously to queries and requests for help while I was writing it. In particular I would like to thank Daniel Andersen, Jo Berry, Ingolfur Blühdorn, Gideon Calder, Stephen Coleman, Nick Couldry, Carolyn Cusick, Brian Doherty, John Dryzek, Yogi Hendlin, John Horton, Mat Humphrey, Kasia Klein, Richard Luther, Karen Mitchell, Monica Mookherjee, Concha Pérez Moreno, John Durham Peters, Hans-Jürgen Puhle, Angel Rivero, Lucy Sargisson, and Mike Saward.

I would also like to thank participants in seminars I gave on listening and democracy at the universities of Keele, Leeds, Nottingham, and Salford between 2010 and 2013, and at the European Consortium for Political Research Joint Sessions in Reykjavík in 2011. Dominic Byatt at Oxford University Press has, as ever, been very supportive in getting the book to this point, not least in conjuring up three anonymous readers at the proposal stage, each of whom provided me with food for thought which I have spent the last two years trying to digest. I hope I have, in some measure, repaid both Dominic for his faith in the project and the readers for their thoughtful reflections on my early plans for the book.

I could not have completed this project without the generosity of the Leverhulme Trustees who awarded me a research fellowship from 2011 to 2013 (grant number RF-2011-572). In these days of large grant consortia it is a great pleasure to record my thanks for this lone scholar support. I am grateful to staff at Keele University who have managed the grant and its consequences, and, of course, to my colleagues in Keele's School of Politics, International Relations and Philosophy who have supported my work in myriad ways—often without realizing it.

Finally I thank the *Political Studies* journal for permission to use material from 'Democracy and nature: speaking and listening', *Political Studies* 58 (2010), no. 4, pp. 752–68, and 'Listening: the new democratic deficit', *Political Studies* 60 (2012), no. 4, pp. 843–59, and to Routledge for permission to use material from 'Do we need (to protect) nature', in Jef Huysmans, Andrew Dobson, and Raia Prokhovnik (eds), *The Politics of Protection: Sites of Insecurity and Political Agency* (London: Routledge, 2006).

Andrew Dobson
Keele University, UK
May 2013

Contents

Introduction

On 22 May 2013 a member of the UK armed forces, Private Lee Rigby, was killed by two attackers on the streets of south London. The assault was carried out in broad daylight in full view of the passing public, and the now ubiquitous camera phone ensured that the aftermath of the attack was captured by passers-by and made available for all to see. One citizen journalist recorded the extraordinary scene of a witness, Ingrid Loyau-Kennett, apparently engaging one of the assailants in conversation as he held a bloodied meat cleaver in his hand. When asked later why she did this, she replied: 'Instinctively, and through my scout training, I like to keep calm and respectful. So I thought, OK, let's listen to what he has to say. I tried to engage him in a conversation.'[1] No one knows exactly what would have happened if Loyau-Kennett hadn't got off her bus to attend to Rigby, only to find him dead and, instead of tending him, listen to his alleged killer; but she was widely credited with having calmed the situation down and avoided potential further bloodshed.

Rigby's killing set off a wave of anti-Muslim actions around the UK, at the head of many of which was the English Defence League (EDL), a far-right protest movement. One of these actions was a protest outside a mosque in the city of York in late May 2013. Once they learnt of the imminent protest, members of the mosque sat down to work out what to do. They decided that confrontation was inappropriate and determined, instead, to provide a calm space in which they could listen to, and hear, one another.[2] The result? 'When we listened, we realised the EDL may have thought that we supported extremist behaviour and the Taliban. We

---

[1] Leo Hickman, 'Woolwich attack witness Ingrid Loyau-Kennett: "I feel like a fraud"', *The Guardian*, 27 May 2013, available at <http://www.guardian.co.uk/uk/2013/may/27/woolwich-witness-ingrid-loyau-kennett> (accessed 29 June 2013).

[2] Mohamed El-Gomati, 'Invite the EDL to tea', *The Guardian*, 1 June 2013, p. 42.

pointed out that we condemned both in the strongest terms. Assumptions
are dangerous, untested assumptions can be lethal. They were surprised,
and they understood. The day ended in a game of football.[3]

These vignettes illustrate the power of listening—a power we have
not, and do not, make enough of. Although much prized in daily conversation, good listening has been almost completely ignored in political conversation, and particularly the form we know as democracy.
Speaking has garnered the lion's share of attention, both in terms of
the skills to be developed and the ways in which we should understand
what improving it might entail (for instance, getting more people to
speak). In this book I aim to examine the reasons why so little attention has been paid to the listening aspect of democratic conversation,
to explore the role that listening might play in democracy, and to outline some institutional changes that could be made to make listening
more central to democratic processes.

Two obvious objections to this prospectus need to be discussed at
the outset. First, while listening might properly be regarded as a virtue in the private sphere of daily conversation, we should not automatically assume that it is a public virtue too. There are indeed some
theorists of democracy—but not many—who relate everyday conversational practices to the manners and methods of democracy. Anthony
Giddens, for example, writes that, '[T]here are remarkable parallels
between what a good relationship looks like, as developed in the literature of marital and sexual therapy, and formal mechanisms of political democracy.'[4] With this, Giddens erases the distinction between the
public and the private by arguing that there is a 'good practice' common to them both—the practice of dialogue. Similarly, Robert Goodin
brings the everyday and the political into contact when he says that,
'[D]eliberative democrats redouble the demands of sheer good conversational manners...Listening attentively to one another is part
and parcel of what it is to deliberate together. Discursive engagement
requires interlocutors to pay attention to what one another is saying
and to adjust their own positions and their own remarks accordingly.'[5]
Michael Oakeshott is another who avers that when we come together

[3] El-Gomati (2013).
[4] Antony Giddens, *Beyond Left and Right: The Future of Radical Politics*
(Cambridge: Polity Press, 1994), pp. 118–19.
[5] Robert Goodin, *Innovating Democracy: Democratic Theory and Practice after the
Deliberative Turn* (Oxford: Oxford University Press, 2008), p. 110.

to discuss big issues, 'the image of this meeting place is not an inquiry or an argument, but a conversation'.[6]

Machiavelli, however, reminds us that effective politicians should treat private virtues with great care in the public sphere. Private virtues are all very well, he says, but 'human nature being what it is, princes cannot possess those qualities, or rather they cannot always exhibit them'.[7] Of course, Machiavelli is hedging his bets here. He is not saying that rulers should *never* display private virtues, but only that they should consider their deployment in the context of what they are trying to achieve. If the private virtue will assist a prince in achieving his objectives then he should exhibit it, but, if not, then the objectives take precedence.

One response to Machiavelli is to analyse the public activity in question and ask if it in some way 'demands', by definition, the cultivation and deployment of relevant virtues. On the face of it, democracy might be just this kind of public, political activity. It is hard to think of a definition of democracy that does not, at some level, entail responsive communication. According to one widely held account, democracy is founded on the autonomy of individuals, and in the political context this involves obeying laws one has made oneself (paraphrasing Rousseau[8]). In anything other than a direct democracy we do not make the laws ourselves, and this, of course, was why Rousseau felt that anything less than a direct democracy was an abdication of freedom.[9] Once we are driven in the direction of having someone else represent our will rather than ourselves, the mechanics of responsiveness become extremely important. There is no guarantee that my will will be represented by my representative, but for there to be any chance of this happening, my representative needs to know what my will is. This implies listening, in its broadest sense. Thus democracy—at least of the representative sort, which is the sort that dominates political horizons today[10]—seems definitionally bound up with communication

---

[6] Michael Oakeshott, 'The voice of poetry in the conversation of mankind', in *Rationalism in Politics and Other Essays* (London: Methuen, 1962), p. 198. See also Luke Philip Plotica, 'Deliberation or conversation: Michael Oakeshott on the ethos and conduct of democracy', *Polity* 44 (2012), no. 2, pp. 286–307.

[7] Niccolò Machiavelli, *The Prince* (Harmondsworth: Penguin, 1961), pp. 91–2.

[8] Jean-Jacques Rousseau, *The Social Contract* (Harmondsworth: Penguin, 1968), p. 65.

[9] Rousseau (1968), p. 141.

[10] Another candidate is deliberative democracy, and we will see in Chapter 4 how important listening is in this context too.

in general, and with listening in particular. It is vital, yet relatively unusual, to emphasize that listening is a key part of what it is to communicate. The novelist Sara Maitland is surely right to say that communication for most of us, most of the time, 'means talk'.[11] In sum, viewing democracy as responsive rule effectively erases the distinction between a private and a public virtue in that listening becomes a practice that is integral to the thing we call democracy.

The second objection is that we should not see democracy as a form of conversation in the first place. This objection is most likely to come from the 'agonistic' school of democratic theory,[12] adherents of which believe that so-called conversational approaches to democracy underestimate both the conflictual nature of politics and the difficulties associated with arriving at a rational consensus. But this is to confuse the usual quarry of agonists—deliberative democracy—with the listening approach to democracy that I am discussing here. While it might be true that deliberative democrats underestimate conflict and overestimate the possibility of arriving at consensus (and many deliberative democrats would nowadays dispute this anyway[13]), the listening approach to democracy does neither. The aim is not to wish away conflict but—as we shall see in Chapter 4 in particular—to make it more apparent. A very successful way of damping down conflict, indeed, is by refusing dialogue—which implies refusing to listen—and endorsing monologue. Oscar Wilde catches this perfectly in an exchange between the Frog and the Rocket in his short story 'The remarkable rocket':

> 'Well, goodbye [says the Frog], I have enjoyed our conversation very much, I assure you.'
> 'Conversation indeed!' said the Rocket. 'You have talked all the time yourself, and that is not conversation.'
> 'Somebody must listen,' answered the Frog, 'and I like to do all the talking myself. It saves time and prevents arguments.'[14]

---

[11] Sara Maitland, *A Book of Silence* (London: Granta, 2008), p. 3.

[12] For example, Chantal Mouffe, 'Deliberative democracy or agonistic pluralism', *Political Science Series* 72 (2000), 1–17 available at <http://www.ihs.ac.at/publications/pol/pw_72.pdf> (accessed 31 January 2013).

[13] See, for instance, John Dryzek, *Foundations and Frontiers of Deliberative Governance* (Oxford: Oxford University Press, 2010), pp. 92–3 and 111–13. For an alternative characterization see Plotica (2012), pp. 288–9.

[14] Oscar Wilde, 'The remarkable rocket', in *The Happy Prince and Other Tales* (1888), available at <http://www.online-literature.com/poe/179/> (accessed 17 March 2013).

The Frog is interested only in outcomes—preferably the ones he wants—and he knows that the chances of getting his own way are improved if he pays no attention to what other people are saying. Similarly, the 'consensus rule' of deliberative democracy suggests a consequence- or outcome-driven theory (though, of course, in principle via a more dialogical process than the monological one Frog would wish for). So, in the eyes of agonists, the point of deliberative democracy is to reach a consensus. The listening approach is much more procedural than consequentialist, though, and it neither implies nor argues for any particular decision rule. So the agonist's objection to seeing democracy as a form of conversation is rooted in a particular understanding of conversation: the kind we have with our neighbour over the garden fence. Democratic conversation is—or should be—much more rigorously *dialogic*—a relationship in which listening and speaking are accorded equal weight and in which the effort put into each is carefully organized and regulated. We shall have more to say about dialogic democracy in Chapter 4, and about its instantiation and institutionalization in Chapter 6.

The plan of the book is as follows. In Chapter 1 I explore listening in the context of contemporary theorizing about democracy. I make no claim to comprehensiveness as far as surveying the state of democratic theory is concerned, but I do draw attention to a number of emergent features of contemporary theory that are worthy of note and to which this book closely relates. The first is what we might call 'sensory democracy'. In brief, this refers to what is usually regarded as the 'passive' side of conversation, the *receptive* side. We use our senses—principally our eyes and ears—to receive messages from other people and from the outside world in general. It is a curiosity of democratic theory and practice that, although we might regard democracy as a conversation, as we observed earlier in this Introduction, virtually no attention has been paid to the role that seeing and hearing plays in it. This is being rectified to some degree now, however, and the visual sense in particular is being explored systematically.[15] We might regard the choice of the visual sense as the first port of call as curious, given that the currency of political discourse is usually regarded as speech, whose corresponding receptive capacity is hearing rather than seeing.

---

[15] See, for example, Jeffrey Edward Green, *The Eyes of the People: Democracy in an Age of Spectatorship* (Oxford and New York: Oxford University Press, 2010), which I discuss in some detail in Chapter 1.

Nevertheless, the work done on seeing has opened up interesting lines of enquiry, and I use some of them to structure Chapter 1. There are key questions around power and empowerment, for example. As I suggested earlier in this Introduction, we tend to regard the senses as passive, and this is certainly the line taken by the small but growing number of analysts of the visual sense in relation to democracy. I believe, though, that the sensory approach to politics and democracy can entail empowerment, and I explore the dynamics of this in some detail.

A second theme relates to types of democracy and the question of whether attention to the senses drives us in the direction of any particular conception of democracy. We are used to the idea that practical exigencies make some forms of democracy more likely than others—that issues of scale are said to make representative democracy more viable than direct democracy, for example. In the sensory context Jeffrey Green believes that his theory of spectatorship takes him towards plebiscitary theories of democracy, and I make a parallel case that putting listening at or near the heart of the democratic process leads us in the direction of dialogic democracy.

A third theme in emerging sensory theories of democracy is its non-ideal nature. This is to say that such theories are inductive rather than deductive, aiming less to make democratic practice fit some ideal theory and more to take 'things as they are' and adapt theory to the facts on the ground. I take a similar line here, but I resist the normative defensiveness that seems to accompany much non-ideal inductive thinking around democracy. Far from arguing that we must make the best of a bad job in the belief that the conditions under which politics is practised in late modern societies are compatible with only attenuated forms of democracy, I suggest that proper attention to listening can breathe life into the democratic project and help us to realize some of its objectives.

Finally, in Chapter 1, I discuss the question of why listening has been so consistently ignored as a topic worthy of analysis by political theorists in general and democratic theorists in particular. I offer an answer that takes us back near the dawn of political theory, to the moment at which Aristotle defined the political animal as an animal with the capacity for reasoned speech. This has coloured our understanding of the fundamental currency of politics ever since, and has led to a preponderance of attention being paid to speech and very little to its sensory counterpart(s). I illustrate the powerful hold that speech has on the political imaginary by discussing a theorist who has self-consciously set out to question the presuppositions of political discourse—Jacques Rancière. Yet even Rancière, I show, fails to question the most basic presupposition of all: that the political animal is an animal with the capacity for reasoned speech. This has consequences for listening as a political–theoretical category, and for discussions regarding what we might properly regard as a legitimate political 'noise'. I return to this discussion in Chapter 5.

It quickly becomes clear to anyone working on listening and politics that resources on the topic in the political science and political theory literature are very few and far between. So we have to look elsewhere. There are a number of professions and practices in which listening plays a key role, and in Chapter 2 I draw on some of them to discuss a range of issues that bear on the nature and role of listening in the political context. I consider the different types of listening that are found in the multidisciplinary literature I consult: compassionate, monological, dialogical, interruptive, inattentive, cataphatic, apophatic. This discussion is carried out in the context of a question that threads its way through the chapter: is there such a thing as 'good' listening? It is tempting to think there is—or should be—such a thing, because if we could identify good listening practices we could then implement them in the political process. In Chapter 2 I argue that there is indeed something of a convergence on what good listening consists of, in the person-to-person context at least, and that this goes by the name of *apophatic* listening. The challenge then is to translate the characteristics of this type of listening into the political context—a challenge I take up in the rest of the book. On the other hand, different professions view 'good listening' in different ways, and this raises the questions of (a) whether there is such a thing as political listening (as opposed, for example, to the listening of the therapist or the classroom teacher), and (b) whether *good* political listening is different to good listening in other contexts and professions.

Another route to undermining the claim that good listening can be univocally described is through the recognition that good listening practices may vary with the culture. Thus, what might count as 'paying attention' in one cultural and linguistic context can look very different in another. This introduces another key theme in Chapter 2, which is the relationship between listening and power. It emerges that defining good listening is itself an exercise of cultural power, in that definitions tend to converge on a space of mid-point expectations and behaviours found in dominant majority cultures. More generally, listening and the withholding of listening are exercises of power in themselves. This power can be expressed through the refusal to listen to particular others, or the refusal to listen to whole identities. This latter is especially important, as can be seen from the history of feminism and other expressions of identity politics. Power can also be expressed, of course, through a positive commitment to listen to others and/or to recognize the speech of hitherto silenced identities. If and when this happens, a third face of power and listening emerges: the way in which listening can be a 'solvent' of power. This effect is found, for example, in committees of truth and reconciliation, when the previously powerful are forced to listen to the previously powerless. There is evidence to suggest that this turning of the tables is experienced as power by those who have been systematically marginalized and excluded.

This discussion of the way in which listening and power are bound together is followed by some reflections on the importance of silence. Silence promotes listening, and it can provide the space within which previously unheard voices are recognized. Can silence be institutionalized? Correspondingly, can listening be learnt like a skill, or is it more like a virtue or even a disposition? With half an eye on the final chapter—Chapter 6—Chapter 2 concludes with some thoughts on whether the instantiation of listening in politics is a matter of changing individuals or structures—or both.

Chapter 3 is devoted to the question of how the chances of democracy achieving some of its core objectives can be enhanced by paying greater attention to listening. In this context I explore legitimacy, trust, disagreement, understanding, and deliberation. All types of government require legitimacy, and each type grounds its legitimacy in a different claim. The more this claim is realized in practice—or, at least, the more the claim looks plausible to those who need to be persuaded by it—the more legitimate the government will be or seem to be. The key legitimacy claim for a democracy is that it be responsive to the views or demands of the people. For a decision in a democracy to be legitimate it must be possible to trace its origin back to 'the people'. In the normal democratic scheme of things this is done by claiming a mandate for action which derives from the fact of having been elected. Success in an election can be regarded as evidence of having 'responded' to the electorate's wishes, and evidence of ongoing responsiveness is vital to legitimacy claims. The role of listening in this legitimacy dynamic is clear. Any claim to have responded to the people's wishes is easily vitiated by evidence that the people have not been listened to. Nor is this just a theoretical point. I offer evidence in Chapter 3 that strongly suggests that governments reach for the listening card precisely when they realize that their legitimacy is at a low ebb. Far from regarding listening as an add-on as far as legitimacy is concerned, governments in democracies seem instinctively to know that it is absolutely central, and this is why they go to such great lengths to establish a listening connection with the electorate when things are going badly.

There are two kinds of risk involved in playing the listening card, however. First, the electorate might regard this last-ditch grab for legitimacy as a cynical ploy—and they are likely to be confirmed in this belief if whatever listening exercise carried out looks like a sham. This raises the question of what a 'good' listening exercise in the political context looks like, and here I introduce the distinction between *process* and *outcome*. Given that the exercise is likely to be carried out when the government is proposing a course of action that has come to seem unpopular, there will be a temptation to regard only a change of policy as evidence of good listening. If policy remains the same, despite both evident popular opposition, and a deliberate and obvious effort by the government to listen, then, on the 'outcome interpretation' of good listening, the exercise will be regarded as a failure. But Chapter 2 will tell us that good listening in the person-to-person context has various procedural elements, such as confirmatory questioning, eye contact, appropriate gestures, and so on. Regardless of how these elements might be reproduced in the political context, there is evidence here for a 'procedural interpretation' of good listening. If this interpretation is adopted then the key parameters against which to judge the seriousness of a listening exercise are its length, breadth, and depth. I will expand on this in Chapter 6.

The degree to which governments run the second risk of listening extra hard depends on what they do once the exercise is complete. If the government changes its mind on any given policy then it can expect to be accused by the Opposition of that ultimate political crime: the U-turn. While changing one's mind on the basis of careful consideration of the evidence might be regarded as a strength in the person-to-person context, it is generally taken to be a sign of weakness for governments. Of course, on the basis of the legitimacy points we made earlier in the Introduction, the government in question will claim that it is a strength not a weakness, but given the currently tenuous hold that listening has on the political imaginary this argument is unlikely to cut much ice—especially in adversarial political contexts such as the USA and the UK. One consequence of taking listening more seriously in democracies would be to draw some of the sting from the U-turn criticism and possibly make governments less reluctant to listen in the first place.

This could set in train a virtuous chain of events, leading to an improvement in relations of trust between governments and citizens— and this is the second theme discussed in Chapter 3. Commentators as varied as Richard Sennett, Charles Tilly, and Pierre Rosanvallon have all noted the rise in distrust in contemporary 'advanced' democracies, and, for Rosanvallon at least, this is an endemic feature of political life. He says the best we can do, mirroring the downbeat argument of Jeffrey Green explored and criticized in Chapter 1, is to *manage* distrust. I offer a more hopeful message, arguing that, just as trust is generated between individuals through experiencing the other as a listener who responds to what is being said, so governments can increase levels of trust through meaningful listening. The greater the levels of distrust, the longer, deeper, and broader the listening campaign will have to be—and, of course, the 'campaign' should be merely a step on the way to inserting listening permanently into the DNA of modern democracies. One other key point here is that one-way, monological listening is as unlikely to be an effective generator of trust between government and citizens as it is between individual people. There may even be a case in the political context for a period of 'affirmative action' in which the government listens to citizens exclusively without there being any reciprocal expectation that citizens listen to government. This is because listening, as a solvent of power, works best when the powerful are obliged to listen—without interruption—to the voices of the powerless. Power lies in being listened to. A more mature stage of the process would be represented by *dialogical* listening, in which citizens would listen—as far as possible without cynicism or prejudice—to politicians as well as vice versa.

Disagreement is a fundamental feature of political life, and deep disagreements can be a source of tension and even violence. As such, disagreement can undermine the stability of democracies, and ways to manage it need to be explored. Part of the argument of Chapter 3 is that listening is an underexplored route to managing disagreement. The point is not to claim that listening can do away with disagreement— this is as unlikely as it is undesirable. A dialogical approach to dealing with disagreement aims at understanding rather than consensus, and listening is an integral feature of such an approach. Some evidence is offered showing how careful listening can improve understanding across social differences, and truth and reconciliation committees are presented as ideal type 'events' in which carefully organized and orchestrated listening can lead to understanding in even the most difficult of circumstances. These committees also show that it is possible to go beyond understanding to shifts in power relations. One concern with a listening approach to dealing with disagreement is that the structures that lead to disagreement are left unaffected once some level of understanding and accommodation between the parties has been reached. Yet there are examples where organized listening and deep shifts in power relations are experienced simultaneously. The South African experience of truth and reconciliation, for instance, suggests that orchestrated listening in contexts of deep disagreement can unsettle and disrupt power.

The penultimate theme of Chapter 3 is understanding itself, not so much in the context of managing disagreement but in the more mundane context of representative democracy and the effective representation of people's interests. In this brief section I introduce the notion of silence as a precondition for effective listening. We tend to think of a flourishing public sphere as a noisy place, but a dialogic approach to politics suggests that silence is vital, both as a space within which the other has an opportunity to speak, and as a precondition for reflection on what the other has said, as a prelude to understanding. We should be wary, however, because silence in the political context is hard to interpret. It might be a sign of acquiescence, of resignation, and of defiance, as well as a sign of a willingness to engage with the other in a dynamic and dialogic process of understanding. Much will depend on how silence is deployed and institutionalized. Ultimately, political silence should be a preparation for communication, not a refusal of it.

The final theme of Chapter 3 is deliberation. I deal with deliberative democracy in detail in Chapter 4 and I argue there that listening should feature much more explicitly and systematically in its theoretical architecture. In Chapter 3 my intention is to focus on how people actually deliberate and to show that we should be paying more independent attention to the listening aspect of real-life deliberation. It is curious how little research has been conducted by political theorists on the pragmatics (as opposed to the theoretical analytics) of deliberation, and in the 'Improving deliberation' section of Chapter 3 I offer a detailed commentary on just one deliberative event with a view to exposing the importance that listening played in it. This analysis is intended to be suggestive rather than representative—other analyses of different events might produce different conclusions.

In sum, Chapter 3 deals with the question of how listening is central to some of the key objectives of democracy, and how these objectives would stand a better chance of being realized if systematic attention were paid to listening's potential. In Chapter 4 I turn my attention to the specific form of democracy with which I concluded Chapter 3—deliberative democracy—and show how listening could and should play a crucial role here too. Of all the forms of democracy available to us in theory and practice, one might have thought that deliberative democracy would have paid the greatest attention to listening. The clue is in the name: *deliberative* democracy. How can one deliberate an issue if one is not carefully listening to all the points of view made in respect of it? It will be said—and indeed it is said—that, far from being ignored in deliberative democracy, listening is implicit in it. This defence, however, is no more sound in the deliberative context than it is in other forms of democracy. To say that listening is implicit in deliberation is to imply that no independent attention needs to be paid to it, but, by this point in the book, I hope that enough will have been said to show how much there is to be gained for democracy by taking listening seriously.

If anything, this point is stronger in the deliberative context than in any other, and there are two reasons for this, both of which are discussed in detail in Chapter 4. First, as we have just seen, deliberative democracy's great strength and attraction lies in its focus on deliberation rather than on the simple aggregation of preferences. Deliberative democrats are guided in their decision-making by 'the force of the better argument', and so it seems obvious that deliberative procedures absolutely require careful listening on the part of the participants. How can we know what 'the better argument' is if we haven't listened to all the other ones? So much seems evident. Less immediately obvious, perhaps, is how listening can and should play a vital role in deliberative democracy's other central objective: inclusion. This objective is related to the first one, at least in so far as we can only determine which is the better argument if all the relevant arguments have been presented to us. The deliberative democratic process therefore needs a means of ensuring that, as far as possible, all points of view have been taken into account—and this implies listening out for voices that may not have been heard before. Inclusion for deliberative democrats is, of course, more complicated than that, and I deal with some of the complexities in Chapter 4, but this gloss is enough to show how deliberative democrats' hearing needs to be especially acute. They need to *listen to* their interlocutors very carefully, and they need to *listen out for* arguments, positions, and even identities that may not have been heard before.

One way of conceiving the role of listening in deliberative democracy is as a *producer of difference*. I arrive at this conclusion in Chapter 4 through an analysis of what Anthony Giddens calls 'dialogic democracy'. Dialogic democracy is not as developed either theoretically or practically as its deliberative cousin, but there are disparate and rather inchoate signs of its steady, if uneven, incursion onto the democratic stage. A common theme in this emergent theory of democracy is its determination to resist settled accounts of issues, and to undergird this resistance with a systematic intention to look for difference even where it might not be immediately apparent. Listening is crucial to this intention, since listening hard (listening *out for*) is the mechanism by which difference becomes apparent and is produced. I illustrate this through a detailed commentary of Iris Marion Young's work on inclusion and democracy (for her, inclusion is an absolutely central element of deliberative democracy), in which I aim to show that her mechanism for inclusion—validating alternative forms of speech— absolutely requires careful listening. There are two reasons for this. First, such listening 'produces' the alternative forms of speech (if we weren't listening expansively we wouldn't notice them), and, second, once they are acknowledged, their strangeness means that we will have to listen hard to understand or capture them. None of this should be taken as an argument for replacing deliberative with dialogical democracy. I offer the latter as a corrective to the former—but in the guise of permanent fixture rather than temporary assistant.

In Chapter 5 I take a big step back from the territory thus far surveyed and ask who or what we should be listening to in the first place. Thus far, the answers to these questions have been taken to be obvious: we listen to people with the capacity for reasoned speech, and/ or their representatives. The 'who' is therefore people, and the 'what' is reasoned speech. There is an obvious circularity at work here, in that once one has answered the 'who' question in a particular way, the answer to the 'what' question follows as a matter of logical course. In Chapter 5 I aim to unsettle this circularity by asking what constitutes a 'political noise', and by considering the claims that the non-human realm might have to political considerability (remember that this realm is explicitly left out in the cold in Aristotle's iconic statement of the characteristics required to be considered a political animal). In answering this question I make use of the key notion of 'recognition'. Drawing on work by Nancy Fraser I distinguish between affirmative and transformative recognition, with the former reallocating recognition on the basis of already existing categories and identities, while the latter restructures the categories and identities themselves.

The affirmative strategy has been used successfully to get people admitted to the realm of 'political beingness' simply by arguing that they have the capacity for reasoned speech. This was precisely how Mary Wollstonecraft argued on behalf of women in *A Vindication of the Rights of Woman*. Can the affirmative strategy work for non-human nature though, where claims regarding the capacity for reasoned speech are much harder to sustain? Given this difficulty, I consider the potential of the transformative approach through an examination of the work of Bruno Latour and Jane Bennett, both of whom have provocative things to say about political beingness. I conclude that, while Latour and Bennett might seem, at first glance, to be adopting a transformative strategy, they leave just enough of the mainstream architecture of categories and identities in place to warrant a new description, which I call 'strong affirmation'. This strong affirmative approach asks what humans have in common with non-human nature, rather than the other way round, and this is then the basis for political considerability. For Latour this is a capacity to 'surprise', while for Bennett it is 'vital materiality' or 'thing-power'. Bennett draws on the work of John Dewey to argue that what makes these communities of possessors of thing-power *political* communities is their capacity to constitute a *problem* around which publics coalesce. Her focus is on the event rather than (in the first instance at least) on the characteristics of those who/which gather around it. On this reading, what makes an event political is not that it involves speaking humans but that a public has coalesced around it. At this point we are evidently in the realms of 'more than listening'. Dewey himself talks of receptivity of 'the signs and symbols without which shared experience is impossible',[16] and this receptivity is—or should be—attuned to detection of 'problems'. 'Do glaciers listen?' asks Julie Cruikshank.[17] Probably

---

[16] John Dewey, *The Public and its Problems: An Essay in Political Enquiry* (Chicago: Gateway Books, 1946), p. 142.

[17] Julie Cruikshank, *Do Glaciers Listen? Local Knowledge, Colonial Encounters, and Social Imagination* (Vancouver and Toronto: UBC Press, 2005).

not, but we should perhaps be listening to them. This would amount to heeding the advice of renowned environmentalist and scientist Rachel Carson: 'Hearing can be a source of...exquisite pleasure, but it requires cultivation...Take time to listen and talk about the voices of the earth and what they mean.'[18]

In the final chapter, Chapter 6, I discuss the ways in which this theoretical work might be turned into political practice. I look in some detail at three types of political relationship—between constituents and representatives, between politicians themselves, and between the government and 'the people'—and suggest how listening might be made a structural feature of them. Throughout this discussion I bring forward three key issues that emerge from earlier chapters in the book—the relationship between listening and power (and, in particular, the challenge of how to get the powerful to listen so that the less powerful experience the power that is *being listened to* as a matter of course rather than as an exception), the degree to which listening can be learnt and how the learning of listening might itself be institutionalized, and, finally, the difference between good and bad listening. In this last case, the distinctions between process and outcome and between apophatic and cataphatic listening are especially important. A central conclusion of Chapter 6 is that good political listening requires planning and organization. In this sense political listening is unlike conversation, which is marked by an aimlessness and formlessness. This lack of structure is, indeed, one of the reasons why conversation is sometimes monological. As there is no formal mechanism in conversation to ensure that good listening takes place, such listening is left to serendipity, and, more particularly, to the listening capacities ('skills') of the interlocutors. In Chapter 6 I aim to strip away these contingencies and suggest ways of maximizing the chances of good political listening through *structuring* political encounters in particular ways. To this end I offer and discuss some examples of good political listening, particularly in the 'scaled-up' context, where whatever we learn about good listening from 'face-to-faceness' might seem hard to apply. Finally, I briefly discuss the role that the so-called new social media might play in improving the chances of dialogue between politicians and people. A considerable amount of hope has been invested in this area, but I take a rather more sceptical line driven

---

[18] Rachel Carson, *The Sense of Wonder* (New York: HarperCollins, 1998), p. 84.

by the distinction between speaking and listening, and the concern that while the new social media offer an astonishing array of platforms from which to *speak*, this may work against—rather than in favour of—more and better listening.

As Richard Sennett has pointed out,[19] certain skills are required for effective co-operation, and one of them is listening. The Scottish journalist Deborah Orr regretfully remembers her time with the workers' co-operative *City Limits* magazine in London as being rather anti-co-operative.[20] People wanted to be listened to, not to listen, she writes, and there was no need for empathy because everyone was constitutionally equal so what was there to empathize about? Orr compares her workers' co-op with Alcoholics Anonymous, the fundamental rule of whose meetings is that everybody listens to everybody else. She says that, 'having a speaker who honestly describes their own experience and emotions, to whom everyone listens quietly, and with whom everyone has an opportunity afterwards to express any feelings of recognition or solidarity—is fantastically powerful and soothing'.[21] There is undoubtedly power in being listened to, and that is the thought that animates the rest of this book.

[19] Richard Sennett, *Together: The Rituals, Pleasures, and Politics of Cooperation* (Yale: Yale University Press, 2012).

[20] Deborah Orr, 'Listening is fantastically powerful and soothing—we need more of it', *The Guardian*, 31 March 2012, p. 47.

[21] Orr (2012), p. 47.

1

Why Listening?

I have two aims in this chapter. The first is to locate my enquiry in the field of contemporary democratic theory. To this end I identify two recent turns in democratic theorizing, one towards what I call 'sensory' democracy, and the second towards non-ideal theorizing. Sensory democracy refers to what we might also call the 'receptive' side of the democratic conversation. We are very used to thinking about its speaking side, but much less attention has been paid to the way in which speech is received and processed, and the role that this aspect of the process does, could, and should play in democratic practice. To date, sensory democratic theorizing has focused mostly on the visual sense—'spectatorship'—and the present book adds to the sensory canon by focusing on our auditory capacities.

The second turn is related to the first. Sensory democratic theorizing is 'non-ideal', in that its theorists take democracy and its present social and cultural context as given. These theorists are therefore self-consciously reluctant to take some ideal version of democracy and try to make it fit conditions that militate against its successful instantiation. One result of this stance is a certain defensiveness as far as the potential for democracy is concerned. It seems inevitable that adapting democracy to uncongenial circumstances will result in the former giving way to the latter, with a consequent decline in the quality of democracy. The present book shares the non-ideal character of most sensory theorizing, but not its defensiveness. In fact, I aim to show how attention to listening can add positively to even some of the more transformative and optimistic theories of democracy—for example, deliberative democracy—and that it can contribute to an improvement in democratic practice too.

The second aim is to discuss the reasons why the concept and practice of listening has been so studiously ignored in political theory in general and in democratic theory in particular. One potential answer to this question is power- and interest-based. The general idea is that it is in the interests of those in power not to listen to citizens (unless it is surveillance listening), so attention is not drawn to listening. I explore this explanation and then offer a particular instance of it, relating to feminism, before pointing out its shortcomings. I then canvass an alternative explanation in relation to Aristotle's affirmation that 'man' is a political animal, and the claim on which this is based: that humans have the capacity for reasoned speech. I argue that this—the aligning of speech with political 'beingness'—has powerfully contributed to the eclipse of listening as a concept and practice worthy of political–theoretical attention.

SENSORY DEMOCRACY

A key context for this book is the broader reassessment of democratic theory and practice that is taking place around the theme of performance, or what we might call 'sensory democracy'.[1] A great deal of attention is paid to voice and speech in our reflections on democracy, and very little to the senses, such as sight and hearing. In this connection there is common ground between the rationale for, and subject matter of, this book and Jeffrey Green's important work.[2] Green points out how, throughout much of the history of political theory, popular power has been understood in terms of voice, and democracy has been theorized from this point of view.[3] His claim is not that the emphasis on voice is wrong but that it is narrow, especially as a measure of how politics is experienced by most people. The voice of the people is heard relatively rarely in modern democracies, he argues, but we do spend

---

[1] Including 'olfactory politics': Qian Hui Tan, 'Smell in the city: smoking and olfactory politics', *Urban Studies* 50 (2013), no. 1, pp. 55–71, which explores smoking as a sensorially transgressive practice.
[2] Jeffrey Edward Green, *The Eyes of the People: Democracy in an Age of Spectatorship* (Oxford and New York: Oxford University Press, 2010).
[3] Green (2010), pp. 3 and 66: 'Whatever the diversity of democratic theory in other respects, it is simply the case that the vocal model has shaped the way representative democracy has been theorized from the eighteenth century to the present.'

a lot of time *spectating*. This basic fact is enough, for Green, to set in motion a consideration of the 'the People's *eyes* as an organ ... of popular empowerment'.[4]

Green's analysis is an important moment in the burgeoning discussion around sensory democracy,[5] and four points in it are worth noting. First, as the quotation above suggests, he is interested in power and empowerment. Second, his focus on spectatorship leads him to endorse a particular form of democracy: 'plebiscitary democracy'. I will use this as a platform to sketch out, very briefly, the reasons why I think attention to listening drives us in the direction of 'dialogical democracy', and this argument will receive much more sustained attention in Chapters 3 and 5.[6] Third, as we noted above, Green believes that his analysis amounts to 'non-ideal theory' (by which he means non-idealistic theory), and I use this idea to introduce a more positive and optimistic account than Green's of the possibilities inherent in listening and its democratic counterpart, dialogical democracy. Fourth, Green defines spectatorship very broadly as 'watching and listening to others who are ... actively engaged'.[7] This treats watching and listening as if they are same thing. Of course, they are indeed both forms of spectatorship, but it is more productive to see them as *aspects* of spectatorship, deserving and needing separate treatment. It is worth remembering the argument that 'the historic achievement of literacy [has] resulted in the primacy of the ocular over the aural sense',[8] if only as a reminder that we should consider sight and hearing as quite different senses.

---

[4] Green (2010), p. 3.

[5] John Parkinson, *Democracy and Public Space: The Physical Sites of Democratic Performance* (Oxford and New York: Oxford University Press, 2012) is another important point of reference.

[6] Robyn Penman and Sue Turnbull suggest that listening takes us in the direction of participatory democracy, rather than deliberative or representative forms. My own view is that better listening could improve these last two forms of democracy considerably, as will become clear in subsequent chapters. I also believe that the best alternative to these two is dialogic, rather than participatory, democracy, and for much the same reason that Penman and Turnbull endorse in their article: its capacity to deal with difference. See Robyn Penman and Sue Turnbull, 'From listening ... to the dialogic realities of participatory democracy', *Continuum: Journal of Media and Cultural Studies* 26 (2012), no. 1, pp. 61–72.

[7] Green (2010), p. 4.

[8] Bruce Buchan, 'Listening for noise in political thought', *Cultural Studies Review* 18 (2012), no. 3, p. 38.

POWER AND EMPOWERMENT

So first, power and empowerment. We normally think of empowerment as a function of the right and capacity to speak,[9] and it is not
immediately obvious how a *sense*, like sight, can be an organ of
political power: 'Political science...is hardly accustomed to treating
the faculty of vision as a suitable foundation for political empowerment.'[10] We might say the same of listening since, as Gideon Calder
has observed, 'agency is located on the side of the speaker rather than
listener.'[11] Is listening not a passive, receptive sense only? And if it is,
then how can power be expressed through it? But only a moment's
reflection is needed to see that the listener has power too: 'speakers
are dependent on listeners for communicative success. Listeners can
simply refuse to listen; they can also wilfully misunderstand, confuse the meaning of words or intentions of the speaker, or disrespect
the wishes of the speaker.'[12] Nikolas Kompridis builds on this in the
more explicitly political context: 'we are unaccustomed to thinking
of agency in terms other than mastery [and] are uncomfortable with
the thought that democratic politics might require a different kind of
agency, rooted in *receptivity* rather than mastery.'[13]

Kompridis goes on to argue that, far from being tangential to
democracy, receptivity is a condition for its renewal in that it is alert
to the possibility of hitherto unheard voices. He is clear that this is not
just an 'acoustical failure' but a failure of receptivity more generally—a
failure of 'recognition', if you will: 'we are being reproached for failing to be receptive, or for remaining selectively receptive...The failure
to be reflectively receptive renders voiceless someone with whom we
claim to share a life, a common fate.'[14] Receptivity is thus an *activity*

---

[9] As a consequence, 'liberal political theory reads an absence of political voice as an
absence of agency,' writes Nikita Dhawan from a post-structural perspective: Nikita
Dhawan, 'Hegemonic listening and subversive silences: ethical–political imperatives',
Critical Studies 36 (2012), p. 49. I would only add that this is true of political theory
beyond the liberal, too.

[10] Green (2010), p. 7.

[11] Gideon Calder, 'Democracy and listening', in Mary-Ann Crumplin (ed.),
Problems of Democracy: Language and Speaking (Oxford: Inter-Disciplinary Press,
2011), p. 129.

[12] Carolyn Cusick, 'Speaking, Listening and Communicative Justice: Educating
Epistemic Trust and Responsibility' (PhD thesis, Vanderbilt University, 2012), p. 62.

[13] Nikolas Kompridis, 'Receptivity, possibility, and democratic politics', *Ethics and
Global Politics* 4 (2011), no. 4, p. 3 (emphasis in the original).

[14] Kompridis (2011), p. 9.

that brings previously unheard voices to our attention in the manner of disclosure rather than discovery. This is to say that the voices were already there, and it is simply a question of being open to the possibility of hearing them. Once these voices are present, listening still has an active and agentic role to play: 'it is *doing* something about a problem of misunderstanding or non-communication, creating a space for potential "hearing" across difference'.[15] All too often, activity in politics is associated with speaking and passivity with listening, but these remarks suggest that there is performativity in the latter as well as in the former.[16]

One practice where listening bears a direct relationship to power—and its reclaiming—is restorative justice. In this context John Braithwaite points to Kay Pranis's insight that, 'we can tell how much power a person has by how many people listen to their stories. When the prime minister speaks from his podium many listen; when the pauper on the street mutters his stories we walk past.'[17] This provides the basis for restorative justice, which works by giving voice to those whose voices have previously gone unheard, and—crucially— by obliging others to listen. The evidence from restorative justice is that these voices belong to the 'poor, powerless and young' and that 'women's voices are actually slightly more likely to be heard in restorative justice conferences than men's voices', which, as Braithwaite points out, is a very different voice to that normally heard in the corridors of power.[18] A similar sense emerges from work carried out by Jenny Pearce with community activists in the North of England. Pearce distinguishes between power over, power to, and power as the capacity to act, and suggests that none of these captures the understanding of

[15] Kathy Bickmore and Serihy Kovalchuk, 'Diverse ways of creating classroom communities for constructive discussions of conflict: cases from Canadian secondary schools', in Peter Cunningham and Nathan Fretwell(eds), *Creating Communities: Local, National and Global* (London: CiCe, 2012).

[16] Buchan (2012), p. 52. But, as Bryce Peake shows in his sonic analysis of Gibraltar and colonialism, 'doing listening' can take on a more malign hue—in this case through 'colonizing Gibraltarian subjects and Gibraltarian spaces'; Bryce Peake, 'Listening, language, and colonialism on Main Street, Gibraltar', *Communication and Critical/ Cultural Studies* 9 (2012), no. 2, p. 172. We will look in a little more detail at the role of listening in colonialism in Chapter 2.

[17] John Braithwaite, 'Setting standards for restorative justice', *British Journal of Criminology* 42 (2002), p. 564. See also Jane J. Bolitho, 'Restorative justice: the ideals and realities of conferencing for young people', *Critical Criminology* 20 (2012), pp. 67 and 69–70.

[18] Braithwaite (2002), p. 564.

power displayed by the activists with whom she talked. They spoke, rather, in terms of what Pearce calls 'non-domineering power', a type of power which is especially relevant when it comes to alternative forms of decision-making. One significance of the Occupy movement, writes Pearce, is its attempt to put into practice different ways of making decisions which, crucially, have the key objective of 'facilitating voice': 'Facilitators make use of the "progressive slant" to ensure that race and gender not the order by which people raise their hands are taken into account when people ask to speak.'[19] This tactic amounts to a form of listening—listening out for otherwise unheard voices—and it is significant that activists with whom Pearce talked defined power as 'people listening to you.'[20] This is the kind of power that Michael Ende's central character Momo confers on people in his eponymous story: 'She listened in a way that made slow people have flashes of inspiration. It wasn't that she actually said anything or asked questions that put such ideas into their heads. She simply sat there and listened with the utmost attention and sympathy, fixing them with her big, dark eyes, and they suddenly became aware of ideas whose existence they had never suspected.'[21]

So withholding listening is an expression of power, being heard is a conferring of power, and the evidence from both Pearce and from the broader field of restorative justice suggests that listening plays a key role in rebalancing power relations. The focus on power in restorative justice makes it interesting when it comes to thinking about how listening might be better institutionalized in political practices, and we will return to this in Chapter 6.[22] In sum, the comments Tanja Dreher makes in respect of media are equally applicable to the realm of politics. She refers to:

...the issues at stake in paying attention to listening—the crucial role of listening in engaging across differences, the ways in which listening can

---

[19] Jenny Pearce, 'Power and the activist', *Development* 55 (2012), no. 2, p. 199.
[20] Pearce (2012), p. 198.
[21] Michael Ende, *Momo* (London: Penguin, 1984), p. 18.
[22] There may be an important role for facilitators, together with the skills that good restorative justice facilitators should possess. John Braithwaite, the author of the article we are discussing here, rules himself out because of what he calls his 'deficiencies as a restorative justice conference facilitator'—'communicating encouragement or doubt when all I should be communicating is *attentive listening*'; Braithwaite (2002), p. 574 (emphasis added).

either enable or constrain another's ability to speak freely, the ways in which a refusal to listen can operate as an exercise of power and privilege, and also as protest, the creative and ethical possibilities produced by attentive and respectful listening, the ways in which institutional structures and conventions can shape relations of speaking and listening.[23]

Another political arena where the power of listening is in evidence is peace and reconciliation. On 12 October 1984 a bomb exploded in the Grand Hotel in Brighton (UK), where the ruling Conservative Party was holding its annual conference. The blast killed five people, including Sir Anthony Berry, the government deputy chief whip. The bomb had been planted by Patrick Magee, of the Irish Republican Army, and Magee was subsequently arrested and imprisoned. Under the terms of the Good Friday Agreement Magee was released from Northern Ireland's Maze Prison in 1999. Sir Anthony Berry's daughter, Jo, was 27 when her father was killed, and ever since October 1984 she had been haunted by one question: why did her father have to die? Magee's release from prison opened up the possibility of her putting this question directly to the man who killed her father, and a lengthy series of negotiations led to them eventually meeting in Dublin in November 2000.[24] That meeting was, unsurprisingly, fraught and difficult. Magee and Berry were divided by background and by class, but, above all, by the fact that Magee had killed Berry's father. How would they bridge this chasm? In a word, they bridged it by *listening* to each other. 'Jo's ability to listen deeply gave Pat the space to tell a personal story about his response to the oppression [in Northern Ireland] experienced by himself and his community,' says Dr Scherto Gill of the Guerrand-Hermès Foundation for Peace.[25] Interestingly, Jo herself says that, judging by her own experience, the point is not to try to reach an end state such as reconciliation or forgiveness, but to focus on the process. And a key

---

[23] Tanja Dreher, 'Media, multiculturalism and the politics of listening', in E. Tilley (ed.), *Power and Place: Refereed Proceedings of the Australian and New Zealand Communication Association Conference 2008* (Palmerston North, NZ: Massey University, 2008), p. 4.

[24] This process is documented in an Everyman programme made for the BBC, *Facing the Enemy.*

[25] Quoted in David Miles, 'Love thy enemy', *Huffington Post*, 4 June 2012, available at <http://www.huffingtonpost.com/david-miles/love-thy-enemy_1_b_1568445.html> (accessed 22 August 2012).

part of the process is listening: 'forgiveness is not a prerequisite for
empathy,' says Berry, '[W]hat is more important . . . is being interested in listening to the other perspective and trying to understand
it, even if you are not willing to agree with it.'[26] Crucially, Patrick
Magee also refers to listening when asked what he has learnt from
his meetings with Berry; 'I have become a much better listener
from my conversations with Jo,' he says, '[S]lowing the dialogue
down to ensure you hear properly and explain adequately may be
the best means of engaging with someone you have hurt.'[27]

Returning for a moment to the visual sense, Jeffrey Green is naturally keen to question the idea that spectatorship implies powerlessness, and part of this involves ridding ourselves of the 'dominance of
the vocal model of popular power,'[28] which constructs the spectator as
'outside processes of collective authorship and self-legislation.'[29] Green
acknowledges the potential power of the gaze in connection with a
comment on Jean-Paul Sartre: '[F]or Sartre, the spectator is no merely
passive figure but, as the holder of the gaze, someone with the power,
albeit a perverse one, to undermine the agency of another.'[30] This
indeed is what lies at the heart of Green's notion of ocular power: 'the
genuine and literal surveillance of . . . leaders.'[31] Critically, Green is
aware that there are empowered and unempowered forms of looking, and a key question for him is what distinguishes the two: what is
the difference between merely looking at our leaders, and having the
capacity to scrutinize them?[32] We will explore Green's answer to this
question a little further on, but for now it is worth noting that there is
a parallel question in relation to listening. We are in a position to listen
to politicians and for politicians to listen to us all the time, but this
aural relationship is characterized by a lack of reciprocity. How can
this sense, so often used to establish, cement, and reproduce power
(through surveillance and eavesdropping), be turned to democratic
advantage?

I suggested earlier in this chapter that listening is tied closely to the idea
of recognition, and, in this context, Tanja Dreher has perceptively noted
that what we are dealing with here is perhaps less a matter of 'participation

---

[26] Miles (2012).   [27] In Miles (2012).   [28] Green (2010), p. 8.
[29] Green (2010), p. 8.   [30] Green (2010), p. 10.   [31] Green (2010), p. 11.
[32] Green (2010), p. 13.

and empowerment' and more one of the 'dynamics and difficulties of *recognition*'.[33] The politics of recognition is an important source of theoretical reflection on making visible the invisible, and we will be drawing on it later in the book, especially in Chapters 4 and 5. Of course, listening, like recognition, is something that can be demanded but withheld. In this sense it is no different to any number of *desiderata* that have become the subject of rights-talk—freedom, equality, justice. As John Downing says, what point is there in a 'right to communicate' if no one is listening?[34] Downing suggests that for it to be made good, the right to communicate should be accompanied by an (underspecified) 'right to be understood'.[35] In other words, the promise of democracy is not redeemed by simply conferring the right to speak, though most democratic theory and practice seems to assume that it is. We would do well to remember, with John Dryzek, that, 'the most effective and insidious way to silence others in politics is a refusal to listen'.[36] This suggests that democracy's promise will only be fulfilled when the right to speak and the right to be heard are regarded as two sides of the same coin, when it is understood that one is incomplete without the other, and when this understanding is embedded in institutional practice.[37]

'CANDOUR' AS A CRITICAL IDEAL

Jeffrey Green argues that technological changes have altered the nature of politics by 'cementing spectatorship into the very structure of daily political experience'.[38] This leads to a large spectating class watching a much smaller elite of political actors, with very little rotation between

[33] Tanja Dreher, 'Speaking up or being heard? Community media interventions and the politics of listening', *Media, Culture and Society* 32 (2010), no. 1, p. 99 (emphasis added).

[34] John Downing, 'Grassroots media: establishing priorities for the years ahead', *Global Media Journal (Australia Edition)* 1 (2007), no. 1, p. 12, available at <http://www.commarts.uws.edu.au/gmjau/iss1_2007/pdf/HC_FINAL_John%20Downing.pdf> (accessed 10 April 2012).

[35] Downing (2007), pp. 12–13.

[36] John Dryzek, *Deliberative Democracy and Beyond* (Oxford: Oxford University Press, 2000), p. 149.

[37] 'Equality and inclusion are democratic principles that are as yet unmet when we measure inclusion according to who can speak without paying attention to all the speakers without adequate listeners'; Cusick (2012), p. 11.

[38] Green (2010), p. 4.

the two. Green points out that this undermines the notion of equality that lies at the heart of democratic theory. Given the structural imbalance between spectators and actors and the consequent difficulty with turning spectators into actors in the normal way—that is, by giving them a meaningful voice—is there any way of turning spectatorship into power? Green argues that there is. In his theory of 'ocular democracy' empowerment is something of a zero-sum game in which the empowerment of the people is in proportion to the disempowerment of politicians, and this disempowerment is a function of them 'not being in control of the conditions of their publicity'.[39] In a democracy characterized by spectatorship, politicians exert their control, in part, by carefully structuring their appearances, and this control is correspondingly undermined to the degree that these appearances are subject to risk and uncertainty. Green points to cross-examination in presidential debates, to unexpected moments in press conferences, and to unscripted public gatherings as moments and sites at which politicians are subjected to the gaze of the public in an uncontrolled way.

The 'critical ideal' that emerges from his theory is what he calls 'candour'. This is not to be understood as 'the individual norm that leaders be sincere, but rather the institutional requirement that leaders not be in control of their own publicity. Leaders are candid to the extent their public appearances are neither rehearsed, preplanned, nor managed from above, but rather contain all the risk and uncertainty of spontaneous public events.'[40] Candour is certainly an interesting notion, or tool, with which to analyse contemporary politics. We can all think of examples of the unscripted moments which are iconic of the functioning of candour, and which expose politicians to the uncomfortable glare of publicity. One such moment occurred in the UK General Election campaign of 2010 when the then Prime Minister Gordon Brown was doing a walkabout in the town of Rochdale. He met Gillian Duffy, a lifelong supporter of the Labour Party (Brown's party), who quizzed him about the scale of immigration into Britain. Once back in his car after the encounter Brown's director of strategic communications asked him what Duffy had said, and Brown replied, 'Oh everything, she was just a sort of bigoted woman. She said she used to be Labour. I mean it's just ridiculous.'[41] What Brown

---

[39] Green (2010), p. 13   [40] Green (2010), pp. 13–14.

[41] Patrick Wintour and Polly Curtis, 'Gordon Brown "penitent" after bigot gaffe torpedoes election campaign', *The Guardian*, 28 April 2010, available at <http://www. guardian.co.uk/politics/2010/apr/28/gordon-brown-penitent-bigot-gaffe-campaign> (accessed 25 June 2012).

didn't know was that this comment was caught on a live broadcast feed, and he was forced to apologize to Duffy on the telephone before making a public apology and then visiting Duffy in her home to apologize again.

This is very much the kind of event Green has in mind when developing his notion of candour and the role it might play in empowering people. His proposals for what we might loosely call institutional change under the sign of ocular spectatorship are based on an assessment of the potential for candour in some rather traditional political set-pieces, such as presidential debates.[42] Thus, he argues for, 'A presidential debate with extemporaneous cross-examination, or a public enquiry of a leading politician or senior official, or a lively press conference that places real pressure on the prime minister or president.'[43] An example of this occurred during a debate between the candidates for the Republican nomination for the US presidential election of 2012. In the middle of the televised debate on 9 November 2011 Governor of Texas Rick Perry spent nearly a minute trying to remember the name of one of the three government departments he had promised to abolish: 'It's three agencies of government when I get there that are gone, Commerce, Education and the, er, what's the third one there? Let's see . . .' Eventually he concluded: 'I would do away with the Education, the Commerce and—let's see—I can't. The third one, I can't. Sorry. Oops.' His struggle led to suggestions from the audience and from the other candidates, and 15 minutes later he said, 'By the way, that was the Department of Energy I was reaching for.'[44] It is hard to tell how far this gaffe contributed to Perry's demise as a potential front-runner for the nomination, but it certainly didn't do him any good.

So there is no denying that these moments of candour exist, that it is possible to interpret them as seeing politicians 'in their true light', and that they do indeed turn the tables somewhat in favour of the spectating public. But this turning of the tables involves a rather impoverished form of empowerment, based as it is on the embarrassment of the politician—indeed, on her or his *humiliation*.[45] We might regard

---

[42] Green (2010), p. 182. [43] Green (2010), p. 200.

[44] Toby Harnden, 'Republican debate: Rick Perry forgets key part of policy in major gaffe', 10 November 2011, available at <http://www.telegraph.co.uk/news/worldnews/republicans/8880467/Republican-debate-Rick-Perry-forgets-key-part-of-policy-in-major-gaffe.html#> (accessed 25 June 2012).

[45] Humiliation seems to be an acceptable aspect of candour for Green (2010), p. 162.

this as corrosive rather than constructive, creating a dynamic that is likely to lead to defensiveness rather than openness—a kind of mediatic arms race in which politicians strive for ever greater control over the means of their publicity while the public seek ever more sophisticated ways of prising open the carapace. This is the kind of approach to 'post-democracy' that Colin Crouch criticizes for its negativity: 'the negative activism of blame and complaint, where the main aim of political controversy is to see politicians called to account, their heads placed on the blocks, and their public and private integrity held up to intimate scrutiny.'[46] This is both a cause and an effect of what Crouch regards as a debilitating personalization of politics, in which the personality of politicians takes over from the discussion of the issues as the main substance of politics: 'The increasing exposure of their [politicians'] private lives to media gaze, as blaming, complaining and investigating replace constructive citizenship...Electoral competition then takes the form of a search for individuals of character and integrity.'[47]

In his *Defending Politics*, Matthew Flinders similarly argues that the political culture of 'catching out' (my term not his), is in danger of having exactly the opposite effect to producing politicians of character and integrity. This is not because there are no such politicians, but because spectatorship as surveillance—especially in the 24/7 social media world in which we live nowadays—is turning politics into 'an increasingly hard and brutal business'.[48] The pressures have become more intense, the criticisms harsher, and the attacks more personal.[49] Good people still try to make a difference, says Flinders, but under these permanent surveillance conditions, 'someone with a life, a family, interests beyond politics, the ability to do other things, can feel deeply inclined to stick to them and leave the political storm to itself'.[50] The result is an impoverishment of the pool of potential politicians, with the profession increasingly left to the 'manically ambitious, socially privileged, or simply weird'.[51]

---

[46] Colin Crouch, *Post-Democracy* (Cambridge: Polity Press, 2004), p. 13.
[47] Crouch (2004), p. 28.
[48] Matthew Flinders, *Defending Politics: Why Democracy Matters in the Twenty-first Century* (Oxford: Oxford University Press, 2012), p. 188.
[49] Flinders (2012), p. 188.
[50] Flinders (2012), p. 188. To this list we might add 'something to hide'.
[51] Flinders (2012), p. 188.

In similar vein, Didier Caluwaerts and Min Reuchamps talk of a nervousness among politicians, born of a feeling of being constantly monitored. This, they say, 'leads to a politics in the trenches, a politics in which the least bit of compromise is immediately magnified and considered treacherous. In such a society, politics is about taking positions and sticking with them for fear of being publicly discredited, and no longer about *listening to each other's arguments*.'[52] If surveillance, as the instrument of candour, prompts entrenchment and fear, leading to an impoverishment of debate, then we are surely heading in exactly the wrong direction as far as democracy is concerned. No doubt this is not the outcome that Green wants from his notion of spectatorship, but Crouch, Flinders, and Caluwaerts and Reuchamps make persuasive points about how candour could come across in current conditions. This is not to reject candour as a principle worth exploring, since, as Green himself says, any conversation which does not have sincerity at its heart is more likely to be headed towards strategic manipulation than mutual understanding. More germane to our enquiry into listening, Green is also surely right to say that under conditions of candour, as he defines it, a precondition for being 'forced to listen' to the claims of others may well be that politicians will not be in total control of the means and fact of their publicity.[53]

Yet beyond embarrassing politicians it is hard to see what these moments of candour achieve. Green himself recognizes that even if the precariousness he wants to be injected into these otherwise set-piece occasions could be guaranteed (not at all easy given the tight rein politicians hold on their public appearances) they would 'not serve the autonomy of the everyday citizen (leading to laws and decisions that the citizen could claim as his or her own).'[54] This cannot count as a criticism of Green's project, however, at least internally, as he has given up on 'improving' democracy in the traditional sense of transferring people's autonomy into the realm of political decision-making. One of the problems with the 'vocal model' of democracy, indeed, he says, is that it assumes that 'popular empowerment must involve

[52] Didier Caluwaerts and Min Reuchamps, 'The G1000: facts, figures and some lessons from an experience of deliberative democracy in Belgium', p. 4 (emphasis added), available at <http://www.rethinkingbelgium.eu/rebel-initiative-files/events/seventh-public-event-g1000-european-citizens-initiative-malaise-democracy/G1000-Background-Paper.pdf> (accessed 27 January 2013).
[53] Green (2010), p. 179.   [54] Green (2010), p. 200.

self-legislation.'[55] But I take it that the great advantage of democracy over other forms of rule is precisely that it respects the human capacity for autonomy: whatever form it takes it must be able to trace the origin of a decision back to the people themselves. So, far from being a problem, self-legislation is the beating heart of democracy, and I do not believe we should reject this normative dimension of democracy so quickly. In this respect I take dialogic democracy to mean breathing new life into some long-standing democratic traditions that have become somewhat tarnished as societies have become bigger and more complex, and as people have become more alienated from the political process.

Green draws the classic distinction between those who rule and those who are ruled, and he rejects the idea that measures can be taken, even in today's large-scale democracies, to unsettle that distinction (e.g. through more rigorous forms of representation, or through innovations such as deliberative forums). This leads him to place speaking and listening firmly and fixedly on either side of the 'those who rule/those who are ruled' divide: 'the two virtues of ruling and being-ruled correspond to the two components of a conversation: speaking and listening. The virtue of ruling consists in the making of speeches and persuasive arguments before the Assembly, while the virtue of being-ruled lies in the careful attention and reception to the arguments being made.'[56] While I positively endorse the use of the word 'conversation' here, there are two things missing from Green's account. First, one virtue of *democratic* ruling (rather than just ruling in general) is that those who rule (as well as those who are ruled) should have the capacity to listen, for this is one element that contributes to responsive rule. Second, it is too simplistic to align speaking with ruling and listening with being ruled. First, it is commonplace to think of those who are ruled as a speaking as well as a listening entity (when they vote, when they express their views on the street, in opinion surveys[57]), but we should also recognize that listening is not just a matter of careful attention; it can also be used as an instrument of power, as we saw earlier in this chapter. Green makes it hard for us to think in this way because he regards both sight and hearing as passive senses.[58] In this sense he comes close to falling into a trap that

---

[55] Green (2010), p. 65.   [56] Green (2010), p. 35.
[57] Green concedes as much, but refers to these as 'rare' events; Green (2010), p. 40.
[58] Green (2010), pp. 40 and 200.

he himself sets. He rightly points out that 'democratic theory has not adequately addressed the spectator because it has been incapable of conceiving of popular power other than as a vocal force'.[59] Yet, in suggesting that sight and hearing are passive senses he provides succour to the very position he is seeking to resist. Thus, while *oral* democracy seems to have run into the sands of cynicism as far as this relationship is concerned, *aural* democracy has the potential to 'reboot' it, and to put it on a more equal footing.[60]

So I am not as pessimistic as Green about the normative outcome of this enquiry into the listening aspect of sensory democracy as he is about ocular spectatorship. Pessimism is a word Green himself uses to describe the general tenor of his theory—candour, he says, might be thought of as an 'inherently *pessimistic* political value'.[61] But he makes a virtue out of this pessimism, arguing that it is the only possible response to an imperfect situation, a situation in which we need to recalibrate what we try to do with contemporary democracy, where we are confronted with 'obstacles and difficulties that are…unnavigable'.[62] It is a mistake, he suggests, to hang on to the ideals of direct democracy in conditions that are utterly unsuited to it. What we need is a better *description* of contemporary democracy, taking into account the way it actually functions, and this will lead to more realistic suggestions for 'improving' democratic theory and practice. Under these conditions, he suggests, pessimism (or, as he also calls it, 'realism') is a virtue rather than a vice. The move from vocal to ocular democracy, from speaking to looking, from activity to passivity (as he sees it) means that we must lower our political sights, and this takes us in the direction of plebiscitary democracy.

But while it might be true that we are in the presence of a 'fallen democracy bereft of genuine popular decision-making',[63] this does not automatically entail endorsing theories and practices of democracy that align with this current state of affairs. '[B]y grounding itself on the People's eyes rather than the People's voice, and thus on an organ that carries with it the problems of inequality and passivity rather than the

---

[59] Green (2010), p. 64.
[60] While the distinction between 'oral' and 'aural' democracy works well on paper, the two words are unfortunately homonymous in the English language so the distinction works less well when read out or spoken.
[61] Green (2010), p. 13; emphasis in the original.
[62] Green (2010), p. 14.   [63] Green (2010), p. 122.

perfection of autonomy and representation,' writes Green, 'the plebi-scitary model I shall defend strives for ideals especially suitable to the fallen conditions that shape the way democracy has come to be expe-rienced today.'[64] This surely cedes too much ground to imperfection.

Beyond Green's contribution, it is striking how the move to what I have called a 'sensory democracy' seems to have entailed lowering our sights, as far as our expectations regarding democracy—and par-ticularly democratic conversation—are concerned. In his discussion of democracy and public space, for example, John Parkinson (like Green) draws a clear distinction between speakers and listeners in terms of their relative activity and passivity. He points out that under 'small-N' conditions, engagement between people aimed at mutual understanding is a reasonable expectation, but, as numbers increase, the distinction between 'performers' and 'audience' becomes more marked. 'When that happens,' writes Parkinson, 'communication can become less about achieving mutual understanding with one's interlocutors, and more about persuading the audience.'[65] Then, tell-ingly, he offers this example to illustrate what he means: 'no one, I imagine, would expect a debate between a group of presidential candidates to result in one of the leaders being persuaded by some-thing another said, stroking his chin thoughtfully and responding, "There is something in what you say, I shall have to reconsider my position." '[66]

This rather effectively illustrates how far expectations in the acad-emy have become removed from those of the population at large. One does not have to listen to radio phone-ins for very long before some-one berates politicians for being involved in monologue rather than dialogue, in which the point of conversation seems to be to entrench positions rather than examine them. Part of my determination here to resist Green's spectator position is driven by his own conclusions as to what plebiscitary democracy can give us. In general terms he comes close to endorsing Max Weber's notion of 'leader democ-racy', the intention of which, according to Green, is not to 'realize traditional democratic values such as inclusiveness equality, popu-lar self-legislation, or the cultivation of the intellectual and moral

---

[64] Green (2010), p. 7. See also p. 47, where Green makes it clear that he doesn't believe that 'being ruled' is normatively superior to ruling, but that theoretical atten-tion to the former is justified by its 'actuality'.
[65] Parkinson (2012), p. 44.   [66] Parkinson (2012), p. 44.

capacities of the citizenry, but rather its capacity to produce *charismatic* leaders capable of providing strong, independent and creative direction to the modern, industrial nation-state'.[67] In this context, the role of the 'public gaze' is no more and no less than to contribute to 'the production of charismatic authority'.[68] I am going to argue that spectatorship, understood in terms of listening rather than watching, can do better than this.

So while this book is part of a turn towards non-ideal democratic theorizing, this should not be taken to mean that I am not interested in 'improving' democracy. I take a self-confessedly normative stance here, and thereby, perhaps foolishly, ignore the advice of theorists like Michael Saward, who counsel against a rush to normativity.[69] Like Colin Crouch in his *Post-Democracy* I have in mind an ideal model of democracy towards which I believe we should be working.[70] And, like Crouch, I believe that what passes as democracy in countries like the UK and the USA is a pallid imitation of what he calls 'maximal democracy'. Crouch describes the maximal model as being about opportunities for participation and the capacity of ordinary people to affect public policy.[71] This contrasts with what he calls post-democracy, the characteristics of which include tightly controlled election campaigns managed by professional experts, covering a narrow range of issues determined by political cliques. Citizens play a background role in post-democracy, confined to responding to signals sent out by political elites and their spin doctors. Meanwhile, the real action goes on behind closed doors as business persuades elected governments to make policy favourable to its interests.[72] Crouch argues that the ideal model 'sets a marker' to which we should aspire, rather than take the facts on the ground (dominant elite, quiescent public) and adapt our aspirations, as far as democracy is concerned, to those facts. 'That way,' says Crouch, 'lies complacency, self-congratulation and an absence of concern to identify ways in which democracy is being weakened'.[73]

---

[67] Green (2010), p. 142.   [68] Green (2010), p. 153.
[69] 'I hope to show in the analysis that follows that *delaying* normative questions in favor of a more fine-grained understanding of representation dynamics is highly desirable'; Michael Saward, *The Representative Claim* (Oxford: Oxford University Press, 2010), p. 29 (emphasis in the original).
[70] Crouch (2004).   [71] Crouch (2004), p. 2.
[72] Crouch (2004), pp. 3–4.   [73] Crouch (2004), p. 3.

PLEBISCITARY AND DIALOGICAL DEMOCRACY

Green's reflections on spectatorship lead him to endorse a particular type of democracy—plebiscitary democracy. He is aware that plebiscitary democracy has something of a bad name—a 'politics of the spectacle, dominated by manipulative elites'[74]—but it does offer him a way of theorizing democracy from the spectatorship point of view. Similarly, a focus on listening leads us, I believe, in the direction of a particular sort of democracy—*dialogic* democracy. I will explain this further in Chapters 2 and 3, but two introductory remarks are in order here. First, 'dialogue' captures the reciprocal relationship implicit in bringing listening back into the communication equation. A dialogic relationship is one in which speaking and listening are of equal importance, and the expression is usefully contrasted with a monological situation in which no listening takes place at all. It is an indictment of contemporary democracy that laypeople will often complain about politicians' unwillingness to listen to the 'views of the people' outside election time, and this is what I mean by 'monological democracy'. This type of democracy is characterized by politicians talking to (at) citizens, with the monologue occasionally punctuated by elections, which are the only formal moments during the democratic cycle when politicians are obliged to listen to the electorate. There are other moments that can be characterized as listening, such as public consultations and the 'focus groups' which have become an infamous feature of the UK's political landscape in recent times. We will be looking at these phenomena in Chapter 6 in connection with the institutional arrangements that would help instantiate dialogical rather than monological democracy.

The second introductory point to make is that dialogical democracy aims at increasing the number of voices heard in political debate. Dialogical democracy here is as much about *listening out for* as it is about *listening to*. It has often been pointed out that the history of democracy can be characterized as a progressive widening of the franchise. This process has been uneven across time and space and it has come about as a result of great struggles involving—effectively—the demand to be heard. The onus has always been on those who want to be heard to make their point in the face of a generalized resistance to

---

[74] Green (2010), p. 5, and see pp. 120–39.

inclusion. Dialogical democracy aims to turn the tables on this resistance by installing a presumption in favour of 'listening out for' potential political voices. It is plausible to suggest that if the focus on politics as speechifying had been systematically accompanied by a dialogical understanding of politics, which implies attention to listening as well as speaking, the historical resistance to inclusion and the widening of the franchise would have been more muted. In this sense, dialogical democracy amounts to a countervailing (though by no means determining) power in the hands of the quiet, the mute, and those on the periphery of mainstream interests, practices, and understandings of politics. I will say more about dialogical democracy in Chapter 4 (especially in relation to deliberative democracy), and in Chapter 6 (in relation to its institutionalization).

DISTINGUISHING BETWEEN WATCHING AND LISTENING

This leads me to the fourth point I wanted to make in connection with Green's theory of spectatorship and democracy. Spectatorship focuses our attention on *perception*, and reminds us that speech is only the vocalized form of human communication. Spectatorship is the other side of the coin of communication, as it were—the moment at which what is said becomes meaningful. But perception is not exhausted by the faculty of vision: sight is just one of what we traditionally refer to as the 'five senses' (sight, hearing, taste, smell, touch).[75] Green elides the first two of these when he defines spectatorship, as we saw earlier, as 'watching and listening to others who are … actively engaged',[76] and then goes on to claim that spectatorship is important because 'most people engage with politics primarily with their eyes, rather than their voice'.[77] Green considers the obvious objection that this engagement also takes place through people's *ears*, but this seems to be rather an

---

[75] There is some debate as to how many senses humans have. The idea of five senses is taken from Aristotle's classification, but we might add a sense of balance, of temperature, of pain, and the sense that enables us to detect our body moving. For present purposes, though, the five senses are enough to be going along with.

[76] Green (2010), p. 4.   [77] Green (2010), p. 5.

afterthought as he clarifies the significance of it (or rather the lack of it)—in a footnote—in the following way:

> To avoid misunderstanding, let me indicate at the outset that the *eyes* of the people is intended to designate not just the visual dimension of political spectatorship, but also importantly the audio one. If this synecdoche by which vision refers to the audiovisual field is not entirely precise, neither is it at all uncommon. Both in ordinary parlance and in philosophical discourse, visual processes are invested with an extravisual significance...The important thing is to distinguish the passive, spectatorial processes of vision and hearing (both of which are intended by the 'eyes of the People') from active processes of voice, participation, and decision making.[78]

Besides mistakenly aligning activity with speech and passivity with spectating, the problem with Green's synecdotic approach is that listening has no independent standing in it. Vision and hearing are both seen in terms of the 'eyes of the people' when, in reality, this only applies to the former of the two terms. This is as much as to claim that everything he says about ocular democracy is applicable to aural democracy and vice versa. The rest of the present book calls this claim into question: each of these forms of sensory democracy needs separate treatment, both for the way in which the enquiry is carried out and for the implications for democracy they bring with them. In what follows I devote my attention exclusively to listening.[79]

LISTENING IN 'THE LITERATURE'

Honourable exceptions aside, virtually no attention has been paid to listening in mainstream political science.[80] This includes the area of

[78] Green (2010), p. 213, fn. 2.

[79] Although I extend what we might understand by listening in Chapter 5.

[80] There is only one monograph on the topic of listening in politics: Susan Bickford's *The Dissonance of Democracy: Listening, Conflict, and Citizenship* (Ithaca and London: Cornell University Press, 1996). David Michael Levin has written a more philosophical book on listening, *The Listening Self: Personal Growth, Social Change and the Closure of Metaphysics* (London and New York: Routledge, 1989), as has Gemma Corradi Fiumara, *The Other Side of Language: A Philosophy of Listening* (London and New York: Routledge, 1990). The listening theme is developed strongly in both Nick Couldry's *Listening Beyond the Echoes* (Colorado: Paradigm Publishers, 2006)—on media—and John Forrester's *Planning in the Face of Power* (Berkeley, Los Angeles, and

political science where one might perhaps have expected listening studies to have bulked large—democratic theory and practice. 'Improving'
democracy has historically been seen as a matter of getting more people to speak and getting them to speak more effectively. But, as Gideon
Calder points out, '[T]he disenfranchised are not just denied a *voice*;
they are denied an *audience*.'[81] Thus, 'how one is heard—how clearly
and effectively—depends on the quality of listening... [S]o it is arrest-
ing to notice how little time is spent, in accounts of democracy, considering what it *is* to listen, whether for individuals or institutions—and
how listening might be provided for.'[82] Democracy has been defined
as responsive rule, and this implies that rulers have some idea of what
to respond *to*. Calder correctly points out that if opinions are to count
in a democracy it is 'pre-conditional... that they are listened to, and
listened out for.'[83] But sustained attention to the business of listening in
democratic theory is very rare indeed. Some have claimed, indeed, that
listening has been ignored well beyond the discipline of politics, and
while the evidence suggests that this is not strictly true—as I will show
in Chapter 2—it is worth bearing in mind the general point.[84] Gemma
Fiumara, for example, claims that, '[F]rom one extreme to the other in

London: University of California Press, 1989)—on planning. There is also a special
issue of the *Continuum* journal devoted to the topic of listening (23 (August 2009),
no. 4) but this is more focused on cultural studies, media, and journalism than on
politics. Penman and Turnbull (2012) offer a useful commentary on the *Continuum*
special issue. Lauri Siisiäinen's, *Foucault and the Politics of Hearing* (London and
New York: Routledge, 2013) is one of the small but growing set of monographs devoted
to unsettling received opinion by adopting a listening point of view. Indeed, what we
might loosely call 'post-structuralism' is a rich source of reflection on listening that
deserves separate and sustained attention.

[81] Calder (2011), p. 134. Tanja Dreher makes a similar point in respect of Muslims
in Australia: 'The dilemmas confronting Muslims in the Australian media are not simply questions of speaking—there is no shortage of articulate and savvy spokespeo-
ple and commentators—but more importantly the difficulties of being heard'; Dreher
(2008), p. 7. Carolyn Cusick refers directly the importance of an audience: 'So "having a
voice" needs to be understood as being able to participate in on-going communicative
exchanges that necessarily involve a listening audience'; Cusick (2012), p. 17.

[82] Calder (2011), p. 126.

[83] Calder (2011), p. 128.

[84] It is curious to read of the absence of attention to listening even in some branches
of linguistics. For example, in their analysis of the comprehensibility of foreign accents,
Catriona Kelly and Barbara Fraser write that, 'The act of communicating involves multiple participants working in concert, yet the majority of studies of accented speech
and intelligibility or comprehensibility concentrate solely on speech production in
an ongoing attempt to define a baseline for understandable speech. In these studies the role of the listener is largely overlooked.' 'Listening between the lines: social
assumptions around foreign accents', *Australian Review of Applied Linguistics* (2012),

the vast array of possible social interactions the stress inevitably falls on the irreplaceable value of the expressive capacity rather than on a propensity to listen.'[85] While there might be some truth in this, Fiumara is also surely exaggerating for effect. We only have to think of how tiresome it can be to be involved in a monological conversation with someone who seems incapable of listening to realize that the 'propensity to listen' can actually be rather highly prized. Likewise, the professions on which we will draw for inspiration in Chapter 2, such as education and nursing, have listening close to their heart (ideally anyway). Even so, Katherine Schultz is right in saying that, 'We typically understand words as powerful. Arguments are more frequently won through the force of words, rather than power of silence.'[86]

We might perhaps expect listening to bulk larger where the aim is not so much to win arguments as to reach understanding and accommodation (deliberative democracy, consensus-building, contract theory), but even here the cupboard is largely bare. I will discuss this in more detail later, but Jim Garrison sets out the stall when he writes that, '[L]iberal thinkers from John Stuart Mill to Jürgen Habermas seem to assume that we secure communicative and democratic rationality simply by assuring freedom of speech.'[87] To pick one of these thinkers (I will discuss Habermas in more detail in Chapter 3), John Stuart Mill has what we might call a 'doubt-based' theory of the truth, according to which we can never be sure that the opinion we are suppressing might be the right one: 'To refuse a hearing to an opinion, because they are sure it is false, is to assume that *their* certainty is the same thing as *absolute* certainty. All silencing of discussion is an assumption of infallibility.'[88]

---

p. 74, available at <http://www.nla.gov.au/openpublish/index.php/aral/article/viewFile/2359/2827> (accessed 11 April 2012).

[85] Fiumara (1990), p. 31.

[86] Katherine Schultz, 'After the blackbird whistles: listening to silence in classrooms', *Teachers College Record* 112 (2010), no. 11, p. 2839. See Sean Gray, 'Silent citizenship in democratic theory and practice: the problems and power of silence in democracy', unpublished paper delivered at the 2012 American Political Science Association Conference, New Orleans, 2012, for an analysis of silence as a form of democratic communication.

[87] Jim Garrison, 'A Deweyan theory of democratic listening', *Educational Theory* 46 (1996), no. 4, p. 3.

[88] John Stuart Mill, *Utilitarianism, On Liberty, and Considerations on Representative Government* (London: J. M. Dent & Sons Ltd, 1972), p. 79.

Although Mill has been handed down to us as a defender of freedom of speech, this quotation makes it clear that he is talking not so much about freedom of speech as the conditions for the possibility of *discussion* (as Carolyn Cusick pithily puts it: 'speaking is worth protecting, but worth protecting because we need to communicate, not because we need to make sounds'[89]). This subtle shift of emphasis from speech to discussion has the potential for bringing listening back into focus As theorists of listening never tire of pointing out, speech is only one side of a discussion, a dialogue, a debate, or a conversation, so freedom of speech, in the absence of the possibility for effective listening, is only half of the story. Theorists of listening will also refer us to remarks such as those made by Fiumara and Schultz as explanations for why we regard Mill as an advocate of freedom of speech rather than as a defender of the conditions for discussion—the hegemonic hold that speech, the word, *logos*, has over us: 'In a logocentric perspective the power of language determines a situation in which the incompetent are relegated to what is considered the desolate limbo of listening.'[90]

Indeed, it is when we think of politics in terms of discussion and debate that the importance of listening is especially marked, and given that large swathes of the post-Enlightenment Western political tradition are written in this language it is a surprise that so little political-theoretical attention has been paid to it. As John Uhr points out, social contract theory in Thomas Hobbes and John Locke is at the heart of the liberal–democratic tradition, and very few parts of Western culture are untouched by contract theory as the 'regulative ideal' according to which political practices are judged. Uhr traces the role of listening through the work of Hobbes and Locke and suggests that there are two broad modes of political listening here, corresponding roughly to the kind of listening authoritarian regimes do (top-down), on the one hand, and the kind that citizens do in holding their governments to account, on the other (bottom-up).[91] Within these modes, we can distinguish between top-down listening of the surveillance type that we associate with the East German Stasi, for example, and the 'gauging the public mood' listening that governments in liberal

---

[89] Cusick (2012), p. 97.   [90] Fiumara (1990), p. 67.

[91] John Uhr, 'Auditory democracy: separation of powers and the location of listening', in Benedetto Fontana, Cary J. Nederman, and Gary Remer (eds), *Talking Democracy: Historical Perspectives on Rhetoric and Democracy* (University Park, PA: Pennsylvania State University Press, 2004).

democratic routinely carry out. Similarly, in the bottom-up context, there is a contrast between the 'disciplinary listening' of which Hobbes speaks, the aim of which is citizen compliance, and the listening whose aim is holding the government to account. Uhr describes this auditory move from Hobbes to Locke as follows: 'The people as fearful listener to an undivided sovereign become the people as watchful listener to a government of separated powers.'[92] This 'holding to account' is just one function of listening, as we will see in Chapter 3, but it is surely an important one in the context of democracy.

Joseph Beatty is one who expresses surprise at the way listening has been ignored—Uhr apart—in the context of contract: 'among philosophers concerned about social contract theory, inasmuch as the social contract maneuver is regularly employed to justify allegiance to values that are presumably the result of some sort of interpersonal, consensual process, the failure to give serious consideration to listening is a significant one'.[93] The obvious point here is that one precondition for a meaningful agreement is that the parties to the agreement have understood each other, and this surely entails careful listening. A legitimate social contract presupposes the right and capacity of the interlocutors to speak, of course, but a contract based solely on speech—in which the parties to the contract literally only spoke without listening— would probably be meaningless and would certainly be illegitimate in political terms. Many progressive demands are, of course, couched in terms of the right to speak, but that right is never granted until and unless the claim or demand to speak is heard. In this sense, the refusal to listen is an exercise of power:

> Western modernity's stress on 'rational' self-assertion through the autonomous individual who has the right to speak and be heard, ironically enough, devalues listening and listeners. This irony is felt far more by the oppressed than the oppressors, and by those from cultural traditions that place a greater value on listening...Much of what claims to be democratic, equal, and empowering dialogue, the right to speak and be heard, is really a conduit metaphor monologue.[94]

---

[92] Uhr (2004), p. 250.

[93] Joseph Beatty, 'Good listening', *Educational Theory* 49 (1999), no. 3, p. 282.

[94] Garrison (1996), p. 4. Garrison also speaks of a 'disabling dogma in liberal thinking. The dogma says that all we need for democratic rationality is freedom of speech. This bit of Western ideology devalues those that listen and is oppressive', p. 21.

Garrison makes two important points here. First, listening (and its withholding), as we saw earlier, is an instrument of power. Listening is therefore a site of political contestation, and, while this is an uncommon thought, we need to get used to it. Second, cultures understand listening in different ways, and I will discuss the implications of this in Chapter 2.

WHY NO LISTENING?

The lack of attention paid to listening in politics contrasts vividly with that paid to speech and its cognates. Why is this so? I do not believe there is a determinate answer to this question, but one kind of answer stems from considerations of power. I have argued that listening is related to power in a number of ways, and that the withholding of listening is an expression of power. This suggests an interest-based reason for why listening features so little in analyses of political processes. The argument might run that it is in the interests of those in power to ensure that as little attention is paid to listening as possible, on the grounds that, if its importance were to be recognized, one more front for political agitation would be opened up. The main problem with this argument is that it is too conspiratorial. For it to work, two unlikely preconditions need to be in place. First, those in power would need to be aware of the political significance of listening, and, second, they would need to have come to an agreement to suppress knowledge and discussion of it. Neither of these presuppositions is plausible. And even if these two preconditions were fulfilled, this kind of interest-based reason for ignoring listening could not account for its relative neglect in the academy. When we look at the small number of people who *do* speak up for listening in the academy in the context of politics and political science, though, power and interests turn out to be important *explananda* after all. Typically, we find these calls coming from those without power and who therefore have an interest in seeking explanations for their powerlessness and looking for routes out of it. It is no coincidence, then, the only full-length political science monograph devoted to listening was written by a feminist scholar, Susan Bickford.[95]

---

[95] Bickford (1996).

We should not, though, jump to the conclusion that feminism is either a necessary or a sufficient condition for a political analysis of listening. In her analysis of the so-called 'Montréal massacre' of 1989,[96] Wendy Hui Kyong Chun advocates a 'politics of listening as a necessary complement to the politics of speaking'.[97] But she finds few resources in feminist theory with regard to listening, and the reason she gives is that, like other representatives of previously excluded groups, feminists focus exclusively on speech as the currency of political participation: '[T]o date, feminism has concentrated on consciousness-raising, on producing speech that breaks one's silence and inaugurates one as a feminist. Although important, the question of how to listen and respond to these testimonials has been largely unaddressed,[98] possibly since the question of listening in general tends to be undertheorized and/or undervalued: more often than not, we assume we know how to listen.'[99] Like most others, the feminists of whom Chun speaks abhor a silence (which, as we shall see in Chapter 2, is a precondition for proper listening): 'feminists usually listen to silence in order to break it…Rarely has the question of how to listen, or listening as a political act, been addressed.'[100] So Chun advocates, 'a politics and practice of listening as a necessary complement to a politics of testifying. I am suggesting a politics that does not valorize the act of speaking in and of itself: a politics that listens to a person's speech or silence and then grapples with the question of how to respond to it.'[101] Chun is effectively asking for a politics of listening—just the politics I am trying to sketch in this book.

Rather than think of listening as gendered, we can take a cue from Aristotle and think of it in terms of species.[102] The centrality of speech

---

[96] Wendy Hui Kyong Chun, 'Case study: the Montréal Massacre', gendercide watch, available at <http://www.gendercide.org/case_montreal.html> (accessed 29 June 2012).

[97] Wendy Hui Kyong Chun, 'Unbearable witness: towards a politics of listening', *Differences: A Journal of Feminist Cultural Studies* 11 (1999), no. 1, p. 114.

[98] i.e. the testimonials of the survivors of the massacre.

[99] Chun (1999), p. 114.

[100] Chun (1999), p. 141.

[101] Chun (1999), p. 138.

[102] In doing so, I share the post-structuralist critique of 'Aristotle's definition of humans as political…and speaking beings'—a definition in which the adjectives, when combined, determine the nature of the political being—but without necessarily endorsing the post-structuralist inversion of the 'ontological priority between subject and language'; Dhawan (2012), p. 49.

to politics is established at the dawn of political theory, in Aristotle's definition of the 'political animal'. In Book 1 of his *Politics* he writes that, 'Nature, as we say, does nothing without some purpose; and for the purpose of making man a political animal she has endowed him alone among the animals with the power of reasoned speech.' Speech is what sets 'man' apart from other animals, says Aristotle, and it enables us to do something that mere 'voice' (which is possessed by other animals) cannot do—that is, 'indicate what is useful and what is harmful, and so also what is right and what is wrong'. Aristotle concludes that, 'the real difference between man and other animals is that humans alone have perception of good and evil, right and wrong, just and unjust'.[103] Since Aristotle, speech has become a definitional feature of politics, to the point where the political being is a speaking being: '[T]o anchor politics to the negotiation of interests or the rational formation of consent presupposes the capacity of all groups involved to be recognized as speaking agents who need to be listened to at all.'[104]

So Aristotle makes speech the defining feature of the political animal, and, more or less by default, this simultaneously makes 'man' the only political animal and speech the currency of politics. This is perhaps the most taken-for-granted aspect of Western political thought and practice: that politics is carried out by human beings, for human beings.[105] Because it is so taken for granted it is rarely noticed, and its power to organize our thinking and our practices goes generally unremarked. This is relevant here because the distinction between political and non-political beings, and the use of speech as the characteristic that organizes the distinction, has the effect of valorizing speaking ahead of listening in terms of desirable capacities. It is better to be a political being than a non-political being, as this admits one to the community of justice (in Aristotle's view), and the entry ticket to this community is the capacity to speak. Franz Kafka's famous ape knew this perfectly well. After he painfully learns to drink alcohol for the first time, he reports, 'Well, I did forget to scratch my belly. But instead of that, because I couldn't do anything else, because I had to, because

---

[103] Aristotle, *The Politics* (Harmondsworth: Penguin, 1962), pp. 28–9.

[104] James Martin, 'The rhetorical citizen', *The CSD Bulletin* (London: University of Westminster, 2009). The dominance of speech in politics has left its mark in our language, where 'parliament' (*parlement*) is the name for the democratic assembly, while the 'Speaker' presides over the business of parliament.

[105] The term most commonly used to describe this valorization of the human is 'anthropocentrism'.

my senses were roaring, I cried out a short and good "Hello!" breaking out into human sounds. And with this cry I sprang into the community of human beings, and I felt its echo—"Just listen. He's talking!"— like a kiss on my entire sweat-soaked body.[106] The ape knows that of all the things he could do to persuade his captors of his human-ness, speaking is the most effective of them all.[107]

This division of the spoils between those who speak and those who do not has gone practically unnoticed, even by those who set out to disinter the unexamined assumptions in Western political thought. Few have set themselves up so self-consciously as an inquisitor of these assumptions as Jacques Rancière, especially in his book *Disagreement*.[108] It is striking, then, to find even him failing to see the elephant in the room. It is clear that Rancière's intention is to work on foundations. The first page of his book has all the trappings of a beginning. It is, after all, Chapter 1 (itself entitled 'The beginning of politics'), page one starts with the words 'Let's begin at the beginning', and Aristotle's *Politics* (itself a beginning of sorts, of course) is the main feature. It is hard to think of a page that could present itself more self-consciously as a beginning than this one. On this first page Rancière quotes the passage from the first book of Aristotle's *Politics* on the contrast between the human and non-human realms, to which we have already referred:

> Nature, as we say, does nothing without some purpose; and she has endowed man alone among the animals with the power of speech. Speech is something different from voice, which is possessed by other animals also and used by them to express pain or pleasure; for their nature does indeed enable them not only to feel pleasure and pain but to communicate these feelings to each other. Speech, on the other hand, serves to indicate what is useful and what is harmful, and so also what is just and what is unjust. For the real difference between man and other animals is that humans alone have perception of good and evil, the just and the unjust, etc. It is the sharing of a common view in these matters that makes a household and a state.[109]

---

[106] Franz Kafka, 'A report for an academy' (1917), available at <http://records.viu.ca/~johnstoi/kafka/reportforacademy.htm > (accessed 12 September 2012).

[107] It is almost as though the ape prefigures the postmodern trope that, 'speech functions as the privileged vehicle for realizing freedom'; Dhawan (2012), p. 49.

[108] Jacques Rancière, *Disagreement: Politics and Philosophy* (Minneapolis and London: University of Minnesota Press, 1999).

[109] Quoted in Rancière (1999), p. 1.

Humans speak while other animals have only voice, and humans have conceptions of right and wrong while other animals only feel pleasure and pain. These remarks are, in themselves, perhaps unexceptional and unexceptionable, but the ferocious sting in their tail is that they serve, for Rancière, as a means of defining the political sphere: humans are inside it, and other animals are not. Politics begins, then, where human and non-human nature part company. Rancière assumes with Aristotle, in other words, that political beings must be speaking beings—but nowhere is this defended or argued for. This assumption suggests there is another, unspoken, beginning to Rancière's tale, a beginning before Rancière's, a moment when it is decided that politics is for speaking beings only.

As it happens there is a preface to Rancière's *Disagreement*, a beginning before the beginning. It starts with another quotation from Aristotle: 'The question we must bear in mind is, equality or inequality in what sort of thing?'[110] But in terms of revealing unspoken species-based assumptions, this is not the new beginning we were looking for. In fact, it just compounds the felony, for surely the primordial question is not 'equality or inequality in what sort of *thing*' but 'equality or inequality of what *sort* of thing'. This latter question points us in the direction of a more fundamental question than any that Rancière asks. He proposes an enquiry into the nature of politics without enquiring of what kind of being the word 'politics' can be predicated, whereas if we think about the 'sort of thing' of which talk of equality can be predicated, we are, in effect, asking what kinds of being can be political beings, since the question of equality or inequality only arises in respect of beings admitted to the community of politics. At the very least we must surely admit that the two questions: (1) of what kind of being can 'politics' be predicated and (2) 'what is politics?' are closely related. But the former question is rarely asked in the modern idiom, and this is because Aristotle's answer, captured in the quotation above, is so firmly established as the context for our thinking.

The consequences of Rancière not asking that first question are important. One of his key distinctions is between 'politics' and 'policing'. Policing is defined as 'the organization of powers, *the distribution of places and roles*, and the systems for legitimizing

---

[110] Rancière (1999), p. vii.

this distribution'.[111] Politics is defined as 'antagonistic to policing': 'whatever breaks with the tangible configuration whereby parties and parts or lack of them are defined by a presupposition that, by definition, has no place in that configuration—that of the part of those who have no part'.[112] Thus policing is about the distribution of roles, and politics is about questioning the criteria that determine that distribution. In his own terms, then, we must regard Rancière's book as an exercise in policing rather than politics. By distinguishing between 'speech' and 'voice' and valorizing the former over the latter he is, precisely, 'distributing places and roles'—and is therefore 'policing'. Doing 'politics', on the other hand (and again in Rancière's own terms) would have involved questioning the 'presupposition that, by definition, has no place in that configuration—that of the part of those who have no part'—that is, the presupposition that the condition for belonging to the circle of 'equal beings' is the capacity to speak.

Rancière denies himself the possibility of exploiting the full richness of his conception of politics by beginning where he does. 'Before the logos that deals with the useful and harmful,' he writes, 'there is the logos that orders and bestows the right to order.'[113] But before *that* there is the decision (rarely explicitly argued for, and certainly not by Rancière) that politics—the 'disruption of the natural pecking order'[114]—only occurs among speaking beings: those in possession of the logos. Thus, 'The brilliant deduction of the political animal's ends from the properties of the logical animal' certainly does 'patch over a tear',[115] but not the one Rancière identifies. In truth, the patch hides the move through which the *political* animal becomes identical with the *logical* animal (i.e. the animal in possession of the logos:[116] the human animal). Once this identity is created, we are no longer in the presence of a 'brilliant deduction' but of a self-fulfilling prophecy. In sum, we might argue that the overwhelming attention paid to speech rather than listening in politics is a direct result of defining the political being in terms of the capacity to speak.

---

[111] Rancière (1999), p. 28; emphasis added.   [112] Rancière (1999), pp. 29–30.
[113] Rancière (1999), p. 16.   [114] Rancière (1999), p. 18.
[115] Rancière (1999), p. 21.   [116] Derived from λέγω, 'I say'.

CONCLUSION

In this chapter I have described this enquiry into listening as part of a developing trend of attention to 'sensory' democracy. Most contributions to this trend take a rather defensive approach to the question of whether democracy can be improved, believing that, under current conditions, citizens are reduced to spectators whose positive input to the political process is confined to a form of surveillance whose success is measured by the degree to which politicians' control of their publicity is undermined. In contrast, I argue that listening can be put to positive use as a solvent of power, and in this sense I aim to make a contribution to normative debates regarding democratic theory and practice. Finally, I have offered what we might call a 'species-based' reason why listening as concept and practice has been so studiously ignored by political theorists. Aristotle's claim that 'man' is a political animal, and that what makes him political is his capacity for speech has had an enduring influence on how we conceive the currency of political intercourse. Speech has been dominant, and this has led to the neglect of listening as an object of enquiry. Once we regard speaking and listening as equally important we are led to think of politics and democracy as ideally *dialogical*. Just what this might mean, though, is a question for the rest of the book, and first we must take a step back and think harder about listening itself. Given the lack of attention paid to it in political theory, we need to look elsewhere for a discussion of listening before bringing it into contact with specifically political intentions and concerns.

2

Learning about Listening

In Chapter 1 we saw that very little attention has been paid to listening by political scientists, either empirically or theoretically. This means that if we are to construct a notion of political listening we will have to draw on inspiration and sources outside the discipline of politics.[1] The principal sources for reflections on listening in what follows are education,[2] medicine (including psychotherapy and counselling),[3] and media and communication,[4] with some references to business and consumer relations. Although these turn out to be the main sites of reflection, there are others—as pretty much any profession or practice which involves person-to-person interaction has its analysis of listening. Of course, politics is just such a profession, yet, as we saw in Chapter 1, it lacks its aural experts—circumstantial proof of the hold that speaking rather than listening has on the political imaginary.

---

[1] Jeffrey Green makes a similar point about the lack of attention paid to the gaze: 'This notion of the gaze as an empowered form of looking is almost entirely unfamiliar to democratic theory in its current state, but it is an important aspect of disciplines outside the study of politics, including theology, psychology, philosophy, art and cultural studies'; *The Eyes of the People: Democracy in an Age of Spectatorship* (Oxford and New York: Oxford University Press, 2010), p. 9.

[2] 'Educational interest in traditional philosophies of listening is growing,' writes Megan Laverty. See her, 'Can you hear me now? Jean-Jacques Rousseau on listening education', *Educational Theory* 61 (2011), no. 2, p. 155. The whole of this issue of *Educational Theory* is devoted to listening.

[3] See, for example, Lennart Fredriksson, 'Modes of relating in a caring conversation: a research synthesis on presence, touch and listening', *Journal of Advanced Nursing* 30 (1999), no. 5, pp. 1167–76; Steven Graybar and Leah Leonard, 'In defense of listening', *American Journal of Psychotherapy* 59 (2005), no. 1, pp. 1–18.

[4] *Continuum Journal of Media and Cultural Studies* 23 (2009), no. 4, for example.

GOOD LISTENING, BAD LISTENING

Indeed, the range of contexts in which listening is regarded as important and relevant brings the paucity of political thinking about it into sharp relief.[5] One issue that emerges from these various analyses is that, while there is some agreement about what good listening looks like in general, each practice and profession is likely to adapt these insights to its own needs and necessities, and we can surmise that this will be as true of politics as it is of any other practice.[6] Suzanne Rice and Nicholas Burbules draw our attention to the importance of context: 'Listening well to a client in a counselling session is quite different from listening well in a casual conversation with a co-worker . . . Listening well to a political debate is dissimilar from listening to a poetry reading.'[7] In a counselling session the therapist will be expected to give her patient undivided attention, and the patient would rightfully feel aggrieved if s/he didn't get it. It is *part of what a counsellor is* to listen in this complete way. The casual conversation with a co-worker is different: we might feel annoyed if the attention of our interlocutor wanders but we could hardly demand of them the same level of attention we would demand of our therapist. What kind of listening should we expect from the politician? Might this depend on what the politician is doing? After all, there is a considerable difference between attending to a constituent and participating in a debate in the legislature. And both these are different from listening to 'the people' at election time. These remarks focus on *roles*, and this is the level at which general conclusions about good listening emerge from the literature—the level that lies behind particular roles. Sheila Shipley (from a nursing background) offers an account that would

---

[5] Joseph Beatty, 'Good listening', *Educational Theory* 49 (1999), no. 3, p. 290.

[6] David Hansen's question regarding the education context is one we need to ask in other situations, including politics: 'what are the modes of listening appropriate for teachers?' in 'Horizons of listening', in Kal Alston (ed.), *Philosophy of Education* (Urbana, IL: Philosophy of Education Society, 2003), p. 23.

[7] Suzanne Rice and Nicholas Burbules, 'Listening: a virtue account', *Teachers College Record* 112 (2010), no. 11, p. 2737. Sophie Haroutunian-Gordon and Megan Laverty comment that, '"good listening" occurs in a wide range of contexts. Would the teacher who is a good listener behave the same way as the doctor who is a good listener?'; 'Listening: an exploration of philosophical traditions', *Educational Theory* 61 (2011), no. 2, p. 121. The question for us is whether political listening is a particular kind of listening too.

be endorsed by many of those who have reflected on good listening in different contexts:

> Listening is a planned and deliberate act in which the listener is fully present and actively engages the client in a nonjudgmental and accepting manner. The purpose of listening is to fully understand and appreciate the speaker's perceptions, experiences and messages. The act of listening involves the use of empathy to understand the patient's lived experience. The listener attends to verbal and nonverbal communication, and constantly strives to understand the spoken message as well as perceive the underlying meanings and tones of the encounter. The listener utilises reflection and feedback to clarify information and communicate that the message has been heard and understood.[8]

Shipley refers here to three features of what is generally regarded as good listening in face-to-face contexts. First, she refers to listening as an *activity*. There is a constant refrain through the literature that, while listening might be thought of as passive, good listening entails active engagement with the speaker. Second, this engagement involves checking that the listener has understood the speaker as well as possible through asking questions ('reflection and feedback') designed to bring the listener's understanding into line with the speaker's intentions.[9] Third, Shipley refers to listening as involving attention to verbal and non-verbal communication, or what is commonly known as body language. On this reading, listening is a matter of responding to visual as well as aural stimuli,[10]

---

[8] Sheila Shipley, 'Listening: a concept analysis', *Nursing Forum: An Independent Voice for Nursing* 45 (2010), no. 2, p. 133.

[9] When we ask a question we are making a commitment to listen to the answer, and this in itself can be empowering to our interlocutor. In her study of the after-effects of the 1971 war of Bangladesh on both victims and perpetrators, Yasmin Saikia recounts the words of one victim of rape, violence, and humiliation: 'In the last thirty years nobody asked me how I was doing and what I want from my life', while another laments that 'women are like cattle, we go wherever our men take us…No one asks us what we want…we want to have a human life too'; Yasmin Saikia, 'Insaniyat for peace: survivors' narrative of the 1971 war of Bangladesh', *Journal of Genocide Research* 13 (2011), no. 4, p. 487. It is hard to read these testimonies in any way other than as a plea to be listened to.

[10] 'The good listener…tracks the literal meaning of the other's statements but also attends to the bodily signs, tones, and mood changes; she keeps up an ongoing internal dialogue, interrogating her own tentative constructions'; Beatty (1999), p. 285. See also Andrew Wolvin and Carolyn Gwynn Oakley, *Listening* (5th edn, Madison, WI: Brown & Benchmark Publishers, 1996), p. 96, and Leonard Waks, 'John Dewey on listening and friendship in school and society', *Educational Theory* 61 (2011), no. 2, p. 192. In connection with Martin Buber, Mordechai Gordon comments that, 'Buber made it quite plain that the dialogical relation between persons is by no means limited to speech. In fact, a glance, a look, or a gaze that meets the eye of another person is sometimes enough for dialogue to emerge'; 'Listening as embracing the other: Martin Buber's philosophy of dialogue', *Educational Theory* 61 (2011), no. 2, p. 214.

and this raises one of the key issues with which we will have to deal in this book: the question of scale. For while two of the characteristics of good listening to which Shipley refers are arguably reproducible in a scaled-up context—the active element of listening and the 'reflection and feedback' technique—attention to visual as well as aural stimuli seems impossible to enact in anything other than a face-to-face context.[11]

Of course, some political encounters do involve face-to-face contact: the conversation between a UK member of parliament and her or his constituent in a Friday surgery is a case in point. Another political context in which face-to-face encounters are the norm is in micro-political encounters, such as those found in deliberative democracy, citizens' juries, and so on. It is also true that perhaps the most archetypal of democratic sites—parliamentary chambers—are characterized by (often literal) face-to-face relationships. And, indeed, in these contexts, MPs, deliberative democrats, jurors, and the like could all learn plenty about good listening from Shipley: listening actively and attentively, confirming understanding through asking questions, and attending to body language. Mei Seung Lam outlines some of the non-aural gestures that contribute to promoting a good listening relationship: 'Behaviors such as adopting open postures, facing the parent squarely, leaning slightly forward, interested facial expressions, good eye contact, and the use of silence all help to show that they are paying full attention to parents' issues.'[12] Even this sort of apparently good general advice does not work in all situations, though. How often have we sat listening to a speech or a talk with our eyes closed, the better to concentrate? From the point of view of the speaker this looks like bad manners—I might even look as though I'm asleep. So it is possible to misinterpret the signs of good listening, and there appears to be no definitive suite of positive behaviours on which one can draw. Having said that, Lam's list is a reasonable starting point and it is not impossible to imagine these techniques being employed in the political situations described already, though it would certainly be unusual. We will pay more attention to them in Chapter 6 when we discuss possible institutional innovations for taking listening more seriously in political contexts.

---

[11] Nicholas Burbules and Suzanne Rice, 'On pretending to listen', *Teachers College Record* 112 (2010), no. 11, p. 2882.

[12] Mei Seung Lam, 'The gentle art of listening: skills for developing family–administrator relationships in early childhood', *Early Childhood Education Journal* 47 (2000), no. 4, p. 271.

Good listening of the sort described by Shipley and Lam is often contrasted with inattentive listening, or what Andrew Wolvin and Carolyn Oakley call 'interruptive' listening, where, instead of listening attentively, 'many of us anticipate what the person will say and just eagerly await our turn to chime in with our own tale'.[13] As Jacqueline Aileen Bussie puts it: 'Instead of "listening" to another person express a viewpoint with which we vehemently disagree, many of us are "re-loading" our verbal gun with ammunition so we can fire off our killer rebuttal. The problem with reloading, of course, is that while we are doing it, we don't genuinely hear what the other person has said'.[14] William Stringfellow, American social activist and Christian, fierce critic of his country's social, economic, and military policy, sums this up neatly: 'Listening is a rare happening among human beings. You cannot listen to the word another is speaking if you are preoccupied with your appearance or impressing the other, or if you are trying to decide what you are going to say when the other stops talking, or if you are debating about whether the word being spoken is true or relevant or agreeable. Such matters may have their place, but only after listening to the word as the word is being uttered'.[15]

Inattentive and interruptive listening are familiar to us from everyday conversation: we are all acquainted with the experience of a dawning awareness that the person with whom we are talking is not listening to us. The awareness can be because of inappropriate responses to what we are saying, or that vacant look in the eyes which shows that our interlocutor is 'somewhere else'. These interpersonal examples have their analogues in the political world too: governments are often accused of not listening to citizens, and the inappropriate response or the vacant look are useful metaphors for describing the ways in which such governments are regarded as carrying on the political conversation. The majority of parliamentary encounters might be regarded as exercises in non-listening too. Martin Buber argued that, 'in many conversations the participants do not really listen to each other but rather talk past one another', a phenomenon Buber called

---

[13] Wolvin and Oakley (1996), p. 389.

[14] Jacqueline Aileen Bussie, 'Reconciled diversity: reflections on our calling to embrace our religious neighbours', *Intersections* 33 (2011), p. 31.

[15] William Stringfellow, 'Protestantism's rejection of the Bible', in Bill Wylie Kellermann (ed.), *A Keeper of the Word: Selected Writings of William Stringfellow* (Michigan: Wm. B. Eerdmans Publishing Co., 1994), p. 169.

'speechifying',[16] This neatly captures the way many casual onlookers will regard debates in legislative chambers around the world where, rather than 'paying close attention to the other's words and meaning', legislators are more often 'thinking about and planning [their] own response while the other is still speaking'.[17]

Indeed, some widely accepted aspects of political practice seem to militate in favour of interruptive listening. Collective responsibility and party discipline, for example, both provide scripts from which politicians can and do speak, and they are both regarded as virtuous in their own way. They hide disagreement in the name of strong government, but this advantage is bought at the cost of closing down dissent and debate both within the government and/or the party, and between the government/party and the Opposition. Closing ranks in this way has the effect of creating 'bloc thinking', the greatest threat to which is the possibility of thinking differently. From this point of view 'interruptive listening' is a crucial tool for the survival of the bloc. We might argue that ideologies themselves—the ideas-based building blocks of political conversation as we usually understand it—encourage interruptive listening. Ideologies, quite precisely, constitute a 'tale' (to use Wolvin and Oakley's term) through which people interpret the political world, suggest changes to it, and mark out some plan for transition from the present state to the desired state. Evidently, ideologies are not wholly self-contained, and they do develop through engagement with other ideologies. But their principal purpose is to provide an internally consistent template for interpretation and action rather than a springboard for the kind of conversation implied by Sheila Shipley's remarks, earlier in this chapter.

It is worth referring here to the heterodox (and minority) view that *pretending* to listen is a legitimate part of normal conversation, not least because it points to an important difference between political listening and other forms. Nicholas Burbules and Suzanne Rice suggest that, 'pretending to listen is a perfectly useful, and sometimes an indispensable, feature of the pragmatics of ordinary communication.'[18] They argue that this is because even in professions where listening is prized and important (teaching, therapy, the judicial system), one cannot 'constantly and at every moment' be listening in the attentive

---

[16] Gordon (2011), p. 216.   [17] Gordon (2011), p. 217.
[18] Burbules and Rice (2010), p. 2875.

way outlined by Shipley.[19] They even suggest that pretending to listen can be a feature of good listening—as in nodding one's head at appropriate moments in a seminar, even when one is not actually listening.[20] The Japanese writer Haruki Murakami offers a convincing example of this process at work in his novel *1Q84*:

> 'I'll need to know more about your activities,' Ushikawa said. The lawyer explained how they had started the organization. Ushikawa found this history boring, but he listened carefully, his expression one of devoted interest. He made all the appropriate noises, nodded in all the right places, and kept his expression docile and open. As he did, the lawyer warmed up to him. Ushikawa was a highly trained listener, adopting such a sincere and receptive manner that he almost always succeeded in putting the other person at ease.[21]

Of course, Ushikawa is a 'highly trained listener' in the sense that he knows how to pretend to listen, rather than that—here at least—he is actually listening. Up to a point the idea that pretending to listen is an unavoidable fact of communicative life is plausible, but whether it is a good thing—or whether it might even amount to good listening— is another. In the political context, the default view of many citizens is that governments pretend to listen rather than actually listen, and when this is coupled with a perceived lack of responsiveness, cynicism ensues. It would surely be unwise, then, to advise politicians to pretend to listen, as this produces what Megan Laverty refers to as a 'hermeneutics of suspicion',[22] in which citizens are so convinced that politicians don't listen that they give up trying to engage with the political process.

LISTENING AND POWER

As well as throwing into relief the contrast between what is generally regarded as good listening and some of politics' standard practices, 'interruptive listening' raises a further dimension of the question of whether good listening can be universally defined: that is, the degree to

---

[19]　Burbules and Rice (2010), p. 2881.
[20]　Burbules and Rice (2010), p. 2880.
[21]　Haruki Murakami, *1Q84 (Book Three)* (London: Vintage, 2012) p. 58.
[22]　Laverty (2011), pp. 157–8.

which definitions of good listening are bound up with cultural power. In common with communicative practices more generally there are cultural factors to take into account when considering listening. While the interruptive listening we have just described might well be regarded as bad listening in some cultures, in others it is seen as good manners. Far from being bad practice, 'interrupting' one's interlocutor in Spanish in the form, for example, of offering ways of finishing her/his sentence is regarded as a sure sign that you are listening very carefully to what is being said.[23] At the other end of the socio-linguistic scale we find the northern Scandinavians, for whom good conversational manners entails waiting a while at the end of the interlocutor's sentence, before continuing the conversation secure in the knowledge that the last intervention is indeed complete. These cultural differences can cause misunderstanding and even offence: Scandinavians are likely to regard Spanish conversational *mores* as rude and inconsiderate while the Spanish are simply following their own rules of polite conversation. Likewise, the Spanish find the gaps in Scandinavian conversation excruciating—and may regard the Scandinavian refusal to interrupt (helpfully) as rather bad manners. Those in the middle of this socio-linguistic spectrum are likely to feel uncomfortable in both directions: irritated at not being allowed to finish a sentence by the Spanish, and feeling mild discomfort at what can feel like disjointed conversations with the Scandinavians.

All this should make us wary of any claims that good listening can be universally described, but it is also clear that there is something approaching a dominant view of what good listening consists of—the view articulated by Shipley. Even if this were a majority view it might not necessarily be the right view, but the rules of the game are more obviously dictated by the middle position than by either of the other two. So what 'good listening' consists of is itself an exercise of power, exerted through cultural dominance. This is one way in which listening is bound up with power, and we see shortly that there are two further ways: listening as an exercise of power and as a solvent of power.

---

[23] '[I]n listening relations, we sometimes will finish a sentence that the other has started, as a sign that we are in tune with what he or she is trying to say...and sometimes we are *helping* others to say something they want to say but are struggling to articulate'; Burbules and Rice (2010), p. 2876. Burbules and Rice are right that this can happen, but they fail to locate this practice in any cultural context. Once we do, we see that what might appear to be a helpful practice in some contexts (as Burbules and Rice imply) can be regarded as a faux pas in others.

These remarks suggest that timeless, placeless rules for good listening are impossible to establish. Nicholas Burbules and Suzanne Rice paint a deliberately impossibilist picture of the ideal listener: 'A romanticised view of listening suggests some kind of totally encompassing focus and understanding: the ideal listener is hearing everything, understanding everything, blessed with profound insight and infinite patience on every occasion. Although some people are certainly better listeners than others, this supposedly ideal listener does not exist.'[24] In the latter part of this quotation, though, there is an important concession: even though ideal listening is impossible, there can still be such a thing as better or worse listening. So we can agree with Suzanne Rice that there is no possibility of 'disinterested, neutral perception',[25] yet still suggest that listening can be improved.

Any such improvement will have to take into account a further feature of language and communication that could constitute a barrier to good listening: the distinction between what Basil Bernstein, through Nicholas Burbules, refers to as 'elaborated' and 'restricted' linguistic codes. As Burbules puts it:

> there are, between different linguistic communities, disparities of vocabulary and syntactic or semantic complexity and flexibility that have the effect of making it difficult if not impossible to express certain kinds of ideas within them. These "restricted codes" constitute a particularly insidious form of silence, since it is not a matter of not being able (or willing, or comfortable) to speak, but of being able to speak only within limits that are largely invisible.[26]

This invisibility has both a linguistic and a political component. Burbules is here referring to the former, and it is important to see that there can be surfeits as well as deficits of language capacity (the Sami peoples are supposed to have 300 words for snow and ice, for example). These surfeits and deficits might indeed make transparent communication especially difficult: total transparency would seem to require a universal language used in universally identical conditions. Yet we do not need access to all 300 words for snow and ice to understand a Sami when she tells us that her nomadic way of life is endangered by the rising temperatures associated with climate change. The discipline

---

[24] Burbules and Rice (2010), p. 2875.

[25] Suzanne Rice, 'Moral perception, situatedness and learning to listen', *Learning Inquiry* 1 (2007), p. 109.

[26] Nicholas Burbules, *Dialogue in Teaching: Theory and Practice* (New York and London: Teachers College, Columbia University, 1993), p. 157.

of linguistic anthropology is devoted precisely to decoding the way in which language is culturally mediated,[27] so while what Burbules calls semantic complexity can make communication imperfect, it does not make it impossible. In this case, indeed, the challenge of dealing with it could amount to a call for very careful listening, thus bringing us full circle.

As I say, the 'invisibility' of which Burbules speaks has a socio-political component too. Suzanne Rice comments that characteristics such as, 'gender, class, and race . . . will bear on our perceptions, including our perceptions of others' voices—indeed, even our ability to hear those voices'.[28] Earlier we saw that defining good listening can involve an expression of cultural power, and here we see that power can skew what is heard—what is 'hearable'—in the first place. In this case it is not only the possibility of misunderstanding what is said that we have to contend with, or of not hearing because of linguistic deficits or surfeits, but the way in which political and cultural power determines (in part) what it is legitimate to say, and how to say it. This, in turn, influences what is likely to be heard. So, however good our translations are, or however aware we are of the possibility that we might not 'hear' another's speech because we lack the concepts they use, the possibility remains that our capacity to listen will be affected by the contours of cultural and political power and how they shape what we are attuned to hear. As Jim Garrison says of quotidian communication, 'Those that have the power are most likely to create the cultural norms of correct conversation',[29] and this applies to political conversation too—that is, when we are talking about what is right and wrong, just and unjust, good and bad (to paraphrase Aristotle). It is not enough to say that these cultural norms turn only on what is *said* or *spoken*, for the norms can only become norms through the filtering process that is *listening*. The social and political world is filled with a babble of voices but only some of them are the currency of political and social life. Most of them

[27] Alessandro Duranti (ed.), *Linguistic Anthropology: A Reader* (2nd edn, Malden, MA, Oxford, and Chichester: Wiley Blackwell, 2009): 'If we want to understand the role of languages in people's lives, we must go beyond the study of their grammar and venture into the world of social action'; Duranti (2009), p. 1.

[28] Rice (2007), pp. 109–10. Stanton Wortham argues that political listening precisely 'involves attention to the social identities inevitably communicated through speech', in 'Listening for identity beyond the speech event', *Teachers College Record* 112 (2010), no. 11, p. 2851.

[29] Jim Garrison, 'A Deweyan theory of democratic listening', *Educational Theory* 46 (1996), no. 4, p. 3.

are filtered out by the cultural power exercised by the ear rather than the tongue. In this sense it is listening, not speaking, that creates the norms: 'a refusal to listen might be seen as a manifestation of privilege and power—it is not simply absence or lack or indifference but rather an active exercise of the privilege not to hear'.[30]

To make better sense of this apparently counter-intuitive conclusion we need to rid ourselves of the idea that listening can only ever be passive while speaking can only ever be active, as we pointed out in Chapter 1. This interpretation of the relationship between the ear and tongue is very common, yet it can blind us to the active significance of listening and the way in which it can materially affect the terms of political trade. This is where we can see listening acting as a solvent of power. Following his comment on how the powerful create the cultural norms of correct conversation, Garrison writes that, '[I]n confrontational contexts often only the oppressed are forced to listen.'[31] While there is undoubtedly truth in this we learn more from the much less common alternative situation, when (for example) perpetrators of political violence are forced to listen to their victims' testimony. This is a striking case of a case in which the polarities of political power are reversed. In mainstream terms the sign of this reversal—what makes us see that a reversal has taken place—is that the victims are speaking, safely and securely. In reality they have always been speaking; what has changed is that they are now being listened to. It is worth recalling here Jenny Pearce's finding (mentioned in Chapter 1) that the social activists she talked to defined power as 'people listening to you'.[32] In this case, the currency of political power is not speech but listening: it is aural not oral. Listening is, at one and the same time, an expression of power and a means of redistributing it.

The difficulty here lies in *obliging* the powerful to listen. If Tanja Dreher is right to say that, 'attention to listening shifts the focus and responsibility for change from marginalized voices and on to the conventions, institutions and privileges which shape who and what can be heard',[33] then the political problem lies in persuading those who take advantage of these privileges to give them up. Dreher argues that, in the media context, 'the ability to speak... is surely shaped by the

[30] Tanja Dreher, 'Speaking up or being heard? Community media interventions and the politics of listening', *Media, Culture and Society* 32 (2010), no. 1, p. 100.

[31] Garrison (1996), p. 3.

[32] Jenny Pearce, 'Power and the activist', *Development* 55 (2012), no. 2, p. 199.

[33] Dreher (2010), p. 85.

perceived interests of the audience and what media producers assume the audience will listen to'.[34] But how are the tables to be turned on the producers—the power-holders—so that alternative voices are heard? The passive voice used in the phrase 'being granted an audience'[35] neatly expresses the direction of travel of power, *from* those with the power to grant or withhold a hearing *to* those without it. It is an important step to recognize that the focus on listening, 'poses the question of change in terms of learning new ways for the centre to hear rather than simply requiring the marginalized to speak up'[36], but it is only a first step. Two further steps are required: first, to offer a normative account of why those at the 'centre' *should* listen to the periphery, and, second, to map out ways in which these normative claims can be made good in practice.

Susan Vice grapples with these questions in the incendiary context of her condition as a 'post-apartheid' white South African. Her answer to the first question rests on a notion of what it is to be 'a good person and live well under...morally dubious conditions'.[37] The 'morally dubious conditions' of which she speaks are, of course, relatively extreme, and it would be wrong to claim that the systemic inequality of the apartheid regime is present in all societies. What drives her argument, though, is a commitment to equality, and, in the context of democracy especially, there is surely a case for arguing that it is incumbent on those with power to listen well and regularly to those without it. Vice's answer to the second question of the kind of commitment that this might entail for the powerful points us in the direction of the next section of this chapter, 'Listening, difference—and silence'. She argues (again from the South African context), that, 'recognizing their damaging presence, whites would try, in a significantly different way to the workings of whiteliness, to make themselves *invisible and unheard*'.[38] This striking strategy of silence has come in for considerable criticism,[39] but it does raise the question of the connection between listening, power, and the space where listening can take place.

---

[34] Dreher (2010), p. 99.   [35] Dreher (2010), p. 99.

[36] Dreher (2010), p. 99.

[37] Susan Vice, 'How do I live in this strange place?' *Journal of Social Philosophy* 41 (2010), no. 3, p. 326.

[38] Vice (2010), p. 335 (emphasis added).

[39] See, for example, Kevin Whitehead and Brett Bowman, 'The professional consequences of political silence', *Journal of Social Philosophy* 43 (2012), no. 4, pp. 426–35.

LISTENING, DIFFERENCE—AND SILENCE

One key concept in both the normative and practical contexts is difference—differences in language, in culture, in political power. What is
listening's relationship to difference? One of the potential strengths of
good listening would seem to be its capacity to heighten our sensitiv-
ity to difference. In more political terms, listening can help to lay bare
disagreement: attentive listening to the other makes us more aware
of conflict and contestation where it exists. This is not to say that listening on its own can help us to overcome disagreement nor that it
is always desirable to do so. (Indeed, I will argue in Chapter 4 that
one aim of good listening is to *produce* disagreement.) Sharon Todd
writes that, 'Listening...does not have as its aim understanding difference ("getting to know the other")...Instead, listening always already
occurs because of the presence of difference, and it lies prior to any
understanding that we can make of the Other's speech...listening is
implicated in the very revelation of difference that speech engenders.'[40]
Todd's point is that without difference, listening would not need to
exist, as every moment of listening would simply be a reconfirmation
of what we already know. In the political context, though, difference
is ever present and unlikely to be effaced or erased. And here, despite
what Todd says, the point seems precisely to 'get to know the other'
with a view to generating greater understanding.

We tend to think of extending the capacity to speak as the best way
to allow differences to emerge and be expressed. Less often do we take
account of the fact that, for speech to be heard, it must be accompanied by its opposite: silence. In democracy's normal terms of trade this
seems counter-intuitive, for we usually think of democracy as being
at its best when the public sphere is filled with the sound of voices.
Yet all too often those voices will be those of the powerful engaged
in an active *silencing* rather than enacting a silence in order to hear
new voices (a 'colour-blind discourse' can simultaneously be very
noisy *and* unrespecting of difference[41]). Carolyn Cusick refers to four
modes of silencing: intentional (active prevention of speaking), inci-
dental (content of speech is not regarded as meaningful or requiring

---

[40] Sharon Todd, *Learning from the Other: Levinas, Psychoanalysis, and Ethical
Possibilities in Education* (New York: SUNY Press, 2003), p. 135.

[41] Katharine Schultz, *Listening: A Framework for Teaching Across Difference*
(New York and London: Columbia University Press, 2003), p. 113.

a response), indirect (speaking is misheard or misunderstood), and selective (speaker adjusts what is said to what is acceptable and therefore likely to be heard).[42] All of these are relevant for the notion of political silencing and all of them are obstacles to effective dialogue. But we can take active control of silence too, to the point where it can act as a strategy of resistance.[43] Drawing on the experience of students in the classroom and in school more generally, Nicholas Burbules writes that:

> Silence can...be a form of protest, wilfully withdrawing from a discussion that has become irrelevant or offensive. Sometimes silence is actually a sign of thoughtful listening where such listening and reflecting are forms of active participation that can help sustain an ongoing dialogue...In still other cases, silence on the part of some persons might be an active choice, because speaking out may simply be too risky for them. [44]

Vincent Jungkunz tells the story of a female student who—to the increasing consternation of her teachers and classmates—practised silence for a day at university in protest at the harassment of her lesbian, gay, bisexual, and transgender (LGBT) classmates. He goes on to develop the notion of 'insubordinate silences' of empowerment, protest, resistance, and refusal.[45] What is common to these silences is that, for all their disruptive effect, they amount to a refusal to communicate. In this light there is no difference between

---

[42] Carolyn Cusick, 'Speaking, Listening and Communicative Justice: Educating Epistemic Trust and Responsibility' (PhD thesis, Vanderbilt University, 2012), pp. 68–9. See also Sean Gray, 'Silent citizenship in democratic theory and practice: the problems and power of silence in democracy', unpublished paper delivered at the 2012 American Political Science Association Conference, New Orleans, 2012, for an extended analysis of the role of silence in democratic theory and practice. For an account of the role of silence in pornography debates see Cusick (2012), pp. 63ff. As Charlotte Brontë wrote in her novel *Villette*, 'Silence is of different kinds, and breathes different meanings'; available at <http://www.literature.org/authors/bronte-charlotte/villette/chapter-29.html> (accessed 21 August 2012).

[43] Nikita Dhawan, 'Hegemonic listening and subversive silences: ethical–political imperatives', *Critical Studies* 36 (2012), p. 58. Dhawan discusses Friday's refusal to speak in Daniel Defoe's *Robinson Crusoe* in this light.

[44] Burbules (1993), p. 156; see also Katherine Schultz, 'After the blackbird whistles: listening to silence in classrooms', *Teachers College Record* 112 (2010), no. 11, pp. 2834 and 2837. This suggests that Arundhati Roy jumps too quickly to the conclusion that 'silence suggests shame'; Suzanna Arundhati Roy, *Listening to Grasshoppers: Field Notes on Democracy* (London: Penguin, 2009), p. 136.

[45] Victor Jungkunz, 'The promise of democratic silences', *New Political Science* 34 (2012), no. 2, pp. 127–50.

the LGBT activist and the refusal (also recounted by Jungkunz) of Condoleezza Rice and Donald Rumsfeld to participate in a film documenting the early post-invasion days in Iraq.[46] Of course, the silence of the relatively weak and the silence of the strong have different meanings, and Jungkunz is right to say that the latter cannot be 'insubordinately' silent. But, as I shall suggest in the next chapter, in general silence should be a preparation for communication, not a refusal of it.

Silence is potentially politically dangerous for those with power as it amounts to an empty space waiting to be filled by the unpredictable. Jeffrey Green makes a similar point in connection with his ocular approach to democracy. As we saw in Chapter 1, his paradigm of empowerment from an ocular point of view is 'candour', and he argues that, '[L]eaders are candid to the extent their public appearances are neither rehearsed, preplanned, nor managed from above, but rather contain all the risk and uncertainty of spontaneous public events.'[47] In a similar way, silence is uncontrolled and unnerving, and this is perhaps why the powerful abhor the vacuum of political silence and fill it with the noise of decision-making. Noise is typically accompanied by speed in today's frantic polities, and this is another reason why silence is a challenge to business as usual. It is likely to be difficult to enact silence as it has the tendency to slow down the political process, and in this sense speed is the friend of the powerful and an enemy of the powerless—or at least of those whose voices are typically not heard. In this context Schultz talks of the overweening imperative to reach agreements too quickly, with the effect of 'masking dissenting opinions',[48] and she claims that it is usually dominant groups which do this. Schultz herself argues for a type of silence with inclusionary intentions: '[L]istening for silence implies listening for words that are not spoken and for the missing voices of those who are silent.'[49] Silence, then, can be the space where power is put into question but may be a space in which power is reaffirmed. In the context of democracy,

---

[46] Jungkunz (2012), p. 129.
[47] Green (2010), pp. 13–14. Green somewhat undermines his argument by referring to Prime Minister's Questions (PMQs) in the UK House of Commons as an example of candour in action. In fact this is a stage-managed encounter which is controlled to the utmost. Certainly, from the point of view of listening, PMQs are an example of very bad practice rather than good.
[48] Schultz (2003), p. 131.   [49] Schultz (2003), p. 113.

writes Gemma Fiumara, '[T]he highest function of silence is revealed in the creation of a coexistential space which permits dialogue to come along.'[50]

We might suggest that the quieter the unheard voices, the more silent this coexistential space needs to be, and the more attuned the listener needs to be to the possibility of hearing a political voice. This raises the question of what a political voice is—what *counts* as a political voice. This question will be addressed later in the book (especially in Chapter 5), but it is worth noting here that foregrounding 'silence' and 'listening' rather than speech or voice opens us up to a range of new, potentially political, signals. One context in which this issue is especially acute is that of the sounds and signals emanating from the non-human natural world. As Suzanne Rice notes, 'it is important to note that where people live very close to nature, hearing and accurately interpreting its rumblings and silences is no doubt highly valued.'[51] Can we call these 'rumblings' and 'silences' political? And if we can, why should we restrict the value attached to good listening to those who live 'very close to nature'? Put differently, as ecological problems of all sorts press upon us with ever greater weight, perhaps we are *all* close to nature nowadays. This certainly seems to be the import of Gemma Fiumara's assertion that climate change, depletion of the ozone layer, and acid rain,[52] 'all send news coming across from nature...we hear *nothing* until the damage inflicted by our deaf logic...concerns the planet we inhabit. There must be some problem of listening if we only hear from earth when it is so seriously endangered that we cannot help paying heed.'[53] There is certainly a stark contrast between those who think that non-human nature is dumb and those who think that it speaks, just as long as we are attuned to listen to it.[54] We shall have more to say on this in Chapter 5. Suffice to say at present that a focus on spaces of silence and on listening opens up the

---

[50] Gemma Corradi Fiumara, *The Other Side of Language: A Philosophy of Listening* (London and New York: Routledge, 1990), p. 99.

[51] Suzanne Rice, 'Toward an Aristotelian conception of good listening', *Educational Theory* 61 (2011), no. 2, p. 150.

[52] These were the key ecological problems at the time Fiumara was writing (1993). Climate change is clearly still with us as a political issue, though acid rain and ozone layer depletion are less salient now than they were in the nineties.

[53] Fiumara (1990), p. 6.

[54] Christopher Manes, 'Nature and silence', in Cheryll Glotfelty and Harold Fromm (eds), *The Ecocriticism Reader: Landmarks in Literary Ecology* (Athens, GA, and London: University of Georgia Press, 1996).

possibility of incorporating new actors into the political game—actors who would not be regarded as even potentially bona fide political agents from a 'capable of speaking' point of view.

TYPES OF LISTENING: COMPASSIONATE, CATA-PHATIC, APOPHATIC

In this section I outline different types of listening, with a view to identifying one 'ideal type'—apophatic listening—that I will develop in the political context in the rest of this book. The first type to discuss is sometimes called 'compassionate listening', which, according to Jim Garrison, 'requires that we dispossess almost (but not quite) all of our thoughts, judgements, and feelings to simply offer hospitality to another's pain'.[55] Listening of this type can benefit both parties in the conversation. It can benefit the listener in a therapeutic way, especially if s/he hasn't been listened to before. And it can benefit the speaker in terms of developing the virtues associated with good listening, which are widely endorsed outside this context. For the listener, there is importance in the creation of a space in which to be heard for perhaps the first time. In this sense compassionate listening can be regarded as a form of political listening in which the power to listen is exercised rather than withheld. But, in a broader compass, there are two problems with compassionate listening as a form of political listening. The first is that the compassionate listener is in danger of undermining the preconditions for a meaningful dialogue. 'Dialogue' presupposes two points of view, but, in effacing her/his thoughts, judgements, and feelings, this type of listener is in danger of turning two points of view into one (that of the person to whom one is listening). This turns dialogue into monologue, and becalms the conversation in the silence of attempted total comprehension.[56]

---

[55] Jim Garrison, 'Compassionate, spiritual, and creative listening in teaching and learning', *Teachers College Record* 112 (2010), no. 11, p. 2773.

[56] As Nikolas Kompridis says: 'The common conception of receptivity is one which makes it synonymous with indiscriminate openness, as though we are equally open to any all [sic.] new possibilities; such a conception leads not only to untenable relativism, it also leads to impassivity. A mind that is equally open to all possibilities would be a mind unminded, a mind rendered incapable of judging anything, precisely because a mind to which everything mattered equally would be a mind to which nothing mattered'; 'Receptivity, possibility, and democratic politics', *Ethics and Global Politics* 4 (2011), no. 4, p. 8.

The second problem follows from the first in that the exercise of listening implies nothing regarding taking action as a consequence of what is heard. We might call this 'therapeutic listening', the objective of which is achieved if the speaker feels better as a result of being listened to; the only changes that have taken place are in the mind of the person being listened to. This might be perfectly defensible in the therapeutic context itself, since the experience of not being listened to is, according to Graybar and Leonard, at the heart of many psychological problems: '[I]n psychotherapy we frequently encounter people who have been listened to far too little in their lives. They present for therapy feeling unseen, unheard, and unknown.'[57] It follows, then, that '[L]istening and being listened to are the cornerstones of psychological development, psychological relatedness, and psychological treatment.'[58] It might even be true that being listened to is something like a human need,[59] but there is a problem when this is transferred to the socio-political context, and when listening becomes a balm to soothe the anxieties of citizens without changing anything in the circumstances that generate the anxieties.

For example, Sachiko Mineyama and his colleagues describe how 'active listening' can improve relations between supervisors and subordinates on the shop floor, but in a way that implies little in terms of changing working conditions. Mineyama refers to the 'person-centred attitude' that lies at the heart of active listening—'initially developed as a core technique of counselors listening to their clients in the Person-Centred Therapy of Carl Rogers... [and]... later applied to non-therapeutic situations as a tool for better communication including supervisor–subordinate relationships'.[60] This transfer of therapeutic listening techniques to the world of work has the effect, in this case, of reducing psychological stress reactions in the workplace and of making subordinates 'feel' greater decision authority[61]—and all this without any changes in the structures that produced the anxiety and the alienation from decision-making in the first place. Nothing has

---

[57] Graybar and Leonard (2005), p. 3.   [58] Graybar and Leonard (2005), p. 3.
[59] Graybar and Leonard (2005), p. 3.
[60] Sachiko Mineyama, Akizumi Tsutsumi, Soshi Takao, Kyoko Nishiuchi, and Norito Kawakami, 'Supervisors' attitudes and skills for active listening with regard to working conditions and psychological stress reactions among subordinate workers', *Journal of Occupational Health* 49 (2007), p. 81.
[61] Mineyama, et al. (2007), p. 86.

changed except the mindsets of subordinates.[62] In other contexts we read of organizers and facilitators responding 'thoughtfully and conscientiously' to subordinates,[63] and building 'psychological safety'.[64] 'Like therapeutic counsellors,' write Tanya Drollinger and her colleagues, 'salespeople need to understand their customers thoroughly and completely',[65] and the reason for all this effort by managers, superiors, and others is that they know that, '[B]eing listened to has been linked to feelings of value, care, intimacy, and involvement with others'.[66]

In fact, it seems that being listened to has such a powerfully positive effect on the 'patient' that the result appears to be independent of whether there is an identifiable human listener present at all. Burbules and Rice note that, '[R]esearch on computerized counselling systems . . . [shows that people] . . . report that they gain significant benefits from these counselling sessions regardless of whether there is a real person there'.[67] This is the *reductio ad absurdum* of compassionate listening: there is no need even for a real live listener. In political terms, compassionate listening runs the risk of contributing to a type of false consciousness through which the subordination of the subordinate is reproduced through (the impression of) being listened to, and the absence of change. Here, listening is deployed as a tool for the reproduction of power rather than its redistribution.

At the other end of the scale from compassionate listening lies what Leonard Waks calls 'cataphatic' listening,[68] which 'involves the use of

[62] This suggests that Stickley and Freshwater are not wholly correct when they say that, 'Effective listening is not of any therapeutic value unless it is acted upon'; Theodore Stickley and Dawn Freshwater, 'The art of listening in the therapeutic relationship', *Mental Health Practice* 9 (2006), no. 5, p. 16.

[63] Joseph Raelin, 'Dialogue and deliberation as expressions of democratic leadership in participatory organizational change', *Journal of Organizational Change Management* 25 (2012), no. 1, p. 15.

[64] Raelin (2012), p. 15.

[65] Tanya Drollinger, Lucette Comer, and Patricia Warrington, 'Development and validation of the active empathetic listening scale', *Psychology and Marketing* 23 (2006), no. 2, p. 163.

[66] Christine Jonas-Simpson, Gail Mitchell, Anne Fisher, Grazia Jones, and Jan Linscott, 'The experience of being listened to: a qualitative study of older adults in long-term care settings', *Journal of Gerontological Nursing* 32 (2006), no. 1, p. 47.

[67] Burbules and Rice (2010), p. 2883.

[68] Leonard Waks, 'Two types of interpersonal listening', *Teachers College Record* 112 (2010), no. 11, pp. 2743–60, and Leonard Waks, 'Listening and questioning: the apophatic/cataphatic distinction revisited', *Learning Inquiry* 1 (2007), pp. 153–61.

prefigured categories'.[69] This bears a family resemblance to inattentive and interruptive listening in that the cataphatic listener is not listening attentively to the speaker but is organizing what is said through categories imposed by the listener. This implies that the listener is not listening properly, in the sense of allowing the speaker to speak for her/himself. Cataphatic listening verges on not listening at all. In political terms it is a very powerful form of listening in that it amounts to what we might call monological listening—effectively a refusal to listen, and therefore a refusal to enter into dialogue. The novelist William Boyd plays on this failure to listen to portray a character—Blanche—in his *Waiting for Sunrise* as a self-centred person lacking empathy. Boyd's protagonist, Lysander Rief, has just received a letter from Blanche, who is his lover:

> He [Rief] put the letter down, deciding to finish it later, and noticing with some irritation that Blanche hadn't bothered to answer any of his questions. Writing letters to each other was meant to be a form of dialogue, a conversation—but Blanche wrote as if the traffic was one way, a declamation about her feelings and what she was up to that paid not the slightest attention to his replies. When he wrote to her he always had her latest letter by his side. A correspondence should feed off its two parts; monologues—however lively and intimate—were not necessarily interesting.[70]

Rief knows that dialogue implies—requires—attention to what one's interlocutor is saying, and his irritation with Blanche stems from her wilful ignoring of his point of view—her failure to listen, in other words. Cataphatic listening appears to be the polar opposite of the compassionate listening we discussed earlier in this chapter, yet they share the likelihood of collapsing dialogue into monologue. In the case of compassionate listening this occurs because the listener immerses her- or himself in the meaning of the other to the point where the distinction between speaker and listener disappears. Cataphatic listening, on the other hand, is always in danger of collapsing into monologue because of the listener's tendency to read everything in terms of prefigured categories. This is politically significant, for, as Garrison says, '[R]igid cataphatic listening and thinking controlled by fixed categories, concepts and principles of identity lies at the core of all kinds

---

[69] Waks (2007), p. 154, and see also Waks (2010), p. 2749.
[70] William Boyd, *Waiting for Sunrise* (London, New Delhi, New York, and Sydney: Bloomsbury Publishing, 2012), pp. 66–7.

of colonialism'.[71] Cataphatic listening is a tool of colonial domination in that the colonizing power can offer the appearance of listening but in such a way as to reproduce relations of power rather than have them challenged. So neither of these ideal type versions of listening—compassionate or cataphatic—will produce the dynamic dialogue we associate with political life.

Waks himself contrasts cataphatic listening with 'apophatic' listening, in which the listener lays aside these categories and is 'still'.[72] In line with much theorizing around what constitutes good listening, Alexandra Michel and Stanton Wortham think that Waks's formulation hits on an important point: '[G]ood listeners must do some of what Leonard Waks calls "apophatic" listening, opening the self to the other and holding one's own categories in abeyance. If a listener reacts to another by immediately categorising the experience and the information using pre-existing categories, it is impossible to learn something genuinely new'.[73] The key point about apophatic listening, which makes it more suitable as a basis for dialogue than either compassionate or cataphatic listening, is that it involves a *temporary* suspension of the listener's categories in order to make room for the speaker's voice and to help it arrive in its 'authentic' form. The listener then processes what has been heard, making sense of it in her/his own terms, perhaps corroborating her/his understanding through asking questions for clarification—and all this before making her/his own intervention. As Rosencrantz puts it: 'Given the importance and vehemence of beliefs... [we should]... suspend our beliefs and preconceptions for a while. That will enable a better examination of not only the basis of our beliefs, but also allow a better understanding of the beliefs, needs and motivations of others in the world'.[74] The 'for a while' is important. This is neither a total immersion in the world of the listener, nor a 'cataphatic' determination to process everything through the listener's categories, but an attempt to hear one's interlocutor in her/his own

---

[71] Garrison (2010), pp. 2770–1. Contrast the role of this 'closed ear' listening in colonialism with the more dynamic picture discussed in Bryce Peake, 'Listening, language, and colonialism on Main Street, Gibraltar', *Communication and Critical/Cultural Studies* 9 (2012), no. 2, pp. 171–90.

[72] Waks (2010), p. 2749.

[73] Alexandra Michel and Stanton Wortham, 'Listen beyond the self: how organisations create direct involvement', *Learning Inquiry* 1 (2007), p. 89.

[74] Lawrence Rosencrantz, *America Adrift: Restoring the Promise of our Democracy* (ebook ISBN 978-1-61916-174-0, 2011), p. 14.

terms while maintaining the distance required for dialogue rather than monologue. As Carolyn Cusick says: 'If we only listen to others' stories, and not also compare and contrast them with our own and with other facts and stories about the world, then we are not actually understanding others' stories, we are simply believing those others'.[75]

Drollinger, Comer, and Wallington make a similar point when quoting C. F. Rogers on empathy: '[E]mpathy is defined as the ability "to perceive the internal frame of reference of another with accuracy, and with the emotional components and meanings... as if one were the other person, but without ever losing sight of the 'as if' condition"'.[76] The 'as if', here, performs the same function as the 'for a while' in Rosencrantz: a temporary suspension of the listener's categories to 'draw' her or him into the orbit of the speaker, yet leaving space for the critical distance between speaker and listener to enable dialogue.[77] We might refer to this as the 'co-creation' of meaning. The point is not to 'reproduce the other's meaning', which is what 'sympathetic listening' aims to do according to Garrison: 'the listener is not simply "open to what the other means" so that he or she can reproduce it; instead the listener is open to the meanings that are being developed between oneself and one's partner'.[78] Through dialogue, meaning is always in the process of being developed, and listening is vital to the development of meaning.

I suggest that we take *apophatic listening* forward as our ideal type. While this notion has been developed almost exclusively in the person-to-person context, my aim is to put it to work in political theory and practice. Wendy Hui Kyong Chun offers an example of the difference that an apophatic approach can make in connection with the 'Montréal massacre' of 1989 which we discussed briefly in

---

[75] Cusick (2012), p. 40.

[76] Drollinger, Comer, and Warrington (2006), p. 162. John Dewey suggests that empathy is a condition for communication itself: 'To formulate the significance of an experience a man must take into conscious account the experiences of others. He must try to find a standpoint which includes the experience of others as well as his own. Otherwise his communication cannot be understood'; Dewey, *Democracy and Education* (London: Macmillan, 1916), ch. 17, section 2.

[77] As Megan Laverty puts it, 'philosophical dialogue is *convergent*... Participants are both *inclusive* and *critical*. They strive to understand what the other is saying but want to test its plausibility too'; 'Dialogue as philosophical inquiry in the teaching of tolerance and sympathy', *Learning Inquiry* 1 (2007), p. 127.

[78] Garrison (1996), p. 9.

Chapter 1. On 6 December 1989 25-year old Marc Lépine entered the École Polytechnique, systematically separated the women from the men in two classrooms, and murdered 14 women students. Lépine had applied for entry into the Engineering faculty and had been refused— just at the time when more women were being accepted onto so-called 'non-traditional' courses such as engineering. In a suicide note Lépine explained his actions as follows:

> Please note that if I am committing suicide today...it is not for economic reasons...but for political reasons. For I have decided to send Ad Patres [Latin: 'to the fathers'] the feminists who have ruined my life.... The feminists always have a talent for enraging me. They want to retain the advantages of being women...while trying to grab those of men.... They are so opportunistic that they neglect to profit from the knowledge accumulated by men throughout the ages. They always try to misrepresent them every time they can.[79]

To call this a traumatic event is an understatement, both for those closely involved and for Canadian society as a whole. Inevitably, it led to a series of competing explanations for what Lépine had done, based on what Chun refers to as differing 'testimonies' of the event. Testimonies are complex, she says, as they can be 'multiple and infelicitous'.[80] This creates problems of interpretation. 'What happens,' she asks, 'when an event seems to invoke testimony not only from its survivors (who are eerily silent), but also from those who were never physically present, from those who seem to be testifying belatedly to another event? What happens when those witnessing the event seem called by the *proximity* of this event to their own real or imagined experiences?'[81] Chun says that the best way of approaching these multiple testimonies, as we saw in Chapter 1, is via a 'politics of listening'. For her, and in terms we used earlier in this chapter, this means 'apophatic' listening: 'opening the self to the other and holding one's own categories in abeyance', as Stanton and Wortham put it. The key thing, writes Chun, is to avoid being a listener who 'knows it all',[82] because this 'forecloses[s] the possibility of listening to the survivors' testimonies'.[83] In articulating her

---

[79] Wendy Hui Kyong Chun, 'Case study: the Montréal Massacre', gendercide watch, available at <http://www.gendercide.org/case_montreal.html> (accessed 2 July 2012).

[80] Wendy Hui Kyong Chun, 'Unbearable witness: towards a politics of listening', *Differences: A Journal of Feminist Cultural Studies*, 11 (1999), no. 1, p. 114.

[81] Chun (1999), p. 114 (emphasis in the original).

[82] Chun (1999), p. 137.   [83] Chun (1999), p. 137.

understanding of the best way to deal with multiple and conflicting testimonies, Chun employs the ideas and language associated with apophatic listening: the notions of empathy, of maintaining a distance between testifier and listener, and of the 'co-production' of meaning:

> The important task in listening, then, is to feel the victim's victories, defeats and silences, know them from within, while at the same time acknowledging that one is not the victim, so that the victim can testify, so that the truth can be reached together. In this model, distance must be maintained between speaker and listener... Such a contract is based on *lack* of comprehension.[84]

Lack of comprehension is both the bedrock for and guarantor of Chun's political listening. Any claim to 'understand' must be provisional and temporary. We will follow up these themes in more detail in Chapter 4, where political listening, as Chun describes it here, becomes a key aspect of 'dialogical democracy'.

FORCED LISTENING

On the face of it, being forced to listen is as bad as being forced to do anything one doesn't want to do. While we normally think of the power of propaganda as lying in its transmission (speech, posters, films), we can easily miss the point that it also entails a particular type of listening—forced listening. Leonard Waks contrasts his apophatic listening, whose aim is to promote dialogue, with what John Dewey calls 'one-way, straight-line listening': 'The passive listening that is characteristic of one-way, straight-line listening... leads to negative uniformity, the absence of vital interchange, and the swallowing up of individuals in an undifferentiated mass.'[85] This 'negative uniformity' is the opposite of the uniformity that theorists like Waks and Dewey believe to be possible through dialogue. In the former case uniformity is *imposed* while in the dialogic case of apophatic listening uniformity has the potential to be *created*.[86] Negative

---

[84] Chun (1999), p. 139 (emphasis in the original).

[85] Waks (2011), p. 201.

[86] Krystyna Górniak-Kocikowska presents the evolution of Karl Jaspers' thought on listening quite precisely as a move from being listened to, to listening out for; the proximate cause of this evolution was the experience of the Nazi regime; ' The factor of listening in Karl Jaspers' philosophy of communication', in Helmut Wautischer, Alan M. Olsen, and Gregory J. Walters (eds), *Philosophical Faith and the Future of Humanity* (Heidelberg, London, and New York: Springer, 2012).

uniformity is the product of propaganda: 'Propaganda messages…can be endlessly and mechanically repeated to captive audiences forced to "listen" passively to one-way messages, while spy networks monitor and effectively prevent any frank private face-to-face discussions.'[87] And it is worth pointing out here that while we might instinctively think of listening as a virtue, we need to take into account the uses to which listening is put before deciding how virtuous it is: 'It would be difficult to argue that listening per se is a virtue—after all, listening can serve bad as well as good ends.'[88] Like truth-telling, the moral status of listening varies according to whether one adopts a deontological or utilitarian perspective. Gemma Fiumara puts Waks's point in a wider context of a general culture in which listening is a form of force-feeding: 'A large part of the linguistic interaction that underlies human coexistence is certainly not listening so much as endurance or forced feeding, hypnotic induction or epistemic violence.'[89]

But is forced listening necessarily a bad thing? While the answer to this might seem obvious, we should first consider an example of forced listening offered by David Doorey: 'captive audience meetings' (CAMs), which are enshrined in Canadian labour law.[90] At these meetings, 'employees are held "captive" in the practical sense that leaving may have negative implications for their employment security. The subject matter of employer speeches in these meetings vary, but one of the most controversial uses of CAMs is to proselytize anti-union, anti-collective bargaining messages to employees during union organizing campaigns.'[91] It might surprise us to learn that CAMs have legal status anywhere, let alone in Canada,[92] but their legitimacy has two plausible foundations: the right of employers to free speech, and the reasonable expectation that employees should be required to attend occasional meetings called by management to explain company policy.

---

[87] Waks (2010), p. 201. This brings to mind a joke in *Private Eye*, a satirical weekly magazine published in the UK. A constituent is visiting his MP and says, 'I'm very concerned about the surveillance society.' The MP replies, 'I know'; Ian Hislop (ed.), *Private Eye Annual 2008* (London: Private Eye Productions, 2008), p. 56.
[88] Rice and Burbules (2010), p. 2729.
[89] Fiumara (1990), p. 93.
[90] David Doorey, 'The medium and the "anti-union" message: "forced listening" and captive audience meetings in Canadian labor law', *Comparative Labor Law and Policy Journal* 29 (2007), no. 2, pp. 79–119.
[91] Doorey (2007), p. 80.
[92] With the exception of the Canadian Federal Board; Doorey (2007), p. 87.

In the particular case discussed by David Doorey, these provisions are in tension with so-called 'interference prohibitions', which prevent employers interfering with 'the selection of formation of a union'.[93] Importantly, Doorey notes that, '[T]he Free Speech provisions are usually drafted so as to create an exception to the Interference Prohibition provisions',[94] so the free speech of employers in the guise of captive audience meetings in which employers are effectively forced to listen takes precedence over employees' uninhibited freedom to select and form unions.

In our context there are two things to be said about CAMs. First, they are an expression of power: the currency of domination here is not the speech used by the employers, but the fact that the employees are *forced to listen* without comeback. So, as Doorey says, 'the employer's implied right to convene CAMs is at once an expression of employer power and a reminder of employee subordination'.[95] Thus, CAMs themselves are a *political act*, or, as Doorey puts it, 'a distinct form of employer expression'.[96] The second point has to do with 'forced listening' and whether we regard it as a bad thing or not. On the face of it, being forced to listen is repugnant in a democratic society,[97] but when we analyse what is repugnant about it, it is not so much the being forced to listen that is anti-democratic (though it might be anti-liberal) but the fact that there is no reciprocal obligation on employers to listen to their employees—in other words, that there is no dialogue. Interestingly, the Canadian Supreme Court has ruled that freedom of expression can be curtailed where, 'the "method" of expression undermines the core values that … [it] … is intended to protect, namely, democratic discourse, truth-finding, and self-fulfilment'.[98] This exception is designed to cover cases such as the expression of points of view through violence, and the reason the Court gives is: '[V]iolence prevents dialogue rather than fostering it'.[99] It seems obvious that captive audience meetings prevent dialogue too, but this does not lead to them being banned.

So, crucially, CAMs prevent dialogue not because of the forced listening element but because of the lack of the aural reciprocity that

---

[93] Doorey (2007), p. 85.   [94] Doorey (2007), p. 87.
[95] Doorey (2007), p. 103.   [96] Doorey (2007), p. 108.
[97] Doorey (2007), p. 107.   [98] Doorey (2007), p. 93.
[99] Doorey (2007), p. 93.

is a precondition for dialogue.[100] Canadian courts have apparently
suggested that freedom of expression should include a right not to be
compelled to listen, but this perhaps takes us in the wrong direction.[101]
Justice George Adams, relates Doorey, argued that, 'forced listening
"destroys and denies...that unfettered interplay and competition
among ideas which is the assumed ambient of communicative free-
doms"'.[102] But it is not so much the forced listening that is the problem
here—after all it is perfectly possible for the absence of listening to
be the culprit as far as unfettered discussion is concerned. From this
point of view forced listening might not be such a bad idea, and, in
cases of restorative justice, forced listening is precisely the lubricant
that gets the whole process moving. So, in analysing what is wrong
with 'captive audience meetings' we should perhaps focus less on the
'captive' and more on the fact that the employees are only ever a passive 'audience'.

LISTENING: CHANGING STRUCTURES OR EDU-
CATING INDIVIDUALS?

Some argue that dialogue has a particular purpose in the political—
and particularly the democratic—context. According to this reading,
listening has an instrumental value in democracies—and particularly
in plural democracies. Katharine Schultz writes that, '[D]emocratic
communities depend on dialogue and the honouring of individual
voices that may clash as people work together toward identifying
common beliefs'.[103] This view is sometimes rooted in an instrumental
view of democracy itself—that the purpose of democracy is 'the broad
achievement of unity or harmony in action'.[104] From this point of view,
listening is the means by which plural societies (can) become democratic: '[I]t is in and through such communication practices that larger
multigroup society becomes democratic'.[105] Walter Parker makes a

---

[100] The point, then, is not so much that, 'the union has no comparable opportunity
to address workers at the workplace' (Doorey (2007), p. 94, fn. 55), but because there is
no comparable opportunity to address the *employers* at the workplace.
[101] Doorey (2007), p. 96.   [102] Doorey (2007), p. 97.
[103] Schultz (2003), p. 74.   [104] Waks (2011), p. 199.
[105] Waks (2011), p. 200.

similar point: '[L]istening deserves to be singled out for several reasons, but a key *political* reason is that democratic community based on...[the]..."wholeness" principle requires it. Equitable and trustworthy conjoint living is not only a matter of being heard, but also of hearing others. Agency resides in both roles—speaker and listener.'[106]

It is equally clear, though, that the kinds of good listening practices we saw described by Shipley and Lam earlier cannot be uncomplicatedly imported into the entirety of the political realm. We are still faced with the scaling-up problem: many political encounters do not involve face-to-face contact, and the gestural and other strategies suggested for improving listening seem hard—if not impossible—to reproduce at these other scales. It is a relative commonplace to think of democracy as a form of dialogue, but it is unusual to *start* with dialogue and to think how democracy might be constructed in order to meet dialogic aspirations. Of course, this is one way of reading what the so-called 'deliberative turn' in democratic theory and practice is about: a determination to return democracy to its dialogic roots. In Chapter 4 we will discuss the role of listening in deliberative democracy in more detail, but for present purposes it is enough to say that these are usually regarded as relatively small-scale experiments designed to insert dialogue into present democratic practices. This contrasts with institutional designs that would put democracy *at the service* of dialogue.

One theorist who starts with dialogue and ends up with democracy rather than the other way round is the educationalist and philosophical pragmatist John Dewey. For Dewey the aim of democracy is to generate a 'public opinion' and this can only be achieved through effective communication. As we saw earlier in this chapter, Dewey drew a distinction between 'negative one-way or straight-line listening' and 'positive *transactional* listening', in which the latter aims at 'coming to a shared action orientation, not reproducing prior meanings of speakers in the minds of listeners.'[107] For Dewey, listening well is not simply a matter of attending to the meaning of the speaker and capturing it exactly; this, rather, is a step on the way to shared and agreed action—or the fully formed 'public opinion' that he regards as democracy's objective. This has implications for institutional design, and it brings

---

[106] Walter Parker, 'Listening to strangers: classroom discussion in democratic education', *Teachers College Record* 112 (2010), no. 11, p. 2827.

[107] Waks (2011), p. 194.

into sharp relief the scaling-up problem to which we referred earlier. Dewey's answer is not to insert small-scale 'transactional listening' events into current democratic practices, but to work up from local levels in the belief that a combination of appropriate school education and the 'social learning' involved in transactional listening at the local level will promote similar kinds of listening, aimed at shared action orientation, at bigger scales. In developing his theory of democracy, writes Leonard Waks, Dewey:

> started from the simplest case—person-to-person conversation result-ing in personal cooperative friendship. He progressed to the somewhat more complicated case of many-to-many conversations in local com-munities generating communal feeling, which is cooperative friendship on a group level. He concluded by analysing the complex group-to-group exchange patterns that can generate democratic solidarity among citizens of multicultural industrial nation-states.[108]

For Dewey, the biggest challenge in the modern states of his time was overcoming the centrifugal tendencies inherent in their size and their (what we would now call) multicultural make-up. In his view, good communication lay at the heart of a solution to this challenge, but such communication was (and is) made more diffi-cult by the very conditions which it is designed to overcome—size and cultural difference. The irony, therefore, is that in small-scale *gemeinschaft* societies, where 'face-to-faceness' gives rise to the pos-sibility of listening across difference, there is less need for it, whereas in large-scale plural societies it is both more necessary and less likely. Dewey argued that the solution to the problem of cohesion in large-scale plural societies lay not so much in improving individu-als' listening skills as in structural social and political change: '[T]o create a modern society grounded in cooperative friendship, local communities must ... be restored.'[109]

All this seems to point to a particular sort of politics, an anti-utopian politics in which meaning is slowly, and perhaps painfully, arrived at over long periods of time. There is no *tabula rasa* on which to inscribe

---

[108] Waks (2011), p. 198.
[109] Waks (2011), p. 203. Nel Noddings comments that Dewey, 'saw conjoint liv-ing...as a way of creating common values and understandings, whereas [Robert Maynard] Hutchins saw common values and understandings as necessary precursors of cooperative (or democratic) life', in ' Why should we listen?' *Philosophy of Education 2003* (Urbana, IL: Philosophy of Education Society, 2003), p. 19.

and invent political projects; the listener is 'thrown into' a world which already has meaning, and s/he works to understand alien points of view and to promote structures and conditions in which dialogue overcomes monologue. '[I]f we are apprentices of listening rather than masters of discourse,' writes Gemma Fiumara, 'we might perhaps promote a different sort of coexistence among humans: not so much in the form of a utopian ideal but rather as an incipient philosophical solidarity capable of envisaging the common destiny of the species.'[110] The general point here is that politics is about relations between strangers, and this is especially true in plural societies when the ties that bind, in the form of common identities, are weak or non-existent. We cannot assume a utopian solution to these schisms and ruptures. Listening has a role to play here in being the precondition for dialogue leading to—at least—a better comprehension (if not understanding) of the other. As Walter Parker says, where identities are not given, the *demos* needs to be forged or created: 'This is the heterogeneous "we the people" who are citizens and comrades—not a species or an identity group, not *homo sapiens* or an *ethnos*, but a *demos*.'[111]

So Dewey's view is that listening can only be improved by changing the structures in which it takes place—to the point where those very structures should be put at the service of improving listening. The far more common point of view is to focus on teaching individuals to listen better. This in turn, of course, raises the question of whether listening can be taught and learnt. There seems little dispute that people can become better listeners, though exactly what is required for this is a matter of debate. Carolyn Cusick suggests that one obstacle to learning how to listen better is that people already think they listen well, but that while their optimal levels of listening might be good, their habitual levels leave something to be desired.[112] Anecdotally, this is borne out by my experience of trying to persuade a House of Commons committee to work with me on improving members' capacity to listen to one another during debates.[113] The project foundered on the members' conviction that they were already very good at listening. Perhaps they were, but perhaps they weren't—and we will never know. Cusick also points out how little attention is paid in formal education to teaching good listening—one piece of research suggested that, 'in classrooms only

---

[110] Fiumara (1990), p. 57.   [111] Parker (2010), p. 2817.
[112] Cusick (2012), p. 134.   [113] The committee will remain nameless.

7% of instruction is about improving listening and only 5% of curricula have dedicated time for teaching listening.[114]

To some degree the question of whether listening can be taught rests on whether one believes listening to be a skill or something more akin to a virtue. Mei Sung Lam, for example, takes the uncomplicated view that, 'listening skills can be practiced and learned by everyone'.[115] This does not mean that learning to listen better is an easy matter but it is easier to cultivate skills than it is to cultivate a mode of being,[116] which is what Martin Buber's theory of dialogue demands of us: 'deep listening, in Buber's account, is not really a skill that can be displayed or modelled but rather a mode of existence towards others'.[117] Gemma Corradi Fiumara,[118] Theodore Stickley and Dawn Freshwater,[119] and Sharon Todd are all opposed to the idea that listening is a skill that can be learnt.[120] Listening, says Todd, for example, is 'not a matter of adherence to rules about what constitutes "good listening"...it does not involve practices such as tilting or nodding one's head, repeating back what the speaker says, or leaning forward to indicate attentiveness'.[121]

These theorists believe that it is more productive to think of good listening as a virtue, or at least to couch it in terms of characteristics that are thought of as virtuous. Suzanne Rice associates the following characteristics with the good listener: 'attuned, attentive, engrossed, empathetic, understanding, patient, caring, discriminating, astute, open-minded, curious, persistent, and courageous',[122] and these stand in obvious contrast to Joseph Beatty's counter-list: 'laziness, inattention, egoism, narcissism, desire for self-comfort or self-consoling rationalization,

---

[114] Cusick (2012), p. 174. This draws on Melissa Beall, Jennifer Gill-Rosier, Jeanine Tate, and Amy Matten, 'State of the context: listening in education', *International Journal of Listening* 22 (2008), no. 2, p. 128.

[115] Lam (2000), p. 267.

[116] 'In actuality, active listening skills are quite difficult to master because of the complex nature of communication: accurate comprehension often requires one to understand the nuances of non-verbal cues, recognize implicit emotions, and tease out personal meaning', in Jongpil Cheon and Michael Grant, 'Active listening: web-based assessment tool for communication and active listening skill development', *TechTrends* 53 (2009), no. 6, p. 24.

[117] Gordon (2011), p. 218.   [118] Fiumara (1990), pp. 160–1.

[119] Stickley and Freshwater (2006), p. 14.   [120] Todd (2003).

[121] Todd (2003), pp. 136–7.

[122] Rice (2011), p. 151; Stickley and Freshwater (2006), p. 15: 'the best listener is often the one with fewer ego needs. Good listening may be associated with humility rather than talkativeness.'

dogmatism, and resistance to change and self-rationalization'.[123] The view that good listening is a virtue rather than a skill leads to the conclusion that learning to listen involves cultivation rather than teaching. This takes time, says Beatty, as well as the opportunity to spend time with people who themselves exhibit the required virtues.[124] '[H]ow much easier it is,' writes Beatty, 'to "train" someone to be a *skilful* listener than to cultivate the *virtue* of good listening. For...skills...make no necessary demands on genuine respect for others, self-honesty, openness, honesty, or love of truth.'[125] Whether we regard listening as a skill or a virtue, the idea that listening for democracy can be improved by teaching individuals to do it better contrasts with Dewey's view that structures rather than people need changing—or rather that the quality of communication is affected by structures as well as by the skills and virtues of the people who inhabit them. I suggest that there is something to be learned from both these positions, but that the structural focus should be on the conditions under which listening takes place rather than on political structures as such. This will become clearer in Chapter 6.

CONCLUSION

In this chapter we have discussed a number of different notions of listening: compassionate, cataphatic, apophatic, monological, and dialogical. It seems obvious that, whatever the context, we should prefer good listening to bad listening. Drawing on practices and disciplines outside of political science and political theory we have seen that there is something of a convergence on what constitutes good listening, organized around the aim of understanding as fully as possible the meaning of what is being said by one's interlocutor, and using a range of techniques both to signal that one is paying close attention, and to ensure that one has indeed understood what is being communicated. In the terminology we have introduced in this chapter this is

---

[123] Beatty (1999), p. 291.

[124] Beatty (1999), p. 296. Walter Parker recommends *reciprocity*, which 'ventilates the listener's ego'; *humility*, which 'undermines the listener's arrogance'; and *caution*, which 'moderates the listener's speed and recklessness', in Parker (2010), pp. 2829–30.

[125] Beatty (1999), p. 296. See also pp. 2728–42. As far as learning to listen is concerned, Rice and Burbules (2010) follow the Aristotelian dictum that one learns to be virtuous by being virtuous—through what they call 'habituation' (p. 2735).

'apophatic' or 'dialogical' listening. But we also saw that listening is a tool for wielding power. Power is exercised through defining what good listening is, through withholding listening, and through granting it. Once we begin to think of listening in terms of power we see that as well as being an instrument of power it can also—under the right conditions—be what I have called a 'solvent' of power. The best example of this is truth and reconciliation committees in which the tables of power are turned precisely through the agency of listening. Being forced to listen amounts to a ceding of power by the powerful, and being heard amounts to an acquisition of power by those who previously lacked it. We have also seen that listening is closely related to silence. Silence constitutes the space in which listening to previously unheard voices takes place, as well as providing the opportunity to listen out for new political voices: the space, in other words, in which the very notion of what constitutes a 'political voice' is put into question. Listening is thus an important agent for the creation of difference, or for 'recognition', to use the term that has become current in theories of social justice, and which we will discuss in more detail in Chapters 4 and 5. Finally, we have broached the question of whether listening is a skill or a virtue, whether it can be 'learned', and whether its instantiation in political life is a matter of changing individuals or changing structures. We will take up this question in Chapter 6, but first we need to consider the relationship between listening and democracy itself in more detail.

3

Listening and Democracy

In the two previous chapters I have prepared the ground for a discussion of the role that listening might play in improving the quality of contemporary democracy. In Chapter 1 I discussed the absence of listening in political theory and practice, and argued that the adoption of a 'sensory' approach to democracy need not entail fitting democracy to a set of rather depressing 'facts' about a seemingly unrecoverable democratic deficit. Then, in Chapter 2, I mined a number of literatures on listening with a view to establishing the relevance of listening to politics and illustrating some of the challenges of doing so. The complexities will be picked up in subsequent chapters, and here my task is the rather more straightforward one of taking democracy 'as it is' and showing how better listening could enhance and improve it. In what follows I look at legitimacy, trust, disagreement, representation, and deliberation.

LISTENING AND LEGITIMACY

Better listening can improve democratic governments' claims to legitimacy. As John Forrester says in connection with planning: '[F]ailing to listen, we fail to learn, and we also damage our working relationships with others. If they do not listen carefully to members of the public, planners will lose any reputation for responsiveness or fairness, any public trust they might have had.'[1] It is in no democratic

---

[1] John Forrester, *Planning in the Face of Power* (Berkeley, Los Angeles, and London: University of California Press, 1989), p. 109.

government's interest to be seen to be imposing policies on its citizens without the views of citizens having been listened to. Indeed, it is noticeable how, when governments feel they are losing touch with the electorate, they organize something like a 'Big Conversation'—like Tony Blair's of 2003 in the UK—in an attempt to reconnect with them. And the purpose of this conversation is not for the government to talk more—it is to convey the impression that the government is *listening*. Another example is the exercise carried out by the European Commission's Directorate General for External Trade (DG Trade) in 2006–7 in response to complaints from European civil society organizations (CSOs) about the way in which their voice was being taken into account when DG Trade decisions were taken.[2] The title of the DG report is significant—'From hearing to listening'—and these exercises are a belated recognition that listening is indeed important. And it is important in a very particular way in the political—and particularly the democratic—context. All governments seek, and need, legitimacy. Different types of regime have different sources of legitimacy, and democratic regimes ground their legitimacy in the claim that they act in accordance with the will of the people. Of course, it will always be a matter of dispute whether any given democracy actually does act in this way, and not everybody will agree that there is such a thing as 'the will of the people' anyway, but the point is that the currency of legitimacy in a democracy is *responsiveness*—or the degree to which a government can claim that it is responding to wishes of the electorate. In this light it is clear why listening is such an important component of democratic legitimacy: it would be hard for a government to claim responsiveness if it could not simultaneously claim that it was 'listening to the people'. What is striking, indeed, is how governments often reach for the listening card precisely when they are in most trouble. This is a powerful recognition of the foundational role that listening plays in democratic legitimacy claims: when all else fails, governments mount a listening exercise and claim the aural high ground. A problem is that these Big Conversations are usually so poorly conducted that they have the opposite effect to that intended. Citizens often come away from them even more firmly confirmed in their belief that the

[2] Kim Bizzari and Mariano Iossa, 'From hearing to listening: improving the dialogue between DG Trade and civil society', ActionAid, 2007, p. 3, available at <http://trade.ec.europa.eu/doclib/docs/2007/may/tradoc_134642.pdf> (accessed 6 December 2012).

government is not listening to them: '[A] "conversation" that does not look or feel like a real conversation is open to the accusation of being a misleading gesture: more a cultivated appearance of listening than an experience of sharing ideas.'[3] There is a real danger that a listening exercise will come across as a last-gasp attempt to curry favour with a sceptical electorate, as Jennifer Lees-Marshment perhaps unwittingly signals with her advice to the 'reflective political leader' to conduct listening exercises to 'get back in touch'.[4]

In Chapter 6 we will look at ways in which these set-piece listening encounters might be improved, but some general remarks can usefully be made now. As we saw in Chapter 2, in daily life there are ways of telling if someone is listening to us properly. The signals may be visual (is my interlocutor paying attention to me as I speak?) or dialogic (is s/he asking me questions that show s/he really wants to understand what I am saying?). But neither of these signals is easy to work into the relationship between government and the people, so the question of what makes a 'real conversation' in the political context is not at all a simple one. Some of the characteristics of good conversation in the quotidian interpersonal sense are hard to replicate—to 'scale up'— in the political arena. How do we know whether the government is really listening? What we notice about the quotidian signs of good conversation is that they are procedural, as it were; they are part of the conversational process itself. When we think of how to judge good listening in the political context, though, we tend to be driven to think in terms of outcomes: we will know if the government has listened properly if it changes its course of action. But there was no suggestion

---

[3] Stephen Coleman, 'Whose conversation? Engaging the public in authentic polylogue', *The Political Quarterly* 75 (2004), no. 2, p. 118. Coleman asks, 'Can a governing party, with all of its entrenched political interests, ideological commitments and institutional pathologies enter into a genuine polylogue with something as amorphous as "the public", or must such an exercise inevitably descend into a technical, consultative ritual or, worse still, a publicity-driven "monologue in disguise", presented as if it were a conversation?' (p. 115). In Chapter 6 I will take up the challenge implied by this question. There is also the problem of representativeness, since, as a letter writer to *The Guardian* newspaper pointed out, only some 0.008% of the adult population took part in the UK Coalition government's listening exercise on the National Health Service; Mike Squires, 'Final diagnosis of Lansley's health plans', *The Guardian*, 16 June 2011, p. 37: 'Hardly an endorsement to usher in plans to destroy the NHS,' says Squires. Hardly an endorsement to do anything at all, we might say.

[4] Jennifer Lees-Marshment, 'Political marketing and opinion leadership: comparative perspectives and findings', in Ludger Helms (ed.), *Comparative Political Leadership* (New York and Basingstoke: Palgrave Macmillan, 2012), p. 169.

in what we learned in Chapter 2 that we should connect good listening with changed minds: we can hold to our original opinion and still be regarded as having listened well. The outcome-driven judgement of good listening in the political—and especially the democratic—context is understandable. If we define democracy as responsive rule then this implies that governments should respond to the wishes of the electorate—and if they don't, then part of the reason could be that they are just not listening to what the electorate is saying. On the other hand, though, a more procedural account of democracy suggests that when judging legitimacy we should focus less on what decision is actually taken and more on *how* it is taken. This is because the legitimacy of a decision in a democracy is determined not so much by what it is as how it was arrived at.

There is, therefore, a common theme in the analytics of both good listening and good democracy that has perhaps been overlooked: what is 'good' in both cases turns on processes rather than outcomes. It is interesting in this context to see that the authors of the DG report referred to earlier in this chapter say that the shortcomings of the consultation process with civil society organizations derive from 'the lack of clear mechanisms outlining how such a voice is acted upon'.[5] This prioritizes process over outcome and indicates that CSOs judge the degree to which they are listened to by assessing transparency and access to procedure rather than through changed outcomes. Another example is given by analysis of the reforms put in place by President Lula of Brazil in the 2003 to 2010 period.[6] In large measure these reforms aimed to allow social movement voices to be heard during the policy process, and, given their historical experience of marginalization, the new habit of procedural inclusion gave social movements the sense of being listened to: 'Although few concrete policies were introduced, the "ritual" of going to Brasilia to attend meetings, councils and conferences has had a positive effect in comparison with the various forms of [historical] disqualification.'[7]

---

[5] Bizzari and Iossa (2007), p. 3.

[6] Gianpaolo Baiocchi, Einar Braathen, and Ana Claudia Teixeira, 'Transformation institutionalized? Making sense of participatory democracy in the Lulu era', 11 June 2012, available at <http://gianpaolobaiocchi.wordpress.com/2012/04/16/transformation-institutionalized-new-essay-on-the-lula-era/> (accessed 6 December 2012). In their totality, the body of thought and action promoted by President Lula is sometimes referred to as 'Lulismo'.

[7] Baiocchi, Braathen, and Teixeira (2012), p. 8. The 'few concrete policies' rider is important here, as in this particular context the lack of outcomes was a disappointment

In the political arena one person's good listening—judged in terms of a changed policy direction—is usually another person's U-turn, which is a fatal accusation to lay at a politician's door. The UK's Coalition government (2010 to date) appeared to go back on a number of the pledges it made after it came to power: over, for instance, selling off state-owned forests, and reducing the number of coastguard stations—while privatizing the remainder—to save money.[8] Again, in 2012, the Secretary of State for Education, Michael Gove, announced some radical changes in UK secondary school education, including a return to an older-style assessment regime. In subsequent months much was made by him of this policy, but then, in early February 2013, he abruptly announced that the changes wouldn't take place after all. Naturally, the Opposition spokesman called this a 'humiliating climbdown'[9]—while, in riposte, Gove's supporters played the listening card for all it was worth. In Gove's defence, former schools minister Nick Gibb said that, 'Ministers always get accused of that [humiliation] if they listen to a consultation process and then change their minds', while Deputy Prime Minister Nick Clegg said effusively, 'I want to pay tribute to Michael. When politicians actually listen to people—there were serious reservations expressed by the regulator, Ofqual, which oversees the qualification system—he's listened and he's reacted...There is no point having a consultation if you've already made up your mind what you're going to do at the end of it.'[10] In each of these cases the original policy proposal was either watered-down

to social movements: 'There is a feeling of general disappointment on the part of organized civil society, which points to the lack of effective decision-making power linked to these spaces'; Baiocchi, Braathen, and Teixeira (2012), p. 5.

[8] At the time of writing—April 2013—this policy was very much back on the agenda: Steven Morris and Severin Carrell, 'Privatising search-and-rescue service and closing bases "will cost lives"', *The Guardian*, 31 January 2013, available at <http://www.guardian.co.uk/politics/2013/jan/31/privatising-search-rescue-helicopters-risk-lives> (accessed 2 April 2013).

[9] Peter Walker, 'Michael Gove forced into U-turn on GCSE replacement plan', *The Guardian*, 7 February 2013, available at <http://www.guardian.co.uk/politics/2013/feb/07/michael-gove-gcse-replacement> (accessed 18 February 2013).

[10] Peter Walker, 'Government denies humiliating U-turn over GCSE replacement', *The Guardian*, 7 February 2013, available at <http://www.guardian.co.uk/education/2013/feb/07/government-denies-u-turn-gcse-replacement> (accessed 18 February 2013). *The Guardian* keeps a record of government U-turns, which, on 7 February 2013, stood at 35: Paul Owen, 'Every Coalition U-turn: the list is full', available at <http://www.guardian.co.uk/politics/2012/may/31/coalition-u-turns-full-list> (accessed 18 February 2013).

or abandoned altogether, and the government was accused variously of weakness, vacillation, and rudderlessness. In a context in which 'strong government' is praised and admired these are damaging criticisms indeed, and claims by the government that 'these changes just show how hard we are listening' did not cut much ice. Yet it is significant that the defence of these U-turns was invariably couched in terms of listening. The plausibility of this line of defence lies precisely and importantly in the connection between listening and legitimacy: what could possibly be wrong with a democratic government listening to public—as well as expert—opinion? Indeed, is this not exactly what democracy is about?

Another example shows that too much 'muscularity' brings its own dangers. A key plank of the Coalition's policy platform was the opening up of the National Health Service (NHS) to greater competition from various health providers. In this case, and in the face of considerable consternation at the scale and pace of these proposals, Prime Minister David Cameron ordered a very public pause in the policy trajectory and instituted a 'Listening Exercise' called the NHS Forum Review, involving (in principle) the whole population as well as health-care stakeholders. Over a period of two months submissions were received and considered, and despite advance notices which suggested that a scaling back and slowing down of the original proposals would take place, the opening up of the NHS to 'any qualified provider' continued apace. Inevitably, this left the government open to accusations that the 'Listening Exercise' was a sham.[11]

It seems, then, that, as far as listening goes, governments are damned if they do and damned if they don't: they will be accused of weakness if they change their mind and of pig-headedness and a failure to listen if they don't. Note, though, that these judgements are based on determining whether good or bad listening has taken place by looking at outcomes (has the decision changed or not?). If we focus on processes instead, as the analytics of both listening and of democracy suggest we should, then listening stops being a political football and becomes a fixed point—though still discursively disputed—around which

---

[11] For a critical assessment of NHS reform, see Alyson Pollock, David Price, Peter Roderick, Tim Treuherz, David McCoy, and Lucy Reynolds, 'The end of the NHS as we know it', openDemocracy, 27 January 2012, available at <http://www.opendemocracy.net/ourkingdom/allyson-pollock-david-price-peter-roderick-tim-treuherz-david-mccoy-martin-mckee-lucy-rey> (accessed 5 December 2012).

discussions and practices aimed at improving democracy can take place. The focus then would be on improving the listening process, and improvement would be judged according to criteria internal to listening rather than by what the process produces in terms of changed (or not) decisions and outcomes. Naturally, the procedural criteria will be different in the political case compared to the quotidian conversational case—eye contact and regular questions designed to elicit or corroborate interpretations are difficult to replicate at this scale, as we observed earlier in this chapter. So, in the political context, we may look for other criteria, such as the length of the listening exercise,[12] the effort expended on drawing in and reaching out to participants, and the way in which views are taken into account. Quite apart from these details, important though they are to a more fully worked out 'institutionalizing' of listening in democratic processes (which we will tackle in Chapter 6), the key thing to note here is that listening does indeed seem to play a role in the construction of democratic legitimacy.

GENERATING TRUST

In an influential set of lectures on the contemporary state of democracy, Pierre Rosanvallon set out to explain what he regards as the 'major political problem of our time': that while '[T]he democratic ideal now reigns unchallenged... regimes claiming to be democratic come in for vigorous criticism almost everywhere.'[13] The criticism is rooted in a deep disaffection with politics, evidenced by high levels of abstentionism and disengagement from the formal procedures of politics. According to Rosanvallon, democracy is a victim of its own success, in that its promise—combining individual autonomy with equality and a sharing of political power—is never fully realized, and perhaps

---

[12] In the UK at least there is a code of practice as far as the length of public consultations is concerned. The code was apparently breached in the case of the government's consultation regarding its controversial Disability Living Allowance plans in 2012: 'The consultation was two weeks shorter than usual, and the legislation was presented to parliament two days before the consultation closed—making it impossible to take into account.' Sue Marsh, 'The government said it was listening to us: it was a sham', *The Guardian*, 9 January 2012, p. 22.

[13] Pierre Rosanvallon, *Counter-Democracy: Politics in an Age of Distrust* (Cambridge: Cambridge University Press, 2008), p. 1.

never can be fully realized. Democracy is always therefore 'asymptotic'—sometimes coming close to, but never actually achieving—its aspirations. Trust and distrust play an important role in Rosanvallon's analysis of democracy's difficulties.[14] To some extent, distrust of established power is at the heart of the origins of democracy: democracy is, in part, an answer to the question of how to regulate and domesticate power, and this is done by granting power to elected individuals for a given period of time only. Elections are thus a way of regulating distrust: the boil of distrust can be lanced through the electoral process. Rosanvallon sees distrust as a permanent feature of the political scene and he shares a good deal of the pessimism around politics and the democratic process that we saw in the work of Jeffrey Green in Chapter 1. Distrust is not only permanently with us, but there is always a constant amount of it, as it were. According to Rosanvallon, the most we can hope for is to manage distrust, and he offers no advice as to how levels of distrust might be reduced. There is a strong echo of Green in Rosanvallon's distinction between 'the ability to act and the ability to prevent',[15] and his acceptance of citizens' 'inability to compel governments to take specific actions or decisions'.[16] The key role of Rosanvallon's citizen is no longer as voter but as watchdog—once again there are powerful similarities between the 'ocular democracy' of Green and the 'watchful eye of the people' of Rosanvallon.[17]

Even if we accept Rosanvallon's thesis that the voter has been replaced by the watchdog, that distrust is endemic, and that effective vigilance is the highest aspiration of the citizen in contemporary liberal democracies, then the aural—as well as the ocular—sense clearly has a role to play. For vigilance is not only a matter of looking hard but of listening hard too. 'Surveillance' (Rosanvallon's word[18]) arguably requires acute use of all the senses, but particularly the aural and ocular ones, since so much information relevant to managing distrust—in the sense of enabling a sufficient amount of the suspension of distrust for politics to be possible at all—arrives through

---

[14] It is interesting to note how trust is becoming an increasingly important concept in political theorizing, both in the context of democracy and more widely. To Rosanvallon we might add Charles Tilly, *Trust and Rule* (Cambridge: Cambridge University Press, 2005) and Richard Sennett, *Together: The Rituals, Pleasures, and Politics of Cooperation* (Yale: Yale University Press, 2012). We will comment further on trust in connection with the idea of dialogic democracy in Chapter 4.

[15] Rosanvallon (2008), p. 14.   [16] Rosanvallon (2008), p. 14.
[17] Rosanvallon (2008), p. 29.   [18] Rosanvallon (2008), p. 13.

these senses. But I believe that focusing on listening provides us with a more positive approach to the distrust problem, as it potentially furnishes us with a means of reducing levels of distrust rather than simply managing it. Clearly, distrust cannot be palliated by simply talking more. Indeed, the roots of distrust often lie in monological talking and the concomitant impression that no real dialogue is taking place. This can combine with a disconnect between what people say and what they do, or between what they promise and what actually happens. This is especially true in the context of the relationship between politicians and the people, which is the relationship on which Rosanvallon focuses. On the one hand there is the gap between the behaviour we expect of our elected representatives and the behaviour they sometimes exhibit. Leaving aside the debate regarding private and public morality and whether we should trust a politician any less in public life if s/he proves less than trustworthy in her or his private life, scandals such as those surrounding UK members of parliament and their expense claims between 2009 and 2012 have a corrosive effect on the politician–people relationship. Levels of trust decline, and the relationship is not repaired—in fact, it is usually further *im*paired—by politicians trying to 'explain themselves'. So more talking, on its own, is not the answer to the problem of distrust—or, at least, not talking by politicians.

It would be equally naïve, though, to think that listening—on its own—will provide the required balm. It is probably uncontroversial to say that politicians should listen to the electorate's opinion under conditions of distrust (indeed, in relatively open societies it is likely to be virtually impossible for them to ignore it). This is a minimal requirement, given that elected politicians acquire their authority and position from the electorate. But this one-way listening may simply polarize the relationship still further in a mire of mutual incomprehension. Trust (at least where it has to be negotiated rather than assumed) is a function of understanding which is, by definition, a matter of reciprocity. In our communicative connection, reciprocity is best understood as *dialogue*, which is the respectful interplay between speaking and listening. So while it might be uncontroversial to say that politicians should listen to the electorate in situations of distrust, it will be less immediately obvious that the same is true in reverse and that dialogue requires that electors listen to politicians too. In the example referred to above—the MPs' expenses scandal—the MPs' case was never really heard and the possibility of a dialogue aimed at a better understanding of the situation was undermined by the strident tones and polarized opinions that characterized the 'debate'—such as it was. So we should not jump too quickly to the conclusion that, '[D]isappointment is an almost inevitable consequence of a distrustful citizenry'[19] Listening, especially apophatic listening leading to dialogue, can be a route to lowering levels of distrust. Imagine the British public adopting an apophatic listening approach to the MPs' expenses issues—as far as possible bracketing off what they 'already know' and listening to the politicians' case in its own terms. We will explore this potential in more detail in Chapter 4 when we develop the idea of dialogic democracy further.

DEALING WITH DEEP DISAGREEMENTS

One of the key problems in both democratic theory and practice is dealing with deep rifts: 'the centrally most difficult problem of democratic theory and government [is] how to handle deep disagreements'[20] The idea of 'handling', here, is important, since the point is not necessarily to *overcome* disagreement. Disagreement should not always be regarded as a failure since it, 'can signal sociability rather than a breach of civility'[21] and we should also take into account the possible sociocultural factors that determine the degree to which disagreement is shunned or embraced: 'Americans are more inclined to like people who agree with them whereas Australians tend to be more interested in people who disagree with them. For the former, agreement implies liking and disagreement rejection, whereas for the latter, disagreement is a source of lively conversation'[22] The rifts that need to be handled might be ideological, sociological, or religious, and a number of strategies have been suggested for dealing with them. These include

---

[19]   Rosanvallon (2008), p. 254.

[20]   Russell Hardin, 'Deliberation: method, not theory', in Stephen Macedo (ed.), *Deliberative Politics: Essays on Democracy and Disagreement* (New York and Oxford: Oxford University Press, 1999), p. 103.

[21]   Maria Sifianou, 'Disagreements, face and politeness', *Journal of Pragmatics* 44 (2012), no. 12, p. 1554.

[22]   Sifianou (2012), p. 1557. Sifianou recognizes, of course, that this is a 'gross overgeneralisation', but she holds to the general point.

special representation for groups, either in theory or in practice,[23] and attempts at encouraging deliberation between parties who disagree profoundly with one another. The role of listening in these difficult contexts has been underexplored. As Susan Bickford says, 'We cannot suppose that political actors are sympathetic toward one another in a conflictual context, yet it is precisely the presence of conflict and differences that makes communicative interaction necessary.'[24] Bickford recommends 'political listening' as a means of connecting parties in conflict with one another, and she stresses that this is not necessarily a 'caring or amicable' practice but, nevertheless, one that 'makes politics possible' as well as being 'what democratic politics requires'.[25]

Scepticism about the capacity for deliberation to deal with these kinds of problems is rife and apparently well-founded. But the reasons for this scepticism themselves invite reflection on the role that listening might play in improving deliberation's chances.[26] For instance, in his commentary on Gutmann and Thompson's vigorous defence of the deliberative approach to dealing with disagreement, Ian Shapiro argues that deliberation can't deal with fundamentalists. As he says: 'the difficulty here is that the fundamentalist believes exactly what Gutmann and Thompson decry as illegitimate: that it is necessary to adopt her sectarian way of life as a condition for gaining access to the moral understanding that is essential to judging the validity of her moral claims'.[27]

What Shapiro's criticism misses is the possibility that deliberation itself has been underdeveloped and undertheorized in not including systematic reflection on the importance of listening for underpinning effective deliberation. We shall see in Chapter 4 that, despite being the closest approximation in democratic theory and practice to 'conversation', deliberative democracy has paid remarkably little attention to

---

[23] Iris Marion Young, 'Polity and group difference: a critique of the idea of universal citizenship', *Ethics* 99 (1989), no 2, pp. 250–74.

[24] Susan Bickford, *The Dissonance of Democracy: Listening, Conflict, and Citizenship* (Ithaca and London: Cornell University Press, 1996), p. 2.

[25] Bickford (1996), p. 2.

[26] At the root, says Carolyn Cusick, this is a problem of epistemology, and she argues that not enough attention has been paid to listening in the context of how to know 'better': Carolyn Cusick, 'Speaking, Listening and Communicative Justice: Educating Epistemic Trust and Responsibility' (PhD thesis, Vanderbilt University, 2012), pp. 45–51.

[27] Ian Shapiro, 'Enough of deliberation: politics is about interests and power', in Macedo (1999), pp. 30–1.

listening as part of its procedural rules. Of course, it might still be the case that Shapiro's fundamentalist won't want to listen, but we should at least consider the possibility that a process in which people take it in turns to *listen* has a better chance of developing the required 'we' community than that in which people take it in turns to *speak* (where there is no listening).

There is a good deal of evidence to suggest that engaged listening can improve understanding across social difference. Research conducted by Ximena Zúñiga and her colleagues in regard to dialogue between and across gender and racial differences, with a sample involving a 'diverse set of participants from different regions of the country [USA], different social and economic class backgrounds, and different types of hosting institutions',[28] produced the following conclusion: 'Participants reported reflecting and learning about a range of issues from other participants, such as sexual violence, individual experiences with racism, the cost of institutional racism, and the benefits of privilege.'[29] Digging down beneath this general conclusion, white participants reported enhanced awareness of the effects of racism on job prospects ('there really *is* such a thing as institutional racism in America'[30]), while, even within groups, there was evidence of increased understanding of the effects of racism and sexism.[31] We shall see more evidence of this dynamic at work towards the end of Chapter 4, and, indeed, the accumulated corroboration of this point is so strong that the challenge lies less in proving it beyond reasonable doubt, and more in creating the conditions in which listening can—and must—take place. At the root this challenge consists of a challenge to political power, for it is the powerful who need to listen to the marginalized—and why should they? The problem is not one of speaking truth to power, but of getting the powerful to listen.

---

[28] Ximena Zúñiga, Jane Mildred, Rani Varghese, Keri DeJong, and Molly Keehn, 'Engaged listening in race/ethnicity and gender intergroup dialogue courses', *Equity and Excellence in Education* 45 (2012), no. 1, p. 84. It should be noted that all the participants were at institutions of higher education.

[29] Zúñiga, et al. (2012), p. 94.

[30] Zúñiga, et al. (2012), p. 94.

[31] '[A] woman of color discussed her increased awareness of power, privilege, and oppression in society after listening to other students of color. Previously, she had held the belief that if someone worked hard, they could "avoid the effects of racism", but the dialogue had made her "more conscious" of the pervasiveness of its effects'; Zúñiga, et al. (2012), p. 94.

One arena in which the powerful (or previously powerful) have been forced to listen is in truth and reconciliation committees.[32] It is well known that listening plays a crucial role in such committees—without careful listening they wouldn't work. The aim of truth and reconciliation committees is not so different from some of the aims of democratic conversation: relation-building, sharing disparate under-standings, developing reciprocity, perhaps even empathizing with those with whom one disagrees. Yet while listening plays a central role in truth and reconciliation committees—perhaps *the* central role—its absence in democratic theory is marked. Indeed, when such theorists are looking for resources to explain and/or assist what John Dryzek (after Robert Putnam) calls the 'bridging' capacity of democracy,[33] they tend to focus only on the speaking side of the dialogic or conver-sational equation. Dryzek himself talks of 'bridging rhetoric', which reaches out to audiences constituted differently from the speaker. It is true that rhetoric has a listening component, in that, in order for it to function effectively as persuasion, the rhetorician has to *under-stand* her/his audience, and this entails careful listening.[34] But what we learn from truth and reconciliation events is that listening plays a powerful and independent role in the bridging process. Maybe part of the reluctance to take this analogy with truth and reconciliation committees too far is that these are extreme situations which bear little resemblance to the kinds of cleavage and division one finds in run-of-the-mill plural societies. Thus, listening is a key part of the political process when it comes to improving the conditions of asylum seek-ers in Australia,[35] dealing with deep disagreements in the Swat Valley in north-west Pakistan,[36] and resolving conflicts between Mexican

---

[32] For an account of the conditions for success of peace and reconciliation commit-tees, and, above all, of the need for perpetrators to listen to their victims' stories, see Yasmin Saikia, 'Insaniyat for peace: survivors' narrative of the 1971 war of Bangladesh', *Journal of Genocide Research* 13 (2011), no. 4, pp. 475–501.

[33] John Dryzek, *Foundations and Frontiers of Deliberative Governance* (Oxford: Oxford University Press, 2010), p. 76.

[34] Jim Macnamara, 'Beyond voice: audience-making and the work and architecture of listening as new media literacies', *Continuum: Journal of Media and Cultural Studies* 27 (2013), no. 1, p. 161.

[35] Deborah Zion, Linda Briskman, and Bebe Loff, 'Psychiatric ethics and a politics of compassion: the case of detained asylum seekers in Australia', *Journal of Bioethical Enquiry* 9 (2012), no. 1, pp. 67–75.

[36] Urs Geiser, 'Reading political contestation in Pakistan's Swat Valley—from delib-eration to "the political" and beyond', *Geoforum* 43 (2012), no. 4, pp. 707–15.

immigrants and white Americans in Arizona,[37] but these situations are so unlike those which obtain in 'standard' multicultural societies that the lessons learned in them may simply not be relevant.

We could take the opposite point of view, though. If listening proves to be so powerful a lubricant in extreme situations, then surely it can be put to work even more effectively and easily in more quotidian ones. President Obama gave an example of the power of listening in overcoming disagreement at the time of the shooting of House Representative Gabrielle Giffords and others in Arizona in January 2011. US politics at the time was characterized by sharply divided opinions across the political spectrum, with the Tea Party squaring up to liberals and Democrats around a range of issues from health care to foreign policy. Obama saw the shooting of Giffords as a chance to draw the American people together, and he seized the opportunity by referring explicitly to the need to listen to one another better. He began his memorial speech by referring to the 'sharply polarized' nature of American political discourse and appealed to his audience to 'talk with each other in a way that heals, not in a way that wounds'. He then exhorted them to 'listen to each other more carefully', before laying out a classical list of the characteristics and benefits of reconciliation that can be achieved by more careful listening: humility, expanding moral imaginations, sharpening empathy, generosity, compassion. Overall, this was an appeal to 'civility in public discourse' with a view to overcoming the 'usual plane of politics and point-scoring and pettiness that drifts away in the next news cycle'.[38] This was a potent use of a tragedy to try to overcome social and political rift and rupture, and a clear example of an appeal to listening and its attributes and consequences as a means for doing so.

Of course, we (and President Obama) must confront the possibility that better listening might result in no more than a better understanding of the reasons for disagreement rather than a means of 'constantly widen[ing] the circle of our concern so that we bequeath the American Dream to future generations',[39] as he grandiosely put it.

---

[37] Emile Bruneau and Rebecca Saxe, 'The power of being heard: the benefits of "perspective-giving" in the context of inter-group conflict', *Journal of Experimental Social Psychology* 48 (2012), no. 4, pp. 855–66.

[38] Barak Obama, 'Obama speech to Arizona Gifford's memorial', War on Terror News, 14 January 2011, available at <http://waronterrornews.typepad.com/home/2011/01/obama-speech-to-arizona-giffords-memorial.html> (accessed 14 June 2011).

[39] Obama (2011).

It could be that listening hard to Obama might make Tea Party activists even surer that the American Dream is not safe in the president's hands and that he needs to be replaced as soon as possible. In this case listening is not a means of overcoming disagreement but rather of deepening and sclerosing it—even if on a better understood basis. Cate Thill has observed this phenomenon at work in the context of the Australian government's attempts at reconciliation in the guise of its Northern Territory Intervention, where she points out that:

> While listening can figure as a way of responding to the other … it is certainly not always open, empathetic or transformative. On the contrary, I would suggest that public debate about the NT Intervention manifests a range of communicative practices, including argumentation, therapeutic and selective listening, which function to preserve rather than transform established hierarchies of attention.[40]

As an antidote to these kinds of non-transformative modes of listening, Thill, drawing on the work of Charles Husband,[41] recommends 'courageous listening'. This type of listening steers a course between not listening at all on the one hand, and expecting that good listening will automatically result in consensus, on the other.[42] The courageous listener backgrounds her/his own perspective and is prepared for incommensurability, which, in Thill's view, is a precondition for further interaction.[43] Here listening plays the role of not so much overcoming deep disagreements but of foregrounding them, so this is a type of listening potentially well suited to agonistic rather than consensus theories and forms of democracy.

A further caveat to the thought that better listening can help overcome disagreement is offered by Jamil Zaki. Zaki suggests that while 'perspective taking' usually reduces prejudice, the approach sometimes fails.[44] Analysis of where and why it fails reveals that, 'the effects of perspective taking … differ dramatically depending on who is walking in whose

---

[40] Cate Thill, 'Courageous listening, responsibility for the other and the Northern Territory Intervention', *Continuum: Journal of Media and Cultural Studies* 23 (2009), no. 4, p. 541.

[41] Charles Husband, 'Media and the public sphere in multi-ethnic societies', in S. Cottle (ed.), *Ethnic Minorities and the Media* (Buckingham and Philadelphia: Open University Press, 2000).

[42] Thill (2009), p. 539.

[43] Thill (2009), p. 540.

[44] Jamil Zaki, 'The curious perils of seeing the other side', *Scientific American Mind* 23 (July/August 2012), no. 3, pp. 20–1.

shoes'.[45] More specifically, dominant groups turn out to be better disposed to non-dominant counterparts after perspective taking, but 'lower status' groups do not always feel the same way. In fact, 'listening to the point of view of white Americans actually worsened the attitudes of Mexican immigrants towards this group'.[46] Zaki offers a number of reasons for this (non-dominant groups are always perspective taking, so more of the same will not shift their attitudes; it is harder for non-dominants to listen to the views of others because they are so used to their own perspectives being ignored), and then offers the crucial—for us—observation that, 'nondominant people's attitudes about disputes improved not after perspective taking but after "perspective giving"—that is, describing their own experiences to attentive members of higher-ranking groups'.[47] This squares very precisely with Jenny Pearce's discovery (referred to in Chapter 1) that social activists will sometimes define power in terms of being listened to. In Chapter 2 I suggested that listening can act as a solvent of power, and while Zaki's observations offer us no reason for abandoning that view, they do suggest that a demand for strictly reciprocal listening across a power gradient is unproductive. The solvent will only have effect if those who are dominant listen to those who are not.

In the dominant literature there are, therefore, two main approaches to the issue of disagreement: one in which the aim is to overcome it ('consensus'), and the other in which it is an unavoidable and even welcome feature of democratic politics ('agonism'). Joshua Miller steers a course between these two with his notion of 'civic care', which is something citizens display towards one another (and to the polity) when they engage in what he calls 'reasonable disagreement'.[48] Key to Miller's position is his focus on the procedures of debate rather than their outcome. He is less interested in whether agreement is reached or not, and more in how disagreement is handled. Whether I persuade my interlocutor to agree with my position is somewhat beside the

---

[45]　Zaki (2012), p. 20.

[46]　Zaki (2012), pp. 20–1. This conclusion is challenged, though, by the research of Zúñiga and her colleagues referred to earlier in this chapter: '[some] have argued that IGD [Intergroup Dialogue] mainly involves people from disadvantaged groups who educate people from advantaged groups. Our finding...does not appear to support this assertion. Participants from both advantaged and disadvantaged groups...appear to have been interested in and to have learned from both groups in their IGD'; Zúñiga, et al. (2012), p. 96.

[47]　Zaki (2012), p. 21.

[48]　Joshua Miller, 'Caring to disagree: democratic disagreement as civic care', *Polity* 44 (2012), no. 3, pp. 400–25.

point, as what counts—from the point of view of sustaining democracy—is the way my interlocutor and I have treated each other. What is curious is how none of these contenders—supporters of consensus, agonists, or even Miller—seems to have noted how important listening is to each of their points of view. Anything other than a forced consensus requires careful listening: agonists cannot know what they are agonizing about without listening out for contending points of view, and Miller's 'civic care' seems inevitably to involve studied listening between citizens. We should perhaps conclude that research on the nature, role, and desirability of disagreement in democracies should henceforth have an analysis of listening at its heart.

LISTENING AND REPRESENTATION

Dealing with deep disagreements is one thing, and 'understanding' is key to this. But there is a more direct way in which better listening can lead to better understanding in the context of one of modern democracy's principal ambitions: the more effective representation of people's interests. The good representative will want to know what her/his constituents' interests are, and it is sometimes all too easy to get this wrong. Careful listening could help. Indeed, it has the capacity to overturn assumptions about the reasons people act as they do, and can lead the way to more effective resolution of political conflict. I am acutely aware that this is a profoundly unsophisticated approach to representation. Michael Saward is rightly critical of the metaphysics of presence betrayed by the triangular conception of representation in which 'a subject stands for an object that is an account of a referent'.[49] He argues that, 'we need to add to this triangular conception the ideas of the maker and the audience (for claims)'.[50] But the implications of this, particularly in respect of the need to take account of the role of the audience in any representative claim, actually lend some potential support to the notion that listening is a key aspect of the analytics of representation. Saward says that, 'there is no representative claim without its being open to a counterclaim or a denial of claim from part

---

[49] Michael Saward, *The Representative Claim* (Oxford: Oxford University Press, 2010), p. 6.
[50] Saward (2010), p. 6.

of its audience. Audience members, too, are agents and actors. This is a point that runs directly counter to what I called above the undue "unidirectionality" of [Hannah] Pitkin's account of political representation.'[51] This supports the view that I have been at pains to stress: listening is an act of independent agency which, while 'requiring' speech (or noise), can then react to it in the forms of refusal or acceptance. This is Saward's point: that the audience at which the representative claim is aimed can refuse to recognize the claim. But the listening has to be reciprocal. First, the audience must 'listen' to the claim and then the claim-maker must listen out for the fate of the claim—acceptance or rejection.

Seyla Benhabib offers a suggestive example of this dynamic at work—the so-called *affaire du foulard* in France in 1989, when three female students were suspended from school for refusing to remove their *hijabs* in class. This was (and is) generally read as a conflict between religion and the French state, and particularly the issue of whether wearing the *hijab* in school is in conflict with the principles of a lay educational context. Benhabib reports that it wasn't until the girls themselves were *listened* to that a different interpretation of the events emerged. The girls were not striking a blow for their religion but rather making a gesture of political defiance.[52] It wasn't until they were listened to that their refusal of the way their protest had been represented became apparent. A common view is that understanding between political actors requires either shared interests or a pre-existing social bond of some kind. Where this is not the case, careful listening—or what Susan Bickford calls 'a quality of *attention* inherent in the very practice of deliberation'[53]—can help. And, as David Levin points out, the practice of careful listening can contribute to a sharpening of reciprocity between listeners, which can, in turn, lead to new and unexpected understandings: 'In a group or community where all people are committed to the reciprocity of good listening, each participant develops a clearer, more individual *sense* of the matter in question by helping each of the others to do the same. Where there really is such reciprocated listening, what is facilitated is not only the *sharing* of an *existing* understanding, but also the *emergence and formation* of *new*

[51] Saward (2010), p. 54.
[52] Seyla Benhabib, *Another Cosmopolitanism* (New York: Oxford University Press, 2004), p. 56.
[53] Bickford (1996), p. 25; emphasis in the original.

understanding.'[54] Talking tends to be directed to a determinate end (the speaker wants to make a point, to nail down an argument, to convince a listener), while listening *prises open* the content of speech and opens up new avenues for exploration.

Making space for the listening that can lead to understanding is crucial. In this context a surprising feature of attending to listening as well as speaking is that, as we saw in Chapter 2, we come to prize silence as well as noise. We tend to think of a flourishing public sphere as being noisome and full of the sound of voices—the more the merrier. On the other hand, we know that a proper conversation requires attentive silence on the part of those who are not speaking: '*Silence* is frequently mentioned as one of the conditions for, or inevitable correlates of, genuine listening.'[55] While we know this is true for quotidian conversation, we have paid very little attention to it in the political context. Benjamin Barber is one of the few who have:

> one measure of healthy political talk is the amount of *silence* it permits and encourages, for silence is the precious medium in which reflection is nurtured and empathy can grow. Without it, there is only the babble of raucous interests and insistent rights vying for the deaf ears of impatient adversaries. The very idea of rights—the right to speak, the right to get on the record, the right to be heard—precludes silence. The Quaker meeting carries a message for democrats, but they are often too busy articulating their interests to hear it.[56]

This presents something of a challenge, for while we might acknowledge that, 'in order to hear something, we must first *give* it our silence',[57] we need to find ways of incorporating silence in the political process. Guidance as to how we might do this is sparse—in fact, the search for silence sometimes seems like a minority sport practised only by the privileged,[58] or in the religious and artistic realms of society.[59] Just how we

---

[54] David Michael Levin, *The Listening Self: Personal Growth, Social Change and the Closure of Metaphysics* (London and New York: Routledge, 1989), p. 135; emphasis in the original.

[55] Bickford (1996), p. 153; emphasis in the original.

[56] Benjamin Barber, *Strong Democracy: Participatory Politics for a New Age* (Berkeley, Los Angeles, and London: University of California Press, 1984), pp. 175–6; emphasis in the original.

[57] Levin (1989), p. 232; emphasis in the original.

[58] Sara Maitland, *A Book of Silence* (London: Granta, 2008). This is a heartfelt plea for silence, but the means described here for achieving it are beyond most of us.

[59] Stuart Sim, *Manifesto for Silence* (Edinburgh: Edinburgh University Press, 2007). This is an erudite book on the importance of silence but, significantly, the practices where 'silence matters' (religion, philosophy, arts, literature) do not include politics.

are to incorporate silence in politics will vary with the case: the raucous atmosphere of Prime Minister's Question Time in the UK's House of Commons contrasts quite starkly with what is generally the more sedate and considered atmosphere of the committee room.[60] One example is that practised by the English and Welsh Green Party, which has a one-minute period of 'attunement' before each plenary debate. This has the effect of helping to focus delegates' attention on their new surroundings (they might have been doing any number of things before coming to the session) and what is going to happen there. The nature and type of silence required therefore need careful analysis and design, and we will explore some options in Chapter 6. One thing they will have in common is that they are attentive silences, for we should remember, along with Susan Bickford, that, '[W]ords that continually fall into dead silence can have no worldly reality and lead to no joint action. This silent refusal, as deliberate not-listening, is clearly a drastic political act.'[61] Political silence must be a preparation for communication, not a refusal of it.

IMPROVING DELIBERATION

I will be paying more detailed attention to deliberative democracy in Chapter 4, but here I want to say something about the role of listening in deliberative contexts, by way of (a) highlighting the relative lack of attention paid to it by deliberative scholars, and (b) signalling some of the benefits that might be derived from doing so. In an article devoted to discussing how people *actually* (rather than ideally) communicate in deliberative forums, Laura Black points out how little research there

---

Sim does, though, talk suggestively about a 'politics of silence' as involving a state of 'reflection' aligned with 'non-consumerism'. Thus, 'silence can become a political statement, a refusal to accept the swamping of our culture by the imperatives of big business corporations and multinational corporations'; p. 2. There may be much in common between 'slow politics'—e.g. slow food—and the politics of silence.

[60] As the current Labour Party leader Ed Miliband rather plaintively said during a boisterous Prime Minister's Question Time session, when the issue of cancer patients was being discussed, 'it was a "disgrace" that they [the Tory Party MPs] were shouting at all. If ever there was a case for pausing, listening and reflecting, this was it'; reported in Simon Hoggart, 'The unfamiliar sound of Labour cheers', *The Guardian*, 16 June 2011, p. 4.

[61] Bickford (1996), p. 155.

is on actual discursive practices.[62] Where work has been done on this, it is striking how little attention (virtually none, it seems) has been paid by political theorists to the degree to which people do or not listen during the deliberative process itself. Analysis has been carried out on how people state opinions and make arguments, on how they cite sources and tell stories, and on how they express disagreement and ask questions. All of these focus on speech, and even when analysis turns to what Black refers to as the 'building and sustaining social relationships' role of deliberation,[63] where consideration, comprehension, and respect become important, there is still no sustained examination of listening, even though is it a vital component of these three practices. It is as though listening requires no independent research effort, which we might regard as odd in a practice which sells itself as one in which views and information are carefully weighed by participants, and in which differences between participants are respected. We should have learned from Chapter 2 that it is no longer good enough to say that deliberative democrats pay 'implicit' attention to listening because it is somehow 'contained' in the very idea of deliberation. Our analysis in Chapter 2 showed how listening is bound up with power in a number of important ways, so if deliberation's intention is to produce political conversation driven by the forceless force of the better argument rather than by power-based strategizing, specific and systematic attention to listening in the deliberative process is not only warranted but essential.

In what follows I aim to demonstrate how listening can be an independent analytical datum when it comes to interpreting democratic processes themselves—and especially deliberative democratic processes. I can show this by discussing a case that Robert Goodin analyses in some detail in his *Innovating Democracy: Democratic Theory and Practice after the Deliberative Turn*.[64] This is obviously only one case, but I believe that the conclusions I reach could be applied to—and certainly tested against other cases of—deliberative democratic processes. The case Goodin examines is the Bloomfield Track case.

---

[62] Laura Black, 'How people communicate during deliberative events', in Tina Nabatchi, John Gastil, G. Michael Weiksner, and Matt Leighninger (eds), *Democracy in Motion: Evaluating the Practice and Impact of Deliberative Civic Engagement* (Oxford: Oxford University Press, 2012), p. 60.

[63] Black (2012), p. 69.

[64] Robert Goodin, *Innovating Democracy: Democratic Theory and Practice after the Deliberative Turn* (Oxford: Oxford University Press, 2008).

The Bloomfield Track is a road that runs through the Daintree Forest in Cairns, Australia, and the policy decision was whether this road should be improved or not. As an exercise in deliberative democracy, the Far North Queensland Citizens' Jury met to consider the policy options. The deliberative process took four days: Day One involved a visit to the site and background briefings; Days Two and Three were taken up with listening to, and questioning, expert witnesses and community representatives; and Day Four was devoted to the jurors' deliberations.

Deliberative democratic theory has it that deliberation, when conducted properly, has the capacity to change people's preferences. When confronted by a better argument the deliberative democrat should change her/his mind.[65] In the Bloomfield Track case the jurors had five policy options to decide between—and, as deliberative theory might expect, over the course of the process the jurors' minds changed dramatically. In fact, as Goodin says, 'the least popular option at the beginning of the process turned out to be the most popular by the end'.[66] But crucially, says Goodin, and contrary to deliberative expectations, the main shift did not take place during the deliberative phase of the process (Day Four), but during what Goodin calls the 'information phase' (Days 1–3). Goodin's counter-intuitive conclusion (at least from the point of view of deliberative logic) runs as follows:

> we are led to suppose (with contemporary deliberative democrats) that deliberation—in the sorts of settings that characterize political life, anyway—consists principally in interpersonal communications, paradigmatically conversational, dialogic, or discursive in form. This chapter queries that proposition. Its thesis is that much (maybe most) of the work of deliberation occurs well before the formal proceedings—before the organized 'talking together' ever begins.[67]

The jurors themselves were asked which of the phases of the process made the biggest difference to them, and their replies certainly give the deliberative democrat food for thought: 'No one thought the "group

---

[65] It is worth pointing out that at the heart of this belief lies the assumption that people are listening properly to other people's views: 'The riskiness of listening comes partly from the possibility that what we hear will require change from us'; Bickford (1996), p. 149. This assumption, and the absolutely crucial role that good listening plays in it, is virtually never recognized or discussed.

[66] Goodin (2008), p. 46.

[67] Goodin (2008), p. 40.

discussion" was the most important factor in changing their opinion; three-quarters of them thought it was the least important factor.'[68]

Goodin then sets out to discuss this somewhat disconcerting set of results. He offers a series of possible explanations for the conclusion that, 'it is clear that the bigger change, by a wide margin, occurred in the minds of jurors *before* the jury's formal discussions began'.[69] Among these reasons are: the order of the phases (whichever phase comes first will be the most significant), the duration of the phases (the discussion phase was shorter than the information phase), the idea of discussion as a 'corrective' (i.e. not designed to change minds but to come to the 'right' decision), and the cumulative effect of data during the information phase, which made it difficult for the direction of travel to be turned round in the discussion phase.[70] He adds to his list an extension of the last explanation via the notion of the possible path dependency of the discussion—that is, that the path the discussion sets out on, and one's place in the discussion order, can affect the decision eventually reached.

These are all plausible explanations and it is not my job here to choose between them. What I want to do is to *add* to the list of possible explanations by pointing out that the role that listening did or did not play in this particular Citizens' Jury is not discussed at all, yet it might well have been very significant. Take, first, the information phase—the phase in which most of the 'changing minds' work was done. As Goodin himself says, '[T]he simple process of jurors *seeing* the site for themselves, *focusing their minds* on the issues, and *listening* to what experts had to say did all the work in changing jurors' attitudes. Talking among themselves, as a jury, did virtually none of it.'[71] Each of the italicized words/phrases is a key aspect of what was going on in the information phase, and it appears that it was these activities, and not talking, that changed jurors' minds. At the very least, then, we might surmise that both as a normative objective and an explanatory factor, *listening* (in the widest sense of using all our senses to capture information) should receive greater attention from theorists of deliberative democracy. Thus, if it is indeed true that the outcome of this particular exercise in deliberative democracy is, 'contrary to the expectations of discursive democrats who would have us privilege

---

[68] Goodin (2008), p. 51. [69] Goodin (2008), p. 49; emphasis in the original.
[70] Goodin (2008), pp. 52–4. [71] Goodin (2008), p. 58; emphasis added.

conversation over cogitation as politically the most important mode of deliberation',[72] then this is because deliberative democracy has come to be too closely associated with talking and not enough with listening. My suggestion is that deliberative democratic theory, as well as its practice, could advance by opening the 'black box' of deliberation and seeing what goes on inside it. Earlier in the chapter, for example, I discussed the role that listening can play in dealing with deep disagreement. John Dryzek has argued that deliberative democracy is 'of crucial importance...to deeply divided societies and deep disputes in the international system'.[73] My suggestion is that whatever success deliberative democracy has in these contexts will be due to a particular 'moment' in the deliberative process: the moment(s) at which apophatic listening is taking place. Once this is understood, the door is open to improving the deliberative process by focusing on establishing the conditions and preconditions for better listening. I will take this idea forward in Chapter 6.

Something similar might be said in respect of Goodin's path-dependency explanation for the discussion phase of the process not having the decisive effect that deliberative democrats might want. According to Goodin, path dependency is a result of what he calls 'serial updating',[74] that is, each speaker listens to what the previous speaker has to say, then forms a judgement: '[I]f we listen carefully and take fully into account what the previous speakers just have said when forming our own view as to what we should say next, the conversation can be highly path dependent'.[75] Goodin's solution to this problem is to abandon serial updating in favour of a 'wait to update' strategy: '[I]nstead of dynamically updating their own beliefs as others speak, they should wait to revise their beliefs until all the private information is on the table. Only at that point should they engage in "periodic

---

[72] Goodin (2008), p. 50. With this contrast between 'conversation' and 'cogitation' Goodin gets extremely close to recognizing listening as a key part of the deliberative process, since cogitating is a matter of processing information we have received through the senses. Yet speaking still seems to be the engine that drives deliberation, for Goodin: 'by talking together, deliberators pool the information that they bring with them to the process'; Robert Goodin, 'How can deliberative democracy get a grip?' *Political Quarterly* 83 (2012), no. 4, p. 806. Once again, the 'pooling' of which Goodin speaks cannot take place without the participants listening carefully to each other.

[73] Dryzek (2010), p. 5, and see John Dryzek, *Deliberative Global Politics: Discourse and Democracy in a Divided World* (Cambridge: Polity Press, 2006).

[74] Goodin (2008), p. 119.

[75] Goodin (2008), p. 119.

updating" of their beliefs, taking account of all the new information now in the public domain.[76]

This is a very sensible suggestion, but what is significant about it is that it turns the *discussion* phase into something resembling the *information* phase of the process—during which, we remember, jurors were doing much more *listening* than *talking*. What Goodin is, in effect, asking for is more silence. It might appear ironic that discursive democracy could be improved by having less discussion, but it only appears so because we have got so used to thinking of discursive democracy in terms of speaking. Once we remember that good listening is an essential component of effective discussion—that the 'ideal speech situation' requires 'ideal listening' too—then the idea that discursive democracy requires less speech and more silence comes to seem less absurd. This would give rise to a more thoroughgoing *dialogical* understanding of deliberative democracy, with all that this would imply for practising and theorizing it. In general, the implication—once more—is that theories of discursive and deliberative democracy should pay more normative and analytic attention to the theoretical and practical role of listening.[77]

Goodin's work provides evidence that listening is a vital part of the deliberative process, and although it is impossible to be sure in advance of further work, it is plausible to imagine that this would be true of any deliberative process we chose to analyse in detail. Given what we learnt in Chapter 2 about good and bad listening and how listening can be improved, there is scope here for improving the quality of deliberation. A precondition for doing so is a recognition of its importance to the deliberative process, and that is what I hope to have begun to establish here. Among other things, this means moving away from judging the success of deliberation by its outcomes and focusing more on the process.[78] The next step is to think of practical ways in which listening might be given its independent due in this process,

---

[76] Goodin (2008), p. 120.

[77] Goodin (2008) offers us a helpful table indicating 'standards of good discursive practice'; (p. 188), about which he says, 'there seems to be an impressively broad scholarly consensus' (p. 187). If so, then the consensus seems to be that listening is not a fundamental part of good practice. Of the fifteen criteria collected under the three headings of 'maxims of conversation', 'rules of political interlocution', and 'indices of deliberative quality', the only references to anything like listening are, 'attentiveness', i.e. 'pay attention to what is said by other participants'; and 'respect', i.e. 'respect towards counterarguments raised by opponents that contradict their own conclusions' (p. 188).

[78] John Gastil, Katie Knobloch, and Meghan Kelly, 'Evaluating deliberative public events and projects', in Nabatchi, et al. (2012).

with a view to its role and efficacy being enhanced. I will come back to this in Chapter 6.

CONCLUSION

In this chapter I have outlined five ways in which better listening could help democracies achieve their objectives. It could enhance legitimacy claims, increase levels of trust, help deal with disagreements, improve representation, and refine deliberation. What this points us towards is a dialogic notion of democracy. We are most used to thinking of dialogue in the context of a conversation in a book or a play. While this is not quite the meaning of dialogue I have in mind here, it points us in the right direction. This is because while dialogue in a play or a book is supposed to resemble a conversation, it clearly is not a conversation in the quotidian sense of the word. And what distinguishes it from a conversation over the garden fence is that it is more structured and determined. This is an important point for my argument in the book as a whole. In the Introduction I referred to democracy as a 'form of political conversation'. This is superficially plausible, but it is open to the objection that political and democratic intersubjectivity is just so different from the face-to-faceness that characterizes the circumstances of conversation that the word 'conversation' simply cannot be predicated of political intersubjectivity without both stretching the meaning of the word beyond the bounds of definitional acceptability, and seriously misunderstanding the nature of politics. So, although in the Introduction I refer positively to Anthony Giddens, Robert Goodin, and Michael Oakeshott as three of the very small number of theorists who refer to the practices one finds in a good relationship or a good conversation as a model for good democratic practices, we should be wary of pressing the analogy too hard. 'Conversation' tends to refer to a relaxed and informal exchange, nearer to what we might refer to as a 'chat' than a dialogue. Conversation and chat might well be an important prelude to dialogue as they are forms of exchange which can engender trust and assurance, both of which are ingredients of effective dialogue. But conversation is not the same as dialogue. The problem with pressing 'conversation' too hastily into strictly *political* service is that it assumes too much of what actually existing politics cannot provide: rough equality of access to speech and to a receptive audience. 'Voices which speak in conversation do not compose a hierarchy,'[79] says Michael Oakeshott. While we know what he means, we also know that hierarchies of all sorts are present in the circumstances of conversation—especially in the power relations that exist between the interlocutors.[80] Perceptively, Oakeshott remarks that, 'Properly speaking, it [conversation] is impossible in the absence of a diversity of voices'[81]—yet while this diversity of voices is what makes conversation possible, it is also the obstacle to the kind of free, 'civilized',[82] exchange of views that Oakeshott enthusiastically endorses. And this is because the diversity of which he speaks is inscribed in a landscape of power in which hierarchies, far from being the exception, are the absolute rule.

However, conversation can *turn into* dialogue, and it is instructive for us to analyse the moment at which this happens. It typically happens when a *disagreement* arises between the participants in a conversation. Archetypally, a dialogue might therefore be defined as a conversation involving different points of view, and—again archetypally—at the moment a conversation turns into a dialogue, particular rules begin to apply. One key rule is that the participants in the dialogue listen to one another, and, given what we said in the previous paragraph, the important thing is to create the circumstances in which listening becomes an obligation rather than an optional extra. Without this structural undergirding there is a danger that the dialogue will collapse back into the conversation, and once that happens the power relations between the interlocutors are more likely to be reproduced rather than challenged. It is significant that we use the phrase 'a dialogue of the deaf' to describe a dialogue that has failed: a dialogue in which the interlocutors have not respected the basic rule of dialogue, which is to listen.[83] I propose that from now on, drawing on what we learnt in the previous chapter, we understand dialogue as *structured disagreement underpinned by apophatic listening*. 'Structured' refers to

[79] Michael Oakeshott, 'The voice of poetry in the conversation of mankind', in *Rationalism in Politics and Other Essays* (London: Methuen, 1962), p. 198.

[80] Luke Plotica recognizes this blind spot in Oakeshott's theory of political conversation: Luke Philip Plotica, 'Deliberation or conversation: Michael Oakeshott on the ethos and conduct of democracy', *Polity* 44 (2012), no. 2, p. 305.

[81] Oakeshott (1962), p. 198.

[82] Oakeshott's word, not mine: Oakeshott (1962), p. 199.

[83] Of course, we should understand 'listen' in a broad sense here. It is perfectly possible for deaf people to listen to conversations—just as it is possible for them not to listen to them.

the way in which the dialogic encounter is organized so as to encourage apophatic listening, or listening which resists the inclination and temptation to hear what is said through pre-existing interpretive frames, and especially those which are the result of the exercise and reproduction of power. I will take this forward both in Chapter 4 and in Chapter 6, where I discuss some of the institutional implications of taking listening and dialogue seriously.

4

Deliberative and Dialogic Democracy

In Chapter 1 we established that very little attention has been paid to listening in political theory in general and in democratic theory in particular. It is less surprising in some cases than in others that democratic theory has not engaged with listening. The Burkean representative, for example, is explicitly enjoined to focus on her or his own judgement when making decisions, rather than on the opinion of electors: '[Y]our representative owes you, not his industry only, but his judgment; and he betrays, instead of serving you, if he sacrifices it to your opinion.'[1] While this does not amount to a counsel against listening to electors it certainly contrasts vividly with a Rousseauian approach which, strictly speaking, demands that delegates do exactly as their electors would wish. This implies that Rousseau's delegacy 'contains' listening in a way that Burke's theory of democratic representation does not. So we might expect some attention to listening in delegate theories of representation even if not in Burkean theories, but even there we find very little reflection. The general point is that, in theory, we are more likely to encounter listening in some areas of democracy than others—where it is 'demanded', as it were.

In this light one is drawn ineluctably towards deliberative democracy, since it is here that the most strenuous efforts have been made—in principle—to focus on dialogue and conversation in democracy, and in theorizing more inclusive forms of democratic theory and practice. Yet even here the practice of listening receives relatively little attention. So while it may be true that listening is *implicitly* as important as

---

[1] Edmund Burke, 'Speech to the Electors of Bristol', 3 November 1774, available at <http://press-pubs.uchicago.edu/founders/documents/v1ch13s7.html> (accessed 18 August 2012).

speaking in deliberative democratic theory and practice, those who discuss it very rarely feel the need to make the implicit, explicit. There are two reasons why deliberative democracy could benefit from paying more attention to listening. These reasons can be summed up in the distinction between listening *to* and listening *for*. The distinction is important: 'Long before I wrote stories,' says the American writer Eudora Welty, 'I listened for stories. Listening *for* them is something more acute than listening *to* them.'[2] In a deliberative situation in which points of view are being measured in terms of the force of the 'better argument' it seems obvious that there is a premium on listening carefully to the arguments being put forward. If participants in deliberation are to weigh up arguments carefully they obviously need to be listening to each other and to expert witnesses (if there are any) carefully. This is listening *to*. In addition, most accounts of deliberative democracy aim to be inclusive of points of view as well as fair between them, and this amounts to listening *for* voices that may previously have gone unheard. Given that fair deliberation and fairness of inclusion are central to deliberative democracy, and that listening is a fundamental feature of them both, one might have expected some attention to have been paid to it.

But, in general, the listening cupboard is very bare indeed. Proving this beyond all reasonable doubt would involve a complete survey of the vast literature devoted to deliberative democracy, and while that is not possible here I hope that the remarks I make about deliberative democracy in what follows will cumulatively amount to evidence for my claim. And, while the cupboard is bare, it is not entirely empty. One collection on deliberative democracy,[3] for example, contains a suggestive essay by Diego Gambetta.[4] Gambetta quotes Oscar Wilde: '[I]t is a very dangerous thing to listen. If one listens one may be convinced; and a man who allows himself to be convinced by an argument is a thoroughly unreasonable person.'[5] Not only is Wilde's comment prescient as far as a well-known feature of deliberative democracy is concerned—the idea of the force of a better argument—it also reminds us that listening is a key part of the process. Gambetta goes on to point out

---

[2] Quoted in Julie Cruikshank, *Do Glaciers Listen? Local Knowledge, Colonial Encounters, and Social Imagination* (Vancouver and Toronto: UBC Press, 2005), p. 76.

[3] Jon Elster (ed.), *Deliberative Democracy* (Cambridge: Cambridge University Press, 1998).

[4] Diego Gambetta, '"Claro!": an essay on discursive machismo', in Elster (1998).

[5] Gambetta (1998), p. 20.

that, '[A]ttitudes towards conversation do not originate from democratic arrangements even though they can be shaped and controlled by them. They are likely to be by-products of a preexisting culture and may well be antithetical to deliberation.'[6] These antithetical attitudes include, says Gambetta, an unwillingness to listen. He is surely right to draw our attention to the importance of this moment in the deliberative process, and we did indeed see in Chapter 2 that while the notion of good listening may be present in all cultures, there will be differences in how that is expressed. Whatever the culture, though, we can be fairly certain of the presence of listening deficiencies. So Gambetta rather undersells his point by writing as if the listening deficiency is the product of certain cultures—'Claro!' cultures (the Spanish for 'of course!' or 'obvious!'), in which 'while agents are still likely to prick up their ears when threats or promises are voiced and make an effort to sort them out of the general noise, they are unlikely to listen to one another's arguments, let alone be persuaded by them.'[7] My point here is that the lack of attention to cultivating the skills and habits of listening goes much further than the machismo cultures examined by Gambetta, and is in fact present (or absent) in theories of deliberative democracy more generally. This is all the more a mystery when we remind ourselves that deliberative democracy 'results from processes of collective deliberation conducted rationally and fairly among free and equal individuals'.[8] How can analysts of this process so systematically have missed out the listening part of it?

HABERMAS, DELIBERATION, LISTENING

We looked at some of the reasons for speech-dominated approaches to politics in general in the first two chapters, and these all apply as background conditions in the specific case of deliberative democracy. But we can deepen the analysis by looking at a key figure in deliberative democracy's theoretical architecture: Jürgen Habermas. It is

---

[6] Gambetta (1998), p. 20. We discussed this phenomenon in Chapter 2.

[7] Gambetta (1998), p. 21.

[8] Seyla Benhabib, 'Toward a deliberative model of democratic legitimacy', in Benhabib (ed.), *Democracy and Difference: Contesting the Boundaries of the Political* (Princeton: Princeton University Press, 1996), p. 69.

widely recognized that Habermas has been a source of inspiration for deliberative democrats.[9] Habermas's work contributes to what has been described as the 'first generation'[10] of deliberative democratic theory: '[F]irst-generation deliberative democrats thought reason exchange to be the only applicable form of communication, which would result in uniform preference change, ending in consensus.'[11] Habermas's analysis of the nature and purpose of communication has left an indelible mark on deliberative democracy in terms of its aims and intentions, yet what is striking about his theory of communicative action is how little attention he pays to the listening aspect of communication.[12] It is symbolically significant that his theory has come to be referred to as the 'ideal *speech* situation', and although he might claim that listening is implicit in the very notion of communication the fact remains that it receives very little attention—if any—in his work. Here is a description, chosen virtually at random, of the presuppositions we are expected to make when considering the circumstances of unconstrained dialogue:

> [I]t is in this sense that in rational discourse, where the speaker seeks to convince his audience through the force of the better argument, we presuppose a dialogical situation that satisfies ideal conditions in a number of respects, including, as we have seen, freedom of access, equal rights to participate, truthfulness on the part of participants, absence of coercion in taking positions, and so forth.[13]

[9] Although it is fair to say that he is not the only inspiration to deliberative democrats, nor should we assume that some of the imputed characteristics of Habermas's thinking in relation to deliberative democracy, such as the drive to consensus, are shared by all deliberative democrats. See John Dryzek, *Foundations and Frontiers of Deliberative Governance* (Oxford: Oxford University Press, 2010), pp. 4 and 15.

[10] Stephen Elstub, 'The third generation of deliberative democracy', *Political Studies Review* 8 (2010), p. 291. The second and third generations, according to Elstub, are those that deal with deliberative democracy in complex and divided societies, and with the institutionalization of deliberative democracy.

[11] Elstub (2010), p. 291. The second generation, according to Stephen Elstub, is more sceptical than the first regarding the possibility of reaching consensus, largely because cultural pluralism and social inequalities militate against it. We will return to this in the section 'Iris Marion Young, inclusion, and listening'.

[12] For a sustained commentary on Habermas and his relationship to listening see Carolyn Cusick, 'Speaking, Listening and Communicative Justice: Educating Epistemic Trust and Responsibility' (PhD thesis, Vanderbilt University, 2012), pp. 1–43 and 85–112.

[13] Jürgen Habermas, *Justification and Application: Remarks on Discourse Ethics* (Cambridge: Polity Press, 1993), p. 56.

Listening is notably absent from this description of the conditions for ideal dialogue, although we know from Chapter 2 that any number of structural and personality-based issues can militate against effective listening. Thus, as Michael Levin points out,

> Habermas's account of communicative action unwittingly postulates an unproblematic hearing: a listener who always hears all there is to be heard; a listening which is invariably accurate and complete. There is no theoretical recognition of auditory distortion, ideological deafness, institutional noise, the specific ways in which power channels hearing and listening channels power. It is as if, when it comes to listening, a metaphysics of presence still governed his thinking.[14]

A fuller account of communicative action would surely reveal that listening is both a feature and a catalyzer of some of the desirable dispositions associated with 'good' communicative processes. These dispositions include an enhancing of the capacity for dialogue, openness, and the development of empathy. (Very occasionally Habermas himself comes close to endorsing this kind of idea, for example where he quotes Dewey approvingly: '[T]he essential need... is the improvement of the methods and conditions of debate, discussion and persuasion.'[15]) We can easily miss the central role that good listening can play in developing these dispositions. Robert Goodin, for example, refers to the importance in deliberative democracy of 'imagining yourself in the place of another, for purposes of trying to understand what the other is saying'.[16] Listening would seem to be crucial to achieving this kind of empathy. It is easy to forget that talk is only one part of conversation or dialogue, and that, when democratic conversation is properly taking place, good listening acts as a kind of check or bulwark against the strategizing talk that Habermas sees as inimical to uncoerced communication. When the talker listens properly s/he is temporarily silent and is forced to check what s/he is saying against the points or claims being made by the interlocutor. This is why Habermas's theory of undistorted communication is one-sided: it fails to take into account the importance of listening as a check on strategizing speech. Goodin recognizes this in the context of deliberative democracy:

[14] Michael Levin, *The Listening Self: Personal Growth, Social Change and the Closure of Metaphysics* (London and New York: Routledge, 1989), p. 111.

[15] Jürgen Habermas, *Between Facts and Norms: Contributions to a Discourse Theory of Law and Democracy* (Cambridge, MA: The MIT Press, 1996), p. 304.

[16] Robert Goodin, *Innovating Democracy: Democratic Theory and Practice after the Deliberative Turn* (Oxford: Oxford University Press, 2008), p. 42

'[D]eliberative democrats redouble the demands of sheer good conversational manners...Listening attentively to one another is part and parcel of what it is to deliberate together. Discursive engagement requires interlocutors to pay attention to what one another is saying and to adjust their own positions and their own remarks accordingly.'[17] This is one of the very few moments where listening is referred to explicitly by a deliberative democracy theorist, and the curiosity is that this recognition of the importance of the aural moment is not followed up systematically.

In this chapter I want to offer dialogic democracy as a corrective, or as an addition, to deliberative democracy. Nothing in what follows should be taken as a rejection of the intentions of deliberative democracy, although I shall be distinguishing between various types of such democracy, and I will signal my preferences. My argument is that making dialogue central to deliberation—and this means paying independent attention to the practice of and conditions for good listening—will improve deliberative democracy and make it better equipped to realize its promise. I will therefore compare and contrast deliberative and dialogic democracy, and one productive way of doing so is to regard them as different answers to the same contemporary problem: dealing with political, social, and cultural pluralism in the absence of settled background assumptions against which to organize the resolution of disputes. In their revealingly different ways, both Habermas and Anthony Giddens deal with this problem—the former through his theory of communicative action and the latter through a version of what he calls dialogic democracy. Dialogic democracy is not at all developed either in theory or in practice; all we have are fragments scattered throughout social and political theory with no common understanding as to what the term means or how it is to be used. Giddens' use of it is one of the most developed there is, and the context in which he deploys it provides an ideal opportunity to compare deliberative and dialogic approaches to the problem of pluralism.[18] First, though, we need to return to Habermas's deliberative approach.

The core of Habermas's thinking is contained in this single sentence: '[R]eaching understanding is the inherent telos of human

---

[17] Goodin (2008), p. 110.
[18] Another important source is Michel Callon, Pierre Lascoumes, and Yannick Barthe, *Acting in an Uncertain World: An Essay on Technical Democracy* (Cambridge, MA, and London: The MIT Press, 2009).

speech.'[19] Understanding through communication is the beating heart of Habermas's theory. Speech, in turn, is at the core of communication for Habermas (indeed he uses 'speech' and 'communication' without formally distinguishing between them), and the majority of his work is devoted to discussing two sorts of communicative action, which he calls 'consensual action' and 'action oriented to reaching understanding',[20] with the bulk of his attention falling on the second of these. What they have in common is their orientation towards understanding, and the way they differ is in terms of the amount of understanding that already exists. In layperson's terms, consensual action is easier to achieve than action oriented to reaching understanding, and this is because a background consensus already exists. This background consensus consists of a series of 'common values', which orientate people's behaviour, as well as the reaction of the social group to this behaviour. The consensus gives rise to expectations which may or may not be fulfilled, but the key thing for Habermas is that there is an existing normative context through which and against which understanding is possible. As he puts it, 'actions are judged according to whether or not they are right in respect to a normative context recognized as legitimate'.[21]

This contrasts with communicative action oriented towards understanding, where the background consensus does not exist. In this case, 'norms are judged according to whether they can be justified, that is, whether they deserve to be recognized as legitimate'[22]—and this is the thought at the heart of deliberative approaches to democratic decision-making. The legitimacy of norms in this situation derives from their being arrived at through free, unconstrained communication, unsullied by strategizing, manipulation, or distortion. This gives rise to the notion of the 'ideal speech situation': 'uncurtailed communication where speakers and hearers, out of the context of their pre-interpreted lifeworld, refer simultaneously to things in the objective, social and subjective worlds in order to negotiate common definitions of the situation'.[23]

---

[19] Jürgen Habermas, *The Theory of Communicative Action*, vol. 1 (Cambridge: Polity Press, 1991), p. 287.

[20] Jürgen Habermas, *Communication and the Evolution of Society* (Boston: Beacon Press, 1979), in William Outhwaite (ed.), *The Habermas Reader* (Cambridge: Polity Press, 2000), p. 130.

[21] Habermas (1979), in Outhwaite (2000), p. 139.

[22] Habermas (1979), in Outhwaite (2000), p. 139.

[23] Habermas (1991), p. 95.

It is this second case—communicative action oriented to reaching understanding—that has been of particular inspiration to deliberative democrats. For such democrats, as for Habermas, the key to the legitimacy of norms and policies is that they be arrived at through a process of unconstrained communication. The legitimacy of actually existing democratic processes and the decisions that emerge from them is called into question by differences in economic, social, political, and cultural power. These decisions are more likely to serve the interests of those with power than those without. In the ideal speech situation these inequalities are smoothed out as participants discuss arguments on their merits, unaffected by strategizing. A further attraction of deliberative democracy is that it holds open the possibility of people's preferences being transformed during the deliberative process. Rather than democracy being simply a question of aggregating the given and unreflective preferences of people through the vote, deliberation offers the prospect of people's minds being changed as discussion takes place, as they are exposed to 'the force of the better argument'.

The Habermasian approach to the problem of consensus in divided societies works at what Ian O'Flynn describes as a 'high level of abstraction'.[24] There are two problems with this approach. The first is that it is in danger of losing touch with reality: agreement might be reached at such a high level of generality that it has no purchase on the day-to-day reality of the situation in question. The second problem is that the drive towards abstraction could entail leaving behind discordant voices that threaten the required distillation of concrete specificities. In other words, this drive could undermine the second of deliberative democracy's objectives referred to earlier: inclusion in the debating and decision-making process. As Elstub says, 'focusing on "common" interests can exclude the more specific but still relevant interests of excluded and marginalised groups'.[25] This is the point at which a comparison between deliberative and dialogic democracy becomes instructive.

In Chapter 1 we saw how Jeffrey Green's focus on ocular spectatorship led him to endorse a particular type of democracy, which he called plebiscitary democracy. In a similar vein, attention to listening suggests a specific form of democracy, which I here call dialogic democracy. Unsurprisingly, this kind of democracy stresses the reciprocal nature of democratic conversation in which speaking and

---

[24] Elstub (2010), p. 295.   [25] Elstub (2010), p. 296.

listening are of equal value and importance and in which equal attention is paid to them, both theoretically and in practice. Although, as we pointed out earlier in this chapter, dialogic democracy is not a particularly well-developed concept, there are signs that 'dialogue' and 'democracy' are being brought together more frequently, mostly in the context of debates around the development of deliberative democracy. This is where Daniel Andersen locates his sustained examination of the role of dialogue in democracy, with particular reference to the foundational role that Habermas plays in deliberative democratic theory.[26] Along with others, Andersen points out that the transformative effect of deliberation is held to depend on the right sort of communication[27]—the unforced force of the better argument. As we saw above, this conviction draws on Habermas's theory of communicative action, and it is certainly the most common interpretation of the theory as regards drivers for transformation.

But there are alternative interpretations and, along with Axel Honneth, Andersen believes that, 'it is not entirely clear whether the transcending potential is to reside in the normative presuppositions of human language or in social interaction.'[28] Andersen's argument is that, in deliberative situations, what causes to people to change their minds—or at least gives them the opportunity to do so—is less the structure of language and more the fact of being together, face to face, in a relatively controlled environment. This opens up the possibility for dialogue, and it is in dialogue (face-to-faceness) rather than deliberation (structure of language) that the potential for changing minds and opinions resides. Andersen argues that this dialogic account 'does not jettison language and deliberation entirely, but situates these activities within an interpersonal experience that is not reducible to communication.'[29] This interpersonal element is vital to Andersen's notion of dialogue, and it is what grounds the possibility of change and transformation:

A dialogic theory directs us to look at what can happen in the deep connections we sometimes make in our interpersonal relations—where we

[26] Daniel Bryan Andersen, 'From Deliberation to Dialogue: The Role of the I–Thou in Democratic Experience' (PhD thesis, University of Oregon, 2012).

[27] Andersen (2012), p. 12.

[28] Axel Honneth, 'Redistribution as recognition: a response to Nancy Fraser', in Nancy Fraser and Axel Honneth, *Redistribution or Recognition? A Political–Philosophical Exchange* (London and New York: Verso, 2003), p. 247, quoted in Andersen (2012), p. 55.

[29] Andersen (2012), p. 47.

are physically present before a particular other that is fundamentally different from myself, where we can speak without reserve, feel welcomed and/or recognized as a partner in conversation, and interact specifically and irreplaceably as oneself.[30]

The key elements here are 'physical presence' and the uniqueness of the interlocutors—irreducible to the language they use and the normative rules that govern language use. Another key term is 'recognized', and I will come back to this in the section 'Anthony Giddens and dialogic democracy'. Recognition plays an important role in Andersen's theory as a moment of acknowledgement that is the precursor to dialogical communication:[31] without recognition the dialogical exchange would never begin. While I agree entirely with this, I think that Andersen underestimates the importance of enquiring into the mechanics of recognition: it is as though he believes he can assume it to be an uncontroversially achieved basis for dialogue. Yet we know that recognition is hard-won and must be fought for. My argument later in this chapter and in Chapter 5 will be that listening plays a vital role in the process of recognition.

ANTHONY GIDDENS AND DIALOGIC DEMOCRACY

Anthony Giddens develops his version of dialogic democracy in the context of his exploration of the changing meanings of radicalism and conservatism in the 1990s.[32] In Giddens' view, the background to these changes is the decline in the hold that tradition has over us. In Giddens' story, tradition is the basis for the kind of 'consensual action' to which we saw Habermas refer earlier in this chapter. Like Habermas, Giddens sees fewer and fewer opportunities for consensual action grounded in tradition or background consensus. This decline is occurring in all walks of life, from the personal to the political, and, according to Giddens, it is in the latter context that shifts in the meaning of radicalism and conservatism are taking place. Thus, people on

---

[30] Andersen (2012), pp. 86 and 119.

[31] Andersen (2012), pp. 56 and 58.

[32] Antony Giddens, *Beyond Left and Right: The Future of Radical Politics* (Cambridge: Polity Press, 1994).

the right find themselves endorsing a free market economics which has the capacity to disrupt the stable and hierarchical social relations on which traditional conservatism is built, while those on the left find themselves trying to achieve traditional objectives (e.g. equality) through traditional means (e.g. nationalization and unionization), which no longer work. In more general terms these disruptions amount to a decline in predictability, and to an increase in the amount of issues that are 'put into question'.

Giddens calls this a 'reflexive social order', in which nothing can be taken for granted—and certainly not the (unreflexive) acquiescence of citizens around issues of public policy.[33] This constitutes a challenge for democracy—or at least for democracy as we have come to understand it in liberal democratic terms. This is because decision-making in modern liberal democracies takes place in a 'black box', hidden away in the actions of arms' length executives, and of representatives who are only distantly and occasionally accountable to the people they represent. This amounts to a crisis of legitimacy in Giddens' estimation, as people are more sceptical about the decisions taken in their name, and, simultaneously, less able to scrutinize or affect them. What this situation calls for, says Giddens, is a different type of democracy, which can provide legitimacy in these reflexive times. Along with many others, Giddens argues, at this point, that deliberative democracy has the required characteristics, principally because 'deliberative democratization would mean greater transparency in many areas of government'.[34]

But Giddens goes beyond deliberative democracy towards its dialogical counterpart. He contrasts the former with the latter by aligning it (the former) closely with the communicative principles of Habermas's ideal speech situation, and rejecting two of its apparent implications. First, he claims that deliberative democracy (when grounded in the ideal speech situation) is tied to 'a transcendental philosophical theorem' that claims that democratization is 'somehow implied by the very act of speech or dialogue'.[35] Giddens rejects this

---

[33] I will pick up the issue of disputed public policy in connection with a discussion of biotechnology later in this chapter. See Bernice Bovenkerk, *The Biotechnology Debate: Democracy in the Face of Intractable Disagreement* (Heidelberg, London, and New York: Springer, 2012).

[34] Giddens (1994), pp. 114–15.

[35] Giddens (1994), p. 115. This is the point made by Daniel Andersen, which we discussed above.

in favour of a more phenomenological approach in which both the potential and the need for dialogic democracy derive from the disruptions to the social and cultural order described briefly above. As 'all that is solid melts into air', stable, reliable, traditional reference points begin to dissolve, nothing can be taken for granted, and public policy needs continual refounding. This refounding is what dialogical democracy can produce, through keeping lines of dialogic communication open at all times, never closing them down, and never assuming settled agreement.

Giddens' second objection to grounding democracy in Habermas's ideal speech situation creates a yet more marked contrast between deliberative and dialogic democracy. '[D]ialogic democracy,' he writes, 'is not necessarily oriented to the achieving of consensus.'[36] Of course, it is not strictly true that deliberative democratic processes always aim at consensus either; such processes can operate according to a number of decision rules, including a simple majority vote. But the implication of what Giddens says is that the possibility of reaching consensus on the kinds of topics we are considering here is vanishingly small. Thus, this kind of deliberative democracy, at least—the kind oriented towards consensus—is inappropriate for the conditions which obtain in a reflexive social order. As he puts it, 'the most "political" of issues, inside and outside the formal public sphere, are precisely those which are likely to remain *essentially contested*.'[37] For Giddens, then, dialogic democracy is defined, at least in part, in procedural terms, and these terms are, in turn, grounded in the essential contestability of the issues with which we are dealing. Thus, Giddens writes that, '[D]ialogic democracy presumes only that dialogue in a public space provides a means of living along with the other in a relation of mutual *tolerance*—whether that "other" be an individual or a global community of religious believers.'[38] Stripping away the contingencies of particular social relations and identities, Giddens arrives at what he calls a 'pure relationship' in which everything is always in question. He says that such a relationship 'inevitably presupposes dialogue'[39] because, in the absence of settled background agreements, dialogue is the only way of establishing trust between the people in the relationship. We came across trust in Chapter 1 in the context of how listening—as a key

[36] Giddens (1994), p. 115.   [37] Giddens (1994), p.115 (emphasis added).
[38] Giddens (1994), p. 115.   [39] Giddens (1994), p. 118.

component of dialogue—can contribute to establishing trust between politicians and the electorate, and in Chapter 2 when we discussed Megan Laverty's idea of a 'hermeneutics of suspicion', which seemed to capture very well the politician–electorate relationship referred to in Chapter 1. In both cases listening, leading to dialogue, can be seen as a practice with the potential for dissolving the relations of suspicion that characterize mistrust. We will explore the issue of trust in a little more detail in the section 'Dialogic democracy and trust'.

Unfortunately, the one example Giddens gives of the dialogic process in action rather undermines his guiding idea that everything is essentially contested and that consensus is unlikely. He talks of a 'democratic parent–child relationship' and describes it as follows: '[T]he parent in effect says to the child: if you were able to discuss our relationship with me as an adult would do, in a free and open way, you would accept my reasons for treating you as I do.'[40] This is hardly a dialogical relationship. The counterfactual situation points to a determinate answer to the question 'how should the child behave?', and it seems that whatever the child might actually say would make no difference to the outcome of the debate. The child effectively 'becomes' the parent and the dialogue becomes a monologue—two people talking, but of exactly the same mind and therefore heading towards exactly the same answer. The child in this story is in the same position as the person behind Rawls's veil of ignorance, or the citizen who finds her/himself in Habermas's ideal speech situation. Giddens here effectively offers us a good example of the bad cataphatic, or monological, listening we discussed in Chapter 2. In similar vein, Habermas defines what he calls 'practical discourse' as 'the form of communication that secures the impartiality of moral judgment together with universal interchangeability of participant perspectives'.[41] As we saw in Chapter 2, dialogue presupposes two or more points of view, and we criticized both compassionate and cataphatic listening for collapsing dialogue into monologue either through immersing oneself too deeply in the other's position or by hearing the other's speech through ready-made categories that effectively turn the other into oneself. Rawls's veil of ignorance and Habermas's ideal speech situation have the same effect through their 'universal interchangeability of participant perspectives'. The situations are designed to push participants towards the

[40] Giddens (1994), p. 119.   [41] Habermas (1993), p. 50.

same conclusion, either through narrowing the information available to them in such a way that certain conclusions just have to be drawn, or by removing the obstacles (power play, strategizing) that militate against reaching a determinate conclusion. Thus, having started out by rejecting Habermas's ideal speech situation as a basis for democracy, here, at least, Giddens returns to it. Yet, although the example cited above might not be well chosen for Giddens' purposes, this brief discussion of it does allow us to reaffirm that genuine dialogical democracy seems well suited to the conditions of his 'reflexive social order', since, in the real world, what Habermas refers to as 'degenerate forms'[42] of discourse are the norm: exclusions, manipulated agreement, sanctions, and the suppression of contrary ideas. Dialogic democracy thus sets its face against the idea of 'subjectless communications',[43] where real people are dissolved into a 'higher level subjectivity',[44] and replaces it with a situation in which difference exists and dialogue should exist, and where listening across difference becomes a necessary feature of social life.

Giddens' argument suggests that dialogical democracy is the most appropriate form of democracy for post-traditional times. In effect, he is calling for the characteristics and practices we normally associate with 'conversation' in the private sphere to be transposed to the public sphere. Part of his argument—and mine—is that we have not paid enough attention to conversation in democratic theory and practice. This may come as a surprise to people in other practices and disciplines where conversation is a constant point of reference. Thus, John Durham Peters, for example, is able to say that, '[W]e live in an age of conversation. It is one of the unquestioned goods of the moment and a normative ideal of how the media are expected to work in a democracy.'[45] Peters is sceptical about conversation, though, and is concerned that it not be fetishized. He argues that, '[C]onversation is not the only format suited for democracy',[46] and while it is true that many forms of communication are permissible and necessary in a democracy it is important to see that I am using 'conversation' is a quite specific way. Peters thinks of conversation as a question of mimicking the 'speech styles and

---

[42] Habermas (1993), p. 57.   [43] Habermas (1996), p. 299.

[44] Habermas (1996), p. 299.

[45] John Durham Peters, 'Media as conversation, conversation as media', in James Curran and David Morley (eds), *Media and Cultural Theory* (Abingdon and New York: Routledge, 2006), p. 115.

[46] Peters (2006), p. 124 (my emphasis).

genres from everyday life'[47]—whatever these styles and genres might be. This enables him to describe the move from tub-thumping oratory in politics to the register of 'sincerity and self-disclosure' (as exhibited in the speech-making and manner of Ronald Reagan and Tony Blair) as the 'conversationalization of public discourse'.[48] I agree with Peters that we can be too cavalier with the word 'conversation', and that it is inappropriate for use in the context of democracy.

In the democratic context, two elements are essential. First, democratic conversation entails a response, and this rules out 'monological forms'[49] of conversation. Indeed. I would go as far as to say that the very idea of monological democratic conversation is a contradiction in terms. Second, conversation must involve listening, and this listening must be reciprocal (in other words it cannot be simply listening to a monologue). Peters himself confirms that, '[L]istening to others is a profound democratic act',[50] and he agrees—against the grain of most received opinion— that, '[W]atching and listening can be intensely *active* practices.'[51] He also says that, '[D]ialogue presupposes silence, indeed it demands it'[52]— and these are all points (reciprocal listening, listening as active, and the importance of silence) which we have been at pains to make throughout this book thus far. They lie at the heart of conversation as I want to understand it here, and I believe it would be a mistake to cast the definitional net so wide as to lose them. This is why I distinguished between conversation and dialogue at the end of Chapter 3, suggesting that we understand dialogue as 'structured disagreement underpinned by apophatic listening'. This aligns listening with democracy in a more systematic way, while simultaneously creating conceptual space between the 'styles and genres of everyday life' (e.g. 'conversation' as usually understood) and those that are appropriate to the political (democratic) realm.

DIALOGIC DEMOCRACY AND TRUST

Giddens also suggests that dialogical democracy has a role to play in creating what he calls 'social solidarity' under conditions which have seen it decline, and in respect of which traditional (left and right)

---

[47] Peters (2006), p. 117.   [48] Peters (2006), p. 119.
[49] Peters (2006), p. 119.   [50] Peters (2006), p. 124.
[51] Peters (2006), p. 124.   [52] Peters (2006), p. 125.

attempts to recover it have failed and will continue to fail. As the right gropes for an unrecoverable sense and experience of tradition in which to ground solidarity, and the left pins its hopes on solidarity growing out of the 'occupational sphere'[53] or in a reconstruction of civil society, the forces of globalization and detraditionalization militate against success. The problem of solidarity, for Giddens, arises in the context of difference and how we deal with it. Difference, on the standard reading, is a threat to solidarity and a solvent of social glue. But for Giddens it is also an opportunity, a kind of training ground: '[G]etting to know the other, coming to rely on the other, presumes using difference as a means of developing positive emotional communication.'[54] For Giddens it seems that the creation of social solidarity in these post-traditional conditions is a matter of learning dispositions and cultivating virtues. He quotes approvingly from John Dewey, who argued that a democratic order requires a 'socially generous' attitude of mind in which people have developed 'neither more nor less than [a] capacity to share in a give and take experience.'[55]

In Chapter 3 we noted the difficulties of 'scaling-up' good listening from the interpersonal context to the broader political one, and Giddens echoes both the promise and the challenge it implies when he writes that, 'the possible democratization of personal life is of the first importance for many aspects of political reform today.'[56] He seems to be suggesting that good dialogic habits must be learnt at the personal level for there to be any hope of them being deployed in wider contexts. The key to the creation of solidarity under conditions of difference and reflexivity is the development of trust, and this can only be achieved under conditions of transparency in which interlocutors are forced to 'confront issues of responsibility.'[57] This, of course, is a good description of what goes on in situations of truth and reconciliation, where the emphasis is precisely upon transparency and communication (as we saw in the case of Jo Berry and Patrick Magee in Chapter 1). The spaces between people, both in the dramatic circumstances of truth and reconciliation encounters and the more quotidian challenges provided by Giddens' post-traditional order, are—or should be—filled

---

[53] Giddens (1994), p. 124.   [54] Giddens (1994), p. 127.

[55] Giddens (1994), p. 130, from John Dewey, *Democracy and Education* (London: Macmillan, 1916), p. 120.

[56] Giddens (1994), p. 131.   [57] Giddens (1994), p. 129.

with dialogue, where 'mechanisms of active trust'[58] are both designed and practised.

The role of listening and dialogue in the (re)creation of trust is especially important in situations where it has declined or never existed, or where conditions are such that trust has to be continually reinvented (this is the situation Giddens is exploring). One influential study of trust—Charles Tilly's *Trust and Rule*[59]—discusses the role of trust in democratization, but because he is more interested in trust networks than in trust itself, his focus is more on the horizontal relationships between potential members of trust groups than on the problematic political relationship between politicians and the electorate. Tilly does, however, recognize that 'a certain level of trust [is] a necessary condition for democracy', and that 'a significant decline in trust threatens democracy'.[60] He also resists the claim that 'trust networks [are] outmoded leftovers from primeval *Gemeinschaft*',[61] necessarily tied to certain ways of living and to a certain socio-economic stage of development. Thus, he helpfully leaves open the possibility of the creation or revival of trust where it has either been eroded or disappeared.

Tilly agrees with Robert Putnam (paraphrasing him) that,[62] '*within already relatively democratic regimes*, people who engage in civic organizations (or perhaps only in organizations oriented to the public good) are more likely to meet their collective obligations, to press for better government performance, and to trust their fellow citizens'.[63] But, he argues, we can say more than this about the role of trust in democratic processes and regimes.[64] We need also to consider the importance of trust between citizens so that they are confident that if they keep to their side of the bargain (e.g. paying taxes), then others will too. Second, citizens must have a generalized trust in the outcomes of democratic processes or they will begin to defect from those processes. Third, those who are not in power must trust incumbents to give up their power if electoral outcomes go against them, and for incumbents to take non-incumbents' interests into account in the

---

[58] Giddens (1994), p. 131.

[59] Charles Tilly, *Trust and Rule* (Cambridge: Cambridge University Press, 2005).

[60] Tilly (2005), p. 133.

[61] Tilly (2005), p. 14.

[62] Robert Putnam, *Making Democracy Work: Civic Traditions in Modern Italy* (Princeton: Princeton University Press, 1993).

[63] Tilly (2005), p. 133 (emphasis in the original).

[64] Tilly (2005), p. 133.

meantime. And fourth—a variation on the third point—'Democracies are supposed to require higher levels of trust in government than other sorts of regime because the voluntary delegation of powers to representatives and officials can only occur on the basis of extensive trust.'[65]

These are all vital considerations, and we are especially concerned here with the third and fourth since they bear upon the relationship between politicians and the electorate and the role of trust in that relationship. Tilly's answer to the problem of declining trust is deceptively simple: 'integrate trust networks into public politics'.[66] This move will help to give people a stake (not Tilly's language) in democratic politics and make it less likely that they will 'exit' when things get tough for them (i.e. when any of the four benefits of trust move into deficit). No doubt Tilly is right in what he says: the integration of trust networks into public politics will have the effect of infusing those politics with trust and will reduce the trust deficit between professional politicians and civil society. The principal problem with this solution, though, is that it seems to rely on trust networks already existing and, as Tilly himself recognizes, trust networks cannot be taken for granted and, in modern societies, are in a state of constant integration and disintegration.[67]

This virtually takes us back to the situation which Giddens describes: the post-traditional order in which reflexivity and difference rather than taken-for-grantedness and homogeneity are the norm. Trust is no less important under these conditions, but it cannot necessarily be sourced from a set of settled trust networks. What if these networks don't exist or are in short supply? How is trust to be generated? Under these conditions one thing we can say for sure is that, absent dialogue, mistrust will persist. The structural similarity between dialogue and trust is that they both involve relationship and reciprocity. In the event of either listening or speaking breaking down or being absent, dialogue does not exist. Similarly, if either the willingness to take a risk or be bound to perform on the basis of recognizing that the other has taken a risk breaks down, trust cannot exist. The relationship between dialogue and trust goes beyond structural similarity though. If we define trust in terms of risk (as Tilly does[68]) then we can see that dialogue is the bedrock of trust, since communication opens up the possibility (not always fulfilled) of creating a relationship in which risk *itself* becomes relational.

---

[65] Tilly (2005), p. 133.   [66] Tilly (2005), p. 136.
[67] Tilly (2005), p. 17.   [68] Tilly (2005), p. 12.

DIFFERENCE AND DIALOGIC DEMOCRACY

Difference plays a key role here, and it is central to our discussion of the role dialogic democracy plays in relation to the deliberative democratic ideal of inclusion. Broadly speaking, there are three positions in regard to difference. The first is the one we have seen Giddens outlining, where difference is a precondition for learning the give-and-take and the tolerance which Giddens would like to see in the post-traditional societies he describes. Without the give-and-take, without the dialogue, difference can sclerose into fundamentalisms. Thus dialogical democracy becomes the antidote to sclerotic solidarity as well as the pathway to the form of post-traditional solidarity described above. Giddens' dialogical democracy therefore 'channels' difference without ever seeking to efface or erase it. We might call this the management of difference.

An alternative approach is taken by John Dewey, who sees what he calls 'communication' as the mechanism by which people come to see what they have in common as opposed to what sets them apart. According to this view, communication makes society because society is what we have in common, and we can only find out what we have in common by communicating. In Dewey's words:

> Society not only continues to exist by transmission, by communication, but it may fairly be said to exist in transmission, in communication. There is more than a verbal tie between the words common, community, and communication. Men live in a community in virtue of the things which they have in common; and communication is the way in which they come to possess things in common. What they must have in common in order to form a community or society are aims, beliefs, aspirations, knowledge—a common understanding—like-mindedness as the sociologists say. Such things cannot be passed physically from one to another, like bricks; they cannot be shared as persons would share a pie by dividing it into physical pieces. The communication which insures participation in a common understanding is one which secures similar emotional and intellectual dispositions—like ways of responding to expectations and requirements.[69]

Dewey concludes this passage by asserting that, '[C]onsensus demands communication', and it is clear that for him difference is an obstacle to be overcome rather than a circumstance to be tolerated. The role

---

[69] Dewey (New York: Macmillan, 1916), p. 5.

of dialogue is to help people to see what they share rather than what drives them apart, and, in the ideal circumstances, dialogue will result in consensus, even if only ever provisional.

The third view of the role of difference in dialogue and in dialogical democracy is represented by Bruce Caron in his discussion of the Higashi-kujo Madang festival in Kyoto, Japan. The aims of the festival include, 'the transmission of cultural knowledge between generations of Koreans, the acknowledgment of the need for all neighbours in the area to recognize their common problems and provide mutual support, and the recognition by the city and nation of heterogeneity as the basis for the respect of human rights'.[70] The festival and its objectives are therefore recognizable in our context as an approach to dealing with social and cultural difference. Caron makes use of Giddens' notion of dialogic democracy as a way of constructing a public sphere capable of incorporating and achieving these objectives, and he especially notes—approvingly—the contrast we pointed out between Giddens' dialogue and Habermas's ideal speech situation, in the section on 'Anthony Giddens and dialogical democracy'. The outcomes of the two processes are different: the former aims at tolerance and the latter at consensus. Caron sides with Giddens on this, but he goes further. Acknowledging that tolerance is a virtue, he then writes, 'I would take the idea...far beyond its threshold level (i.e., being aware of difference and deciding not to react unfavourably to this) to a point where the differences that are found in and emerge through this dialogue are desired outcomes.'[71] According to this view, dialogical democracy becomes a mechanism by which difference is *produced*, in respectful contrast to Robyn Penman and Sue Turnbull's emphasis on 'listening across differences'.[72] The success of dialogical democracy will be determined by the degree to which it brings previously unheralded voices into the political arena. On this reading, dialogical democracy is a thoroughly procedural affair, and listening out for new

---

[70] Bruce Caron, 'Dancing toward a dialogic democracy', in *Community, Democracy and Performance* (2003), p. 282, available at <http://junana.com/CDP/corpus/pdfs/Chapter_8.pdf> (accessed 24 April 2012). (At the website, this is the 'Citation format example' given: Caron, Bruce. 2003. Community, Democracy and Performance: The Urban Practice of Kyoto's Higashi-Kujo Madang. Santa Barbara: The New Media Studio, available at <http://junana.com/CDP/corpus/index.html>.)

[71] Caron (2003), p. 293.

[72] Robyn Penman and Sue Turnbull, 'From listening...to the dialogic realities of participatory democracy', *Continuum: Journal of Media and Cultural Studies* 26 (2012), no. 1, pp. 61–72.

voices lies at the heart of the procedure. An example of this in action comes from the experience of 'Lulismo' discussed briefly in Chapter 3. It will be remembered that one of the aims of Lulismo was to bring previously unheard voices into the policy-making process. Thus, a deliberate and systematic attempt was made to make the process participatory, 'with literally millions of individual Brazilians participating in one of the many conferences, councils and programmes created to foster dialogue and gather citizen input'.[73] This had the effect of drawing previously excluded actors into the political process, through the creation of new ministries (for women, racial equality, agrarian development, for example) and the deliberate selection of unionized (45%) and social movement actors (46%) for political appointments.[74]

The contrast with Habermas, and with consensual forms of deliberative democracy, is marked. We remember Habermas saying that, '[R]eaching understanding is the inherent telos of human speech', and this is taken up in many theories of deliberative democracy. But this forgets the 'I am here; here I am!' role of speech—not so much aimed at reaching understanding as appealing for a place at the table at which understanding will be reached. As Graham Smith reminds us, '[A]ccording to theories of deliberative democracy, two fundamental conditions need to be fulfilled for the emergence of more legitimate and trustworthy forms of political authority: *inclusiveness* and unconstrained dialogue'.[75] The task of ensuring inclusiveness comes before the unconstrained dialogue and it needs careful, systematic, and independent attention. We cannot, to any degree, assume that the call for unconstrained dialogue will automatically entail inclusiveness, so we need ways of maximizing inclusiveness ahead of deliberation. This suggests that the move towards consensus, which is typical of much deliberative democratic theorizing, may need to be resisted, because, '[S]ome attempts at conflict dialogue, using rational talk to "bridge" differences by emphasising commonalities, may unintentionally

---

[73] Gianpaolo Baiocchi, Einar Braathen, and Ana Claudia Teixeira, 'Transformation institutionalized? Making sense of participatory democracy in the Lulu era', 11 June 2012, available at <http://gianpaolobaiocchi.wordpress.com/2012/04/16/transformation-institutionalized-new-essay-on-the-lula-era/> (accessed 6 December 2012), p. 1.

[74] Baiocchi, Braathen, and Teixeira (2012), p. 5.

[75] Graham Smith, *Deliberative Democracy and the Environment* (London and New York: Routledge, 2003), p. 56 (emphasis added).

function to distance or avoid addressing deeply-lived inequalities.[76] Thus, the role of a dialogical approach to democracy is to produce difference, multiply voices, and ensure that 'closure' is not achieved at the expense of failing to question prevailing relations of power. This is the key role that 'listening out for' plays in the dialogic conception of democracy—listening out for previously unheard and unheralded voices, even if they derail the drive to consensus. This multiplication becomes a key criterion for determining the degree to which the approach to decision-making is dialogic or not. As Michel Callon, Pierre Lascoumes, and Yannick Barthe put it in their discussion of dialogic democracy: 'To what extent are new groups invited to express their views, exchange their points of view, and negotiate? The more groups there are and the greater their diversity, the more meaningful their debate will be.'[77]

We find an example of this at work in a study of biotechnology debates in Australia and the Netherlands. Earlier in the chapter I talked of Giddens' notion of a 'reflexive social order' in which nothing can be taken for granted, and I referred specifically to issues of public policy in modern, plural times. In this context, Bernice Bovenkerk's study of the potential role of deliberative democracy in biotechnology debates is revealing.[78] As she says, '[T]he debate about the genetic modification of animals and plants is...a paradigmatic case for intractable disagreement in today's pluralistic societies.'[79] She refers to a typology of three types of problem—structured, unstructured, and moderately structured[80]—and argues that biotechnology is an unstructured problem because 'no consensus exists on either facts or values'[81] in the debate. She is also fully aware of the different goals pursued by deliberative democrats, much as I have described them in this chapter. To the goals of consensus and inclusion, which we have already noted, she adds a third—quality of debate—and points out that these goals can be in tension with one another. Her suggestion

---

[76] Kathy Bickmore and Serihy Kovalchuk, 'Diverse ways of creating classroom communities for constructive discussions of conflict: cases from Canadian secondary schools', in Peter Cunningham and Nathan Fretwell (eds), *Creating Communities: Local, National and Global* (London: CiCe, 2012), p. 6.

[77] Callon, Lascoumes, and Barthe (2009), p. 159.

[78] Bovenkerk (2012).

[79] Bovenkerk (2012), p. ix.

[80] Bovenkerk (2012), p. ix.

[81] Bovenkerk (2012), p. 3.

is that different kinds of debate prompt different emphases in terms of these goals, and in unstructured debates—like those surrounding biotechnology—the goals of inclusion and quality of understanding are more important than consensus.[82] This is because, as Robyn Eckersley puts it in her Foreword to Bovenkerk's work, 'it is fairer from a pluralist standpoint since there is much less risk of suppression of dissensus.'[83] This amounts to a call for a dialogical approach to democracy as I have been describing it here, particularly in regard to the way that it emphasizes the importance of listening out for potentially discordant voices.

It is especially interesting to see the merits of a dialogical approach to democracy being expressed in situations that *already* seem characterized by multiple voices and riven with dissent. One might have thought that deliberative democracy would have much to commend it in such situations, aiming, as it often does, at consensus and the overcoming of division and disagreement along lines that all can agree to. Nathalia Jaramillo describes a case in point in her study of three schools near Medellín in Colombia, which has, as she says, 'a unique history of ongoing conflict and civil war.'[84] Jaramillo looks to what she calls the critical education tradition (Paulo Freire,[85] for example) for 'a *mediating* tool to transcend the central class-ethic-gendered antagonisms ... that continue to destroy communities, limit the possibilities of human development across class lines, and threaten our conceptions of democracy.'[86] Isn't this precisely the kind of context for which deliberative democracy is designed? As Jaramillo herself says, deliberative democracy focuses on 'shared communication strategies and consensual practices', and this seems to be the ideal approach for dealing with deeply divided societies, such as the one Jaramillo describes. Her concern, though, is that the urge to consensus carries with it the danger that the conversation will be conducted in terms of the dominant partner(s) and that subaltern voices will go missing.

---

[82] Bovenkerk (2012), pp. 13–14.

[83] Robyn Eckersley, 'Foreword', in Bovenkerk (2012), p. vii.

[84] Nathalia Jaramillo, 'Dialogic action for critical democracy', *Journal for Critical Education Policy Studies* 9 (2011), no. 1, p. 73.

[85] Paulo Freire, *Pedagogy of the Oppressed* (30th anniversary edn, New York: Continuum Academic Publishing, 2007).

[86] Jaramillo (2011), p. 73; emphasis added.

For Jaramillo, the problem with adopting the impartiality rule that accompanies the deliberative ideal of 'the force of the better argument' is that the rules for determining what 'better' means will be skewed in favour of the dominant forces. From this perspective, impartiality, in working with the grain of taken-for-granted common sense, can serve to sustain and reproduce rather than challenge existing power relations. So Jaramillo begins with *partiality*: 'the voices of those subaltern subjects who have been traditionally excluded... in the construction of so-called democratic states... [and]... the normative structures that underlie seemingly "impartial" modes of governance and sociability'.[87] Ultimately, '[T]he point here is to question the very paradigms upon which we determine our *reasonable* understandings of democracy as an act of social justice.'[88] Once again, the role of dialogical democracy is to multiply difference by listening out for excluded voices. This is as much as to say that legitimacy ('one of those perennial issues in thinking about democracy that never quite receives a treatment that would satisfy those who worry about it'[89]) from the dialogic point of view will be judged by its success in regard to inclusion. One of deliberative democracy's legitimacy criteria is that the institution, value, policy, decision, or practice in question be 'accepted as proper by those to whom it is supposed to apply'.[90] In its determination to 'listen out for', dialogic democracy can help make good this particular legitimacy criterion of its deliberative cousin.

IRIS MARION YOUNG, INCLUSION, LISTENING

At this point we can pick out a key figure in the development of deliberative democracy—Iris Marion Young—and show how attention to listening should be a vital component of her theory and, by extension, of deliberative democracy in general.[91] Young fits squarely into the second generation of deliberative democrats as described

---

[87] Jaramillo (2011), p. 86.   [88] Jaramillo (2011), p. 86; emphasis in original.
[89] Dryzek (2010), p. 21.   [90] Dryzek (2010), p. 21.
[91] See also Cusick (2012), pp. 26–30 and 35–37.

by Stephen Elstub. Thus, while she would accept that the deliberative democracy is 'formally inclusive', she would argue that it is not 'substantially inclusive because the complete dependence on rational forms of communication privileges dominant social groups'.[92] The title of her seminal book, *Inclusion and Democracy*,[93] is significant. Young is well aware that the Habermasian norms of deliberation and the objective of consensus could have the effect of reducing rather than increasing inclusion. Inclusion is vital to her because she believes it is a way of producing just outcomes from a system that tends to reinforce social and economic equalities.[94] Difference is therefore an important category in Young's thought, and in terms of the three approaches to difference outlined above, Young is somewhere between the first and the third. So she does not see difference as eradicable (in this she agrees with Giddens), and she would concur with Caron that justice entails enabling difference to emerge. She would be much less inclined to go along with Dewey's notion that the point of communication is to overcome difference in favour of a common good: 'my conception ... [of] ... a communicative model of democratic inclusion theorizes different social segments struggling and engaging with one another across their differences rather than putting those differences aside to invoke a common good'.[95]

Young is suspicious of the idea of the common good because of the danger that, in circumstances of unequal power, its definition will tend towards favouring the interests of the powerful.[96] There is also the possibility that, in any drive to define the common good, there will be a temptation to leave aside difficult and disruptive issues.[97] Both of these tendencies are a threat to inclusion, and they are reinforced by what Young refers to as 'privileging argument',[98] and this is her real quarry. Her concern is, of course, not so much with argument as such, but with the norms that constitute good argument. Her claim is that deliberative argument cannot progress unless there are 'mutually accepted premises and frameworks', and that these shared premises may turn out to exclude the expression of some interests.[99]

[92] Elstub (2010), p. 297.
[93] Iris Marion Young, *Inclusion and Democracy* (Oxford: Oxford University Press, 2000).
[94] Young (2000), p. 17.   [95] Young (2000), p. 18.
[96] Young (2000), p. 43.   [97] Young (2000), p. 44.
[98] Young (2000), pp. 37–40.   [99] Young (2000), p. 37.

Connected to this, Young is especially sensitive to the possibility that certain *ways of speaking* will be excluded because they do not meet standard norms. What she seems not to notice, though, is how this exclusion is carried out through the mechanism of *not listening*. Gideon Calder is surely right to say that, 'the establishment of this degree of consensus around political values must entail an advance decision not to listen to certain kinds of voice'.[100] Young refers to this as 'internal exclusion', in which 'the terms of discourse make assumptions some do not share, the interaction privileges specific styles of expression, the participation of some people is dismissed as out of order'.[101] All of these amount to failures of listening, which is the mechanism through which exclusion is achieved, yet to which Young pays no independent analytic attention.

Young's critique leads her to add what she regards as three new modes of political communication to the established one of deliberative argument: greeting, rhetoric, and narrative.[102] These are important because they broaden the range of communicative tools at the disposal of political actors and therefore have the potential for making good the inclusionary claims of deliberative democracy. Greeting is important because it amounts to an acknowledgement and an invitation to the other to participate, and is thus a gesture of inclusion.[103] Rhetoric plays two key inclusionary roles for Young: it can help get previously excluded issues on the political agenda through using precisely the emotionally charged language that is frowned upon in rational argument, and it addresses specific publics rather than general ones (and we should remember that 'general' often, in fact, means those who are countenanced by the beneficiaries of social and political inequality).[104] The value of narrative lies in its capacity to communicate what Young calls 'particularity of experience',[105] which can again go missing in the drive towards consensus, the common good, and shared premises. Young's belief is that adding greeting, rhetoric, and narrative to the accepted range of modes of democratic (and

---

[100] Gideon Calder, 'Democracy and listening', in Mary-Ann Crumplin (ed.), *Problems of Democracy: Language and Speaking* (Oxford: Inter-Disciplinary Press, 2011), p. 133.

[101] Young (2000), p. 53.   [102] Young (2000), p. 57.

[103] Young (2000), pp. 57–60.   [104] Young (2000), pp. 66–69.

[105] Young (2000), p. 71.

especially deliberative) communication would improve the prospects for inclusion.

I do not disagree with this, but I want to argue that Young has only told half of the story, and that telling the other half makes her inclusionary argument more complete and compelling. The overall point is that her insistence on looking at alternative ways of speaking needs to be complemented by attention to listening. The logic seems as obvious as it is often ignored: speaking (in whatever form or register) *is already taking place*; what is missing is the willingness to listen to alternative forms and registers of voice. This is precisely the point made by Gayatri Spivak when she explores the systematic silencing of certain subjects in colonial and anti-colonial discourses.[106] Once again we are reminded of John Dryzek's point that, 'the most effective and insidious way to silence others in politics is a refusal to listen.'[107] Young calls her preferred form of democracy, 'communicative democracy,'[108] and this already seems to me to signal a step in the wrong direction. 'Communication' is about one-way delivery; one communicates a message to someone without any expectation or requirement that they reply to it. 'Dialogic' surely captures Young's intentions better, since she is not only interested in having more people speak, but in having that speech recognized and acted on. And a precondition for this recognition and action is listening, for if there is no listening there will be no recognition and no action. Dialogic democracy stresses the reciprocal nature of democratic conversation in which speaking and listening are of equal value and importance and in which equal attention is paid to them, both theoretically and in practice. In the instance being discussed here dialogical democracy does not *replace* deliberative democracy but enhances it.

As I say, the idea of listening is implicit here, and this is especially apparent in the first of Young's three new modes of communication—greeting. '[I]n the moment of communication I call greeting,' she writes, 'a speaker announces her presence as *ready to listen* and take responsibility for her relationship to her interlocutors.'[109]

---

[106] Gayatri Chakravorty Spivak, 'Can the subaltern speak?' in Gary Nelson and Lawrence Grossberg (eds), *Marxism and the Interpretation of Culture* (Urbana, IL: Illinois University Press, 1988), pp. 271–313.

[107] John Dryzek, *Deliberative Democracy and Beyond* (Oxford: Oxford University Press, 2000), p. 149.

[108] Young (2000), p. 40.

[109] Young (2000), p. 59 (emphasis added).

Greeting is an essential moment of opening up without which, according to Young, no discussion can take place at all;[110] what is specifically important about it is that it signals politeness, deference, and acknowledgement. All of these are, of course, signalled by listening too, so when we analyse what it is about greeting that does the work Young says it is does, listening is the key component of the communication process. In sum it signals *recognition*,[111] which is an absolutely key term in calls for justice in democracy like Young's, and which I will analyse in much more detail in Chapter 5. There are also echoes of listening (if I can put it like that) in her remarks on rhetoric, the second of the 'new' forms of communication she would like to see incorporated into democratic theory and practice. Significantly, she describes the importance of rhetoric in terms of its 'dialogic' nature.[112] This refers to the way in which the rhetorician has to establish a relationship with particular audiences rather than general ones, and how this implies the need for the rhetorician to know the audience, so as to tap in to the 'assumed history or set of values' salient to it.[113] Although Young does not say so, the good rhetorician will therefore have to have listened to her or his audience so as to know these histories and values. Only in this way will the rhetorician's objective of reaching and persuading 'different others' be met.[114] Of course, the use to which the rhetorician puts this knowledge may be malevolent as well as benign,[115] but the point here is to show how listening is implicit in Young's call for the recognition of alternative forms of communication. The theoretical point of making the implicit explicit is to show how listening is essential to the objective of recognition, even though Young does not quite recognize this.

I made a similar point when discussing Daniel Andersen's theory of dialogic democracy earlier in the section, 'Habermas, deliberation, listening'. I pointed out how recognition is important for him as the moment at which dialogue becomes possible, but that he does

---

[110] Young (2000), p. 61.

[111] Young (2000), p. 61.   [112] Young (2000), p. 68.

[113] Young (2000), p. 68.   [114] Dryzek (2010), p. 66.

[115] Young herself says that, 'listeners to greetings, rhetoric, and narrative should be critically vigilant, and should apply standards of evaluation to them as well as to argument'; Young (2000), p. 79. Dryzek (2010), p. 68 draws a contrast between 'heresthetic', which is designed to manipulate an audience's choice sets, and rhetoric, which seeks to persuade an audience.

not pay sufficient attention to how that moment might come about, and how important listening is for that moment. This is a little surprising, as he spends a lot of time analysing the Restorative Listening Project—an innovative project that sought to address racial tensions that had built up in Portland (Oregon) during a process of gentrification of part of the city. There are two striking aspects of Andersen's account of this process. The first is how much listening is implicit in it. Drawn virtually at random, here is one comment he makes: '[T]hey [the meetings] generally featured local African American residents... [who]... were asked to tell their stories before (what turned out to be) largely white audiences.'[116] The key element in this is not really dialogue, in the sense of an exchange of views, but the white audience *listening* to the African Americans. The work is being done by the witnessing, not by the talking. The second striking thing is how little reflection there is here on the importance of listening to the success of the Restorative Listening Project. There are a number of occasions when Andersen has cause to refer to listening in the restorative process,[117] but the opportunity to analyse listening as an independent factor is not taken. The Project's mission statement makes clear the vital importance of listening: 'The Restorative Listening Project is based on the principle of Restorative Justice which says that only when those most impacted are heard, acknowledged and efforts have been made to repair the harm can the community be made whole again.'[118] Having a voice is one thing, but 'being heard and acknowledged' is absolutely vital to the success of any restorative process. Remember that Andersen's intention is to question deliberative democracy's claim that changes of mind or opinion are driven by the normative demands of the structure of language. In this context he interestingly refers to the Restorative Listening Project as 'a deliberative success without deliberation'.[119] This is certainly what it seems to be, since '[N]othing in this institutional design created formal deliberation. In fact, the open challenging of "facts" of presenters or audience members was discouraged—though such challenges did happen and were perceived by many as an interruption of the process.'[120] But what Andersen doesn't say is that this also appears to be a process without *dialogue* either. He does point out that what made

---

[116] Andersen (2012), p. 166.   [117] Andersen (2012), pp. 165, 166, 168, 172.
[118] Quoted in Andersen (2012), p. 165.   [119] Andersen (2012), p. 171.
[120] Andersen (2012), p. 171.

the process effective was a design which had 'speakers present their stories to an audience that, at first, was only supposed to listen',[121] and only afterwards was there a possibility for discussion. Once again, the important work is being done by the listening of the whites, as a vital corollary of the speech of the African Americans. Andersen refers to this moment as 'anti-dialogic', and while at first blush this might seem a surprising way of characterizing a process of restoration and reconciliation, it makes perfect sense once we give listening its independent and indispensable due as creating the conditions within which dialogue—and deliberation—can take place. Neither dialogue nor deliberation can do without listening and silence.

CONCLUSION

The so-called 'deliberative turn' in democratic theory has been one of the most exciting political–theoretical developments of recent times. The twin promise of inclusiveness and unconstrained dialogue is hard for progressives to resist, and when real signs of advance regarding institutional design are included, the package begins to look extremely attractive. In this chapter I have tried to show how deliberative democracy's promise is more likely to be realized if the *dialogic* conditions for inclusivity and free deliberation are taken into account. These conditions take two forms, both of which relate to listening. First, the process of deliberation will be at its best when the rules of good listening learnt in Chapter 2 are followed. This is the discipline of listening *to*. Second, inclusiveness has been shown to be a function of effective listening *out for*. The latter leads to an increase in legitimacy in pluralist societies, as it promises to draw on as wide a range of viewpoints as possible. While this has the potential to increase the centrifugal tendencies of such societies, the injunction to listen well to one's interlocutors acts as a counterbalance and can act as a route to understanding—if not to agreement. Dialogic democracy therefore has the potential to unsettle its deliberative cousin, especially when the latter takes the form in which the object of the process is to reach a consensus. Dialogic democracy takes its time, it engineers silences, it makes sure that all voices have been heard—and then it listens again.

---

[121] Andersen (2012), p. 172.

Listening is obviously key to effective dialogical democracy, but how is it to be institutionalized? Plenty of work has gone in to trying to make deliberative democracy work in practice, and, in this regard, dialogic democracy is way behind the curve. Having done some theoretical catching up in this chapter, in Chapter 6 I will discuss some of the measures that might be taken to introduce listening to actual political practice. First, though, I plan to take a step back and ask two questions—thus far avoided in this enquiry into political listening—to whom, and for what, should we be listening?

5

Listening to Whom? Listening for What?

Thus far in this book we have talked about listening and politics, and listening and democracy, in quite traditional ways. This is to say that the focus has been on aural listening (listening with the ear), and what we have been listening to (or out for) is speech. Speech, though, is just one form of communication, and listening is just one of the senses we use to receive communication. In Chapter 4 we saw Iris Marion Young arguing for a broadening of the types of speech that should be regarded as legitimate in democratic debate—to 'rational' speech she adds greeting, rhetoric, and narrative. In this chapter I follow Young's line of enquiry but take it a stage further by asking whether other forms of communication might be regarded as 'political', and what 'listening' might entail in an even broader context than Young's. If it turns out that political communication involves more than just speech, then we will be enjoined to wonder, too, just what we are listening out for. We introduced the distinction between listening to and listening out for in Chapter 1 and took it up in again Chapter 4 when we were outlining the nature of dialogic democracy. If we take it that political communication involves more than the noises made by human speech then we must necessarily ask what we are listening out for beyond human speech.

It is entirely commonplace to think that communication does indeed involve more than just human speech. We have had several opportunities to point out that the origins of the idea that human speech is the primordial political noise lie with Aristotle. This becomes a recurring theme in Western political thought, and indeed, as we saw in Chapter 1, a key building block of liberal democratic thought—the contract—seems to require speech (or some close analogue) as a pre-condition for it. As Thomas Hobbes put it:

the most noble and profitable invention of all other, was that of SPEECH, consisting of *names* and *appellations*, and their connexion; whereby men register their thoughts; recall them when they are past; and also declare them to one another for mutual utility and conversation; without which, there had been amongst men; neither commonwealth, nor society nor contract, nor peace, no more than amongst lions, bears or wolves.[1]

Apart from establishing speech as a precondition for contract, in the last part of the quotation Hobbes reinforces the Aristotelian trope that animals cannot speak and therefore cannot make contracts. Given that, for Hobbes, the making of a contract is what brings politics into being, this amounts to a principled exclusion of the non-human—and its/their noises—from politics. We recall that in the same passage in which Aristotle establishes that 'man' is a (and the only) political animal, he contrasts 'speech' with 'voice'. Voice is possessed by non-human animals, says Aristotle, and what links speech and voice (though Aristotle does not make this point) is that they are both forms of communication. Beyond this we often refer to non-vocal forms of communication too: gestures and touch, for example. These point us towards senses beyond hearing—to the visual and tactile senses in this case. So while we might not want to argue that all forms of communication are political, or that we need to hone all our receptive senses for political ends, there seems to be a prima facie case for at least considering the possibility that political communication can be non-'voiced'. What both Aristotle and Hobbes are doing is distinguishing 'noise' (as 'unwanted sound'[2]) from politically meaningful communication, and their position is that anything other than human speech is just noise. This is also the rest position of most political theorizing.

RECOGNITION

One way of thinking about what forms of communication might be regarded as political is through the idea of 'recognition'. This is what Iris Marion Young was doing when she argued for greeting, rhetoric, and

---

[1] Thomas Hobbes, *Leviathan* (Oxford: Basil Blackwell, 1946), p. 18.
[2] Bruce Buchan, 'Listening for noise in political thought', *Cultural Studies Review* 18 (2012), no. 3, p. 37.

narrative as legitimate forms of political communication: she wanted them (and those who deploy them) to be *recognized* as political. The notion of recognition has found its way into contemporary political theory principally through debates around the meaning and practice of social justice. Traditionally, social justice is about distribution: the distribution of goods and bads in society (or, more technically, the 'community of justice'). Those in favour of introducing the idea of recognition into justice debates argue that it is important to look for the sources and causes of maldistribution. This is, of course, not a new question in itself, even if recognition theorists might sometimes be read as claiming that it is. Marxism, for example, can be read as an enquiry into the causes of maldistribution. But my point here is not to argue the merits of recognition in comparison with other analyses of maldistribution. Nor am I interested in another key debate internal to the recognition issue: the question of the relationship between material and cultural factors that contribute to maldistribution. This has been argued at length by Axel Honneth and Nancy Fraser, with the former taking the view that, 'even distributional injustices must be understood as the institutional expression of social disrespect',[3] while Fraser argues that, '[E]ven the most material economic institutions have a constitutive, irreducible cultural dimension; they are shot through with significations and norms. Conversely, even the most discursive cultural practices have a constitutive, irreducible political–economic dimension; they are underpinned by material supports.'[4] So Honneth argues for a foundational role for recognition as an explanatory factor in maldistribution, while Fraser maintains that the relationship is dialectical.[5]

We cannot—and nor do I want to—resolve this dispute here. Perhaps we can agree with David Schlosberg that, '*Part* of the problem of injustice, and *part* of the reason for unjust distribution, is a lack of recognition of group difference.'[6] Nancy Fraser regards the focus on recognition as a feature of what she calls the 'post-socialist condition',

---

[3] Axel Honneth, 'Redistribution as recognition: a response to Nancy Fraser', in Nancy Fraser and Axel Honneth, *Redistribution or Recognition? A Political–Philosophical Exchange* (London and New York: Verso, 2003), p. 114.

[4] Nancy Fraser, *Justice Interruptus: Critical Reflections on the 'Postsocialist' Condition* (New York and London: Routledge, 1997), p. 15.

[5] Fraser (1997), p. 15.

[6] David Schlosberg, *Defining Environmental Justice: Theories, Movements and Nature* (Oxford: Oxford University Press, 2007), p. 15; emphasis added.

in which, 'the most salient social movements are no longer economically defined "classes" who are struggling to defend their "interests", end "exploitation", and win "redistribution". Instead, they are culturally defined "groups" or "communities of value" who are struggling to defend their "identities", end "cultural domination", and win "recognition".'[7] What is promising about the concept of recognition from our point of view is that it seeks to uncover 'disguised particularisms'[8]—that is, ideas that claim universal validity but which actually serve particular interests. Fraser makes this point in the context of a reply to the critique that recognition is itself a form of particularism—a claim made on behalf of particular groups with sectional interests. This would be the view that, 'the inherent thrust of such politics is a particularistic self-assertion that rejects the universalism of "common dreams"'.[9] Not at all, writes Fraser: '[I]n fact…those movements arose in the first place precisely to protest the disguised particularisms—the masculinism, the white-Anglo ethnocentrism, the heterosexism—lurking behind what parades as universal.'[10]

As this quotation suggests, claims for recognition have been made principally by and on behalf of groups organized around gender, race, and sexuality, but the means through which misrecognition and non-recognition are exercised makes the notion applicable to any group or community that can claim to have been subjected to them. Fraser describes the mechanics of the process as follows:

> [I]njustice is rooted in social patterns of representation, interpretation, and communication. Examples include cultural domination (being subjected to patterns of interpretation and communication that are associated with another culture and are alien and/or hostile to one's own); nonrecognition (being rendered invisible by means of the authoritative representational, communicative, and interpretative practices of one's culture); and disrespect (being routinely maligned or disparaged in stereotypic public cultural representations and/or in everyday life interactions).[11]

What is striking about this list from our point of view is the crucial role that communication plays in patterns of recognition and misrecognition. Fraser talks of 'alien' forms of communication, and of the

---

[7] Fraser (1997), p. 2.   [8] Fraser (1997), p. 5.
[9] Fraser (1997), p. 5.   [10] Fraser (1997), p. 5.
[11] Fraser (2007), p. 14.

distinction between authoritative and non-authoritative communicative practices. Once again this reminds us of Young's attempt to change the terms of debate by including greeting, rhetoric, and narrative in the legitimate range of forms of democratic communication, and her decision to call her preferred form of democracy, 'communicative' democracy.

While we tend to think of all this in the context of human groups, and while we might think that this is where the power of the critique resides, there is potential in the notion of recognition for examining the apparently ineluctable link between speech and politics as a disguised particularism. Looked at the other way round, the Aristotelian assertion that the political being is a speaking being is universally regarded as being true—outside the theorists and arguments that I will be considering in this chapter anyway. So if recognition is a tool for disclosing disguised particularisms and for making claims on behalf of previously excluded groups and communities, then it has potential for helping us to think through the implications of unsettling the elision between the speaking being and the political being.

Once a case of mis- or non-recognition has been established, what forms of action can be taken to remedy them? Fraser contrasts the distributional and recognitional approaches as follows:

> [T]he remedy for economic injustice is political–economic restructuring of some sort... [T]he remedy for cultural injustice... is some sort of cultural or symbolic change. This could involve upwardly revaluing disrespected identities and the cultural products of maligned groups. It could also involve recognizing and positively valorizing cultural diversity. More radically still, it could involve the wholesale transformation of societal patterns of representation, interpretation, and communication in ways that would change *everybody's* sense of self.[12]

This is a rich passage that merits unpacking. Fraser draws a contrast between, on the one hand, working for the inclusion of excluded groups by positively revaluing their previously derided characteristics and, on the other, changing the rules by which inclusion is determined in the first place. One example of the 'upwardly revaluing disrespected identities' strategy is that deployed by a strand of so-called 'difference feminism', which argues that the differences between men and women

---

[12] Fraser (2007), p. 15.

should be celebrated rather than used as the basis for unfair discrimination. So if is true, for example, that women communicate more through narrative than through what we normally understand by 'reasoned speech', then narrative needs to be revalued positively rather than derided as a somehow less respectable form of communication. There is another strategy related to this one to which Fraser neither refers nor discusses. This is the one adopted by theorists and activists such as Mary Wollstonecraft, whereby women are shown to possess the characteristics required for inclusion rather than positively revaluing any women-specific characteristics. Thus, if the possession of reason is regarded as the entry ticket to political consideration (e.g. the right to vote), then the task of feminists—from this point of view—is to show that women are rational and it is therefore illogical to deny them participation. Both this strategy and the other one of 'positive revaluation' contrast with a third, which involves changing the rules of engagement themselves. So while the first two involve recognition through *affirmation* ('surface reallocations of respect to existing identities of existing groups; supports group differentiations'), the last one involves recognition through *transformation* ('deep restructuring of relations of recognition; destabilizes group differentiation'[13]).

AFFIRMATION AND TRANSFORMATION

Fraser herself offers sexuality as an example of how these different strategies work: '[A]ffirmative remedies for homophobia and heterosexism are currently associated with gay-identity politics, which aims to revalue gay and lesbian identity. Transformative remedies, in contrast, are associated with queer politics, which would deconstruct the homo-hetero dichotomy.' So '[W]hereas gay-identity politics tends to enhance existing sexual group differentiation, queer politics tends to destabilize it—at least ostensibly and in the long run. The point holds for recognition remedies more generally. Whereas affirmative recognition remedies tend to promote existing group differentiations, transformative recognition remedies tend, in the long run, to destabilize them so as to make room for future regroupments.'[14]

---

[13] Fraser (2007), p. 27.   [14] Fraser (2007), p. 24.

The distinction Fraser draws between affirmation and transformation as routes to recognition is crucial in our context, as it suggests different kinds of answer to our overarching questions in this chapter: listening to whom and listening for what? Both feminist affirmation and transformation have their listening components. Take the two circumstances of feminist affirmation first: asserting that women already possess the characteristics required for political considerability, and revaluing positively their specific characteristics as consistent with political considerability. A precondition for these strategies working is that women be listened to, both for the voice they have which is already legitimate, and for the one they would like to add to the list of legitimate voices. The point here is that we already know who we are listening to—women. The transformative strategy, though, demands a different kind of listening—one which is so open-ended that it operates without categories. In Chapter 2 we encountered the distinction between cataphatic and apophatic listening. Cataphatic listeners bring their own categories and expectations to bear when they listen, while apophatic listeners allow categories to emerge from what they hear. In this context, the affirmative strategy is closer to the cataphatic than the apophatic end of the spectrum—the categories 'man' and 'woman' are established and unquestioned. Apophatic listening, on the other hand, is more likely to bring about the conditions in which differentiations are destabilized and 'regroupments' are possible. We will come back to this.

The strategies of affirmation and transformation have their application in environmental political theory and practice, and consideration of this will take us further in our enquiry into whether political communication can and should involve more than human speech. Environmental ethics has long been concerned with the question of who or what should be accorded ethical and/or political considerability, and in this sense the questions—if not the answers—are similar to those asked by feminists. As in Wollstonecraft-style feminism, the search is on for a 'Factor X'—a factor that makes human beings ethically and/or politically considerable, and which is shared by (an)other species. If such a factor can be found then it would be inconsistent to deny the non-human species ethical/political considerability just because it is non-human. The term 'speciesism' has been coined to describe this kind of unjustified discrimination. In our context we have seen Aristotle arguing that the Factor X of political considerability is 'the power of reasoned speech' but there are alternatives. Jeremy Bentham famously wrote that, 'the question is not, Can they reason? nor, Can they talk? but, Can they suffer?'[15] The capacity to suffer is shared by more creatures than the capacity to reason or to talk. So if this is the capacity that determines considerability, the charmed circle is widened at a stroke. Factor X might turn out to be a biological fact, as in the case made by the Great Ape Project (GAP): '[F]rom the biological point of view, between two human beings there can be a difference of 0.5% in the DNA. Between a man and a chimpanzee this difference is only 1.23%.'[16] This leads GAP to the conclusion that, 'the exploitation of great primates in laboratories, circus, entertainment shows and zoos can be considered a kind of slavery, reminding what men used to do with others of his own kind who were considered to be inferior a little bit more than one century ago'.[17]

David Schlosberg employs the affirmation strategy in his discussion of environmental justice. His argument is that a purely distributional approach to justice is inadequate to the environmental context, and he agrees with Young and others that, '[P]art of the problem of injustice, and part of the reason for unjust distribution, is a lack of recognition of group difference.'[18] His is very much an affirmative, Factor X approach to recognition: 'many authors argue...for the consideration and recognition of nature because of the multiple commonalities or similarities between humans and their environment. Here the focus is on various qualities of the essence of being that we share with non-human nature: needs, sentience, interests, agency, physical integrity, and the unfolding of potential.'[19] This leaves the categories 'human' and 'nature' in place, and bases the claim for recognition on the similarities between them—what they have in common. And Schlosberg sees real potential here because, 'there is plenty to recognize in nature. Extending ecological justice into the realm of recognition, we find much to appreciate about the natural world. Recognizing sentience, needs, agency, or integrity in nature gives us avenues to expand our

---

[15] Jeremy Bentham, *The Principles of Morals and Legislation* (Darien, CT: Hafner Publishing, 1970), p. 311, fn.
[16] Great Ape Project, available at <http://www.greatapeproject.org/en-US/oproje-togap/Missao> (accessed 4 October 2012).
[17] Great Ape Project (2012).
[18] Schlosberg (2007), p. 15.
[19] Schlosberg (2007), p. 133.

understanding of the community of justice, and of ecological justice specifically.[20]

Often the affirmation route to recognition is couched in the language of rights. Once a previously excluded group is granted rights it can claim to have been 'recognized', but, as Christopher Stone pointed out in his seminal essay on the possibility of granting rights to trees and the rest of nature, there is a circularity to the rights approach: 'there will be resistance to giving the thing "rights" until it can be seen and valued in itself; yet, it is hard to see and value it for itself until we can bring ourselves to give it "rights"'.[21] So the rights strategy is not, in and of itself, a means of securing recognition; we need to find out what prevents recognition and work out ways of overcoming the obstacles. As Schlosberg says, '[T]he point is to examine the range of social and cultural values and practices that impede the full recognition of a group as an accepted member of the moral and political community.'[22]

So what is it that enjoins us to regard the human being as the political being, and to deny this recognition to the non-human realm? How is this power of recognition exercised? We have already commented on the foundational role that Aristotle's focus on speech plays in this story, and it exerts a powerful influence even on thinkers who question accepted boundaries as much as Jacques Rancière, as we saw in Chapter 1. In Rancière's case, Jane Bennett reports that, '[W]hen asked in public whether he thought that an animal or a plant or a drug or a (nonlinguistic) sound could disrupt the police order, Rancière said no: he did not want to extend the concept of the political that far; non-humans do not qualify as participants in a demos; the disruption effect must be accompanied by the desire to engage in reasoned discourse.'[23] 'Reasoned discourse' really does seem to be the elephant in the room— so obviously there and yet so apparently invisible. Another example comes from Iris Marion Young, and, as we commented in Chapter 4, it is all the more striking in her case, given the careful thought she has lent to the legitimacy of different forms of speech. As she writes in connection with deliberative democracy: '[D]eliberative theorists

---

[20] Schlosberg (2007), p. 138.

[21] Christopher Stone, 'Should trees have standing? Towards legal rights for natural objects', *Southern California Law Review* 45 (1972), p. 456.

[22] Schlosberg (2007), p. 141.

[23] Jane Bennett, *Vibrant Matter* (Durham, NC, and London: Duke University Press, 2010), p. 106. See Chapter 1 for a fuller discussion of Rancière in this context.

tend to assume that bracketing political and economic power is sufficient to make speakers equal. This assumption fails to notice that the social power that can prevent people from being equal speakers derives not only from economic dependence or political domination but also from an internalized sense of the right one has to speak or not to speak, and from the devaluation of some people's style of speech and the elevation of others.'[24]

This comment on the devaluation of some styles of speech and the elevation of others is what leads Young to try to establish greeting, rhetoric, and narrative as legitimate forms of communication. She argues that, '[A] theory of communicative democracy that attends to social difference, to the way that power sometimes enters speech itself, recognizes the cultural specificity of deliberative practices, and proposes a more—inclusive model of communication.'[25] *What this forgets, though, is that speech itself—or at least the capacity to speak—is already power.*

The question this suggests is: can the affirmation route to recognition work for mute nature? This way of putting the question is, of course, tendentious in that it assumes that nature is indeed mute. I hope we can agree that non-human nature is mute in that it lacks the capacity for reasoned speech, and, in this sense, a strict interpretation of the affirmation strategy is not going to work. As Christopher Manes says, 'nature is silent in our culture (and in literate cultures generally) in the sense that the status of being a speaking subject is jealously guarded as an exclusively human prerogative.'[26] As long as reasoned speech is held to be the ideal form of political communication, any other type of communication can only ever be regarded as metaphorical or analogous in relation to it—and thus impure, inadequate, 'not quite up to the mark'. So when Jane Bennett talks of the electricity grid 'speaking' when it blacked out we know she is not using the term in the sense of reasoned speech but as a metaphor for speech: '[T]he electrical grid, by blacking out, lit up quite a lot: the shabby condition of the public-utilities infrastructure, the law-abidingness of New York

---

[24] Iris Marion Young, 'Communication and the other: beyond deliberative democracy', in Seyla Benhabib (ed.), *Democracy and Difference: Contesting the Boundaries of the Political* (Princeton: Princeton University Press, 1996), p. 122.

[25] Young (1996), p. 123.

[26] Christopher Manes, 'Nature and silence', in Cheryll Glotfelty and Harold Fromm (eds), *The Ecocriticism Reader: Landmarks in Literary Ecology* (Athens, GA, and London: University of Georgia Press, 1996), p. 15.

City residents living in the dark, the disproportionate and accelerating consumption of energy by North Americans, and the element of unpredictability marking assemblages composed of intersecting and resonating elements. *Thus spoke the grid.*[27] The fact that this is a metaphor is instructive. On the one hand it shows that the grid is not 'really' speaking, in the sense of reasoned speech. On the other hand, though, it shows that something *like* speech is taking place otherwise the metaphor would have no purchase on our understanding at all. So even if the grid is not actually speaking, we might well regard it as *communicating*. As Bennett goes on to claim, '[O]ne might even say that it exhibited a communicative-interest.'[28] This suggests that a strict strategy of affirmation will be unsuccessful, as non-human nature— let alone an electricity grid—cannot be thought of possessing (even potentially) the power of reasoned speech. But we should not reject affirmation as the route to recognition for non-human nature quite yet. We might still make use of a less strict interpretation of it, but first we must examine the claims of the second route to recognition that Fraser offers us: transformation.

TRANSFORMATION: BRUNO LATOUR

I aim to discuss this option through the work of two theorists who have adopted it—Bruno Latour and Jane Bennett. Neither of them adopts transformation in a self-conscious way, in the sense of being aware of Nancy Fraser's use of the term and offering their work as examples of it in action. But I believe that their work can be read in this light and that is what I propose to do. Both Latour and Bennett begin with 'nature' and 'politics' in two separate spheres and then 'smear' them together in a way that is transformative in the way Fraser describes—almost, anyway. They achieve this in instructively different ways, and I will begin with Latour's approach.

'From the time the term "politics" was invented,' Latour writes, 'every type of politics has been defined by its relation to nature.'[29] This

---

[27] Bennett (2010), p. 36 (emphasis added).
[28] Bennett (2010), p. 36.
[29] Bruno Latour, *The Politics of Nature: How to Bring the Sciences into Democracy* (Cambridge, MA, and London: Harvard University Press, 2004), p. 1.

corresponds to a point we have made on occasions in this book: that politics and nature are regarded as two separate spheres, and that from an Aristotelian point of view the thing that separates them is (the capacity for) reasoned speech. Given this state of affairs we can either:

(a) '*distinguish[ing]* between questions of nature and questions of politics', or,

(b) 'treat[ing] those two sets of questions as a single issue'.[30]

Latour adopts the second, transformative, strategy. At the core of his thinking is the idea of two 'houses' or 'assemblies', which he calls the House of Science and the House of Politics.[31] For Latour, 'nature' inhabits the House of Science, and people inhabit the House of Politics. Epistemologically, the former is generally regarded as a realm of certainty and objectivity while the latter is a realm of doubt and normativity.[32] The consequence of Latour's schema is that we have 'two houses, one of which would have authority and not speak, while the other would have speech and no authority'.[33] Significantly for us, note how the capacity to speak is once again a defining feature of the two-house set-up. As we consider the way in which Latour believes himself to be redesigning ('transforming', to use Fraser's term) the rules of the game, the key thing to remember is that he works in the realm of epistemology. Earlier we saw the affirmative strategy (in the guise of the Great Ape Project) adopting the view that some animals are sufficiently similar to the human animal as to warrant their proxy participation in the political game. This is, indeed, one way of crossing the human/non-human boundary, but it is not the way Latour chooses. He explicitly resists what 'many ecological thinkers have invited us to do ... to extricate ourselves from traditional metaphysics in order to embrace a different, less dualistic, more generous, warmer metaphysics', and this is because 'any metaphysics has the disagreeable characteristic of leading to interminable disputes'.[34] The disputes he refers to are those determining *which* characteristics are required for

---

[30] Latour (2004), p. 1 (emphasis in the original).

[31] Latour (2004), p. 15.

[32] This might be regarded as weak philosophy of science—does anyone any longer really believe in nature or science as a realm of objectivity? But Latour is writing schematically. His aim is to set up two epistemological contrasts with at least some basis in vernacular reality, even if professional philosophers of science have appropriately complicated that reality.

[33] Latour (2004), p. 17.   [34] Latour (2004), p. 60.

'moral considerability'—always pushing beyond the human but never quite sure where to stop, or why.

Latour eschews metaphysics for epistemology, and the epistemological point he makes is this: '[W]e are not witnessing the emergence of questions about nature in political debates, but the progressive transformation of all matters of facts into disputed states of affair, which nothing can limit any longer to the natural world alone—which nothing, precisely, can *naturalise* any longer.'[35] From Latour's point of view, the affirmation route to recognition pays too much attention to 'nature as such' (ontology), and not enough to what we can or cannot *know* about it (epistemology). Epistemologically, he wants us to rid ourselves of the idea that the House of Nature is a realm of objective knowledge—and then to collapse the two houses, or assemblies, not by making anything of the ontological fact that some animals are similar to humans, but by examining the implications of the idea that 'matters of fact' are being (or have been) replaced by 'disputed states of affair'. Thus, the House of Nature is no longer the univocal 'legislator' that some political ecologists claim it to be: it is, rather, a realm of dispute and uncertainty. So: '[P]olitical ecology does not shift attention from the human pole to the pole of nature; it shifts from *certainty* about the production of risk-free objects (with their clear separation between things and people) to *uncertainty* about the relations whose unintended consequences threaten to disrupt all ordering, all plans, all impacts.'[36]

So rather than see politics naturalized by nature—by which Latour understands the 'aborting' or short-circuiting of politics, the cutting-off of debate—he wants to see nature politicized, by which he understands the introduction of the trope which characterizes the House of Humans—uncertainty, doubt—to the House of Nature. Once again, the key thing is that the border crossing between the 'human' and the 'natural' takes place via epistemology rather than via ontology, zoology, ecology, or biology. The striking thing for Latour is not that humans share 99.5 per cent of their DNA with chimpanzees, but that the realm inhabited by chimpanzees can no longer be regarded as a realm of scientific objectivity.

In terms that remind us of Fraser's transformational approach to recognition Latour writes that, ' "nature" and "society" do not

---

[35] Latour (2004), p. 25.   [36] Latour (2004), p. 25 (emphasis in the original).

designate domains of reality'.[37] His aim is to construct a 'new collective'—a 'political ecology of collectives consisting of humans and non-humans'.[38] The way he does this indicates that affirmation and transformation, as routes to recognition, are at two ends of a spectrum rather than an unbridgeable divide. In the first place Latour talks of 'exchanging properties' between humans and non-humans, with a view to exposing characteristics that they have in common. While these are not DNA-type characteristics but, more specifically, *political* characteristics, it is still the case that the 'common characteristic' approach is more affirmative than transformational, and we saw examples of this above. Second, Latour agrees with Aristotle that 'the only way to recognize the "citizenry" within the collective that may be relevant for public life is to define the collective as an assembly of beings *capable of speaking*'.[39] Once again this looks more affirmative than transformational: not only is the new collective to be formed by looking for common characteristics, but the key characteristic has to do with speaking. On the face of it this is not at all promising for the creation of Latour's new collective: such a stipulation seems guaranteed to cement, rather that transform, the distinction between the House of the Things and the House of Humans—because 'things' cannot speak. As Latour says: 'Politics talks and palavers; nature does not, except in ancient myths, fables and fairy tales.'[40]

But there is a significant difference between Latour's use of exchange and of the notion of common characteristics, and what we encountered in Schlosberg in the section 'Recognition'. In Schlosberg and the other examples we looked at, the affirmation strategy proceeds by way of selecting a characteristic found in humans and then looking for it in non-humans. If it is a characteristic to which considerability (ethical or political) attaches, then granting considerability to humans while withholding it from non-humans is unjustifiable. Latour's approach is subtly but significantly different: he looks for characteristics that humans share with non-humans, *but in such a way that it is surprising that the former share it with the latter rather than the other way round.* Let us call this 'strong affirmation', in contrast to the weak version that takes human capacities as the reference point for legitimate recognition. So Latour points out that both humans and non-humans

---

[37] Latour (2004), p. 53.   [38] Latour (2004), p. 61.
[39] Latour (2004), p. 62.   [40] Latour (2004), p. 62.

suffer from 'speech impedimenta',[41] by which he means 'the difficulties one has in speaking and the devices one needs for articulation of the common world'.[42] We do not hear from either things or humans in an unmediated way. Both things and people have 'spokespersons', and it is this that shows the 'profound kinship between representatives of humans (in the political sense) and representatives of non-humans (in the epistemological sense)'.[43] As Latour puts it: '[I]f I speak in the name of another, I am not speaking in my own name. Conversely, if I were to affirm without further ado that another is speaking through me, I would be demonstrating great naiveté, a naiveté that certain epistemological myths manifest ("facts speak for themselves") but political traditions prohibit.'[44]

So Latour sets up an apparent opposition between politics (a realm of doubt and uncertainty) and science (objectivity, certainty)—and then undermines it to the point where the two realms 'meld' into one. His strategy is to drag us away from the naïve belief that 'facts speak for themselves'. After all, we do not believe that in the realm of politics, so why believe it in the realm of science? Much more common, epistemologically, he says, are 'intermediary states', characterized by notions of 'translation, betrayal, falsification, invention, synthesis, or transposition'.[45] His point is that these intermediary states are just as common in the House of Things as they are in the House of People—and it is this that brings the two houses together in what Latour regards as a reconstituted polity. This is Latour's version of the 'deep restructuring of relations of recognition [and of] group differentiation'[46] that characterizes—for Fraser—the transformative approach to recognition. Latour's own words express this transformation: '[W]ithin the collective, there is now a blend of entities, voices, and actors . . . we have discovered the work common to politics and to the sciences alike: stirring the entities of the collective together in order to make them articulable and to *make them speak*.'[47] The entities are 'blended' and 'stirred' to the point where the categories that defined their separateness are undermined.

And it is here that the importance of listening to this kind of recognition becomes apparent. Latour writes that, 'nonhumans are not

---

41 Latour (2004), p. 63.   42 Latour (2004), pp. 249–50.
43 Latour (2004), p. 250.   44 Latour (2004), p. 64.
45 Latour (2004), p. 64.   46 Fraser (1997), p. 27.
47 Latour (2004), p. 89.

in themselves objects, and still less are they matters of fact. They first appear as matters of concern, as new entities that provoke perplexity and thus speech in those who gather around them, discuss them, and argue over them.'[48] He continues: 'nonhumans are not defined by necessity any more than they are defined by mute objectivity. The only thing that can be said about them is that they *emerge in surprising fashion*, lengthening the list of beings that must be taken into account.'[49] He concludes: '[T]o put it crudely, human and nonhuman actors appear first of all as troublemakers. The notion of *recalcitrance* offers the most appropriate path to defining their action.'[50] Latour talks of 'matters of concern', of 'perplexity'. How can we know what a matter of concern is if it can't tell us? The main capacity required is attentiveness on *our* part—openness to the possibility of the emergence of 'matters of concern'. This suggests 'listening' at the apophatic end of the listening spectrum, where categories are placed in abeyance, and where there is no prejudging of what might be a matter of concern or perplexity. We will come back to this after looking at the second theorist I want to consider in this exploration of the nature of transformative approaches to the recognition of nature in politics and democracy— Jane Bennett.

TRANSFORMATION: JANE BENNETT

Bennett asks herself what happens if we stop thinking of matter as 'passive stuff, as raw, brute, or inert', and instead think of it as vibrant, lively and vital?'[51] In this regard, where Latour focuses on epistemology, doubt, and uncertainty as the tools for a transformative recognition, Bennett focuses on ontology.[52] But this is not the 'warmer metaphysics' ontology of which Latour is so critical. Rather than ask the traditional ontological question of what a thing *is*, Bennett asks what things *do*. She refers approvingly to Cyril Smith's work on the history of metallography, where he claims that 'it was the human metalworkers' intense intimacy with their material that enabled *them*,

---

[48] Latour (2004), p. 66.   [49] Latour (2004), p. 79.
[50] Latour (2004), p. 81.   [51] Bennett (2010), p. vii.
[52] Bennett (2010), p. xi.

rather than (the less hands-on) scientists, to be the ones to first discover the polycrystalline structure of nonorganic matter. The desire of the craftsperson to see what a metal can *do*, rather than the desire of the scientist to know what a metal *is*, enabled the former to discern a life in metal and thus, eventually, to collaborate more productively with it.'[53] This signals a move away from regarding non-human things as passive objects on which work is done, towards a view where such things have vitality—and maybe even agency.

The agency point is pressed in one example Bennett gives of her 'vital materialism' at work: Charles Darwin and his observations of worms. Darwin spent many long hours observing worms and the way they made topsoil and vegetable mould. This is what worms do, by instinct, and in doing so they make 'possible an earth hospitable to humans.'[54] Darwin then adds to this commonplace thought by saying that worms have 'played an ... important part in the history of the world',[55] and, of course, in the sense that without them the soil would be less fertile than it is and crop-growing might be harder than it is, they do. But Bennett takes the point a stage further by referring to this wormy activity as '*making* history',[56] and by going on to make the claim that worms are, in some sense, political beings. In favour of the first point she enlists Darwin himself, and his observations that worms seem sometimes to be making choices as they go about their business, and that their activity can therefore be regarded as in some sense purposive—a prerequisite, it is generally regarded, for something to be making history rather than just being a part of it. Interestingly, the force of this point relies to some degree on granting worms human characteristics, or at least those characteristics possessed by humans which make them historical beings. In this sense, humans and their powers and capacities remain the measure of historical and political being-ness, and this sounds very much like the affirmation strategy—and not the transformation strategy—we came across in Nancy Fraser's work. But Bennett's mode of affirmation is very similar to the 'strong' form we encountered in Latour, where the surprise is that humans share characteristics with non-humans rather than the other way round: the latter rather than former are regarded as the standard against which comparisons are made. Bennett's strategy is to point out

[53] Bennett (2010), p. 60.   [54] Bennett (2010), p. 95.
[55] In Bennett (2010), p. 95.   [56] Bennett (2010), p. 95; my emphasis.

that humans are bundles of vital materiality—just as non-humans are. We need, she says, to '*raise the status of the materiality of which we are composed*. Each human is a heterogeneous compound of wonderfully vibrant, dangerously vibrant, matter. If matter itself is lively, then not only is the difference between subjects and objects minimized, but the status of the shared materiality of all things is elevated.'[57] Similarly, she refers to the full 'range of the nonhuman powers circulating around and within human bodies',[58] emphasizing what I am calling the strong affirmative point: that we should pay more attention to the presence of the non-human in the human rather than the other way round. Vitality is thus 'smeared' across the human and non-human spheres. This leads Bennett to want to 'emphasize, even overemphasize, the agentic contributions of nonhuman forces (operating in nature, in the human body, and in human artifacts) in an attempt to counter the narcissistic human reflex of human language and thought'[59]—and the agentic capacity here is revealed in the 'small but irreducible degree of independence from the words, images, and feelings they [objects] provoke in us'.[60] Bennett sums all this up as 'thing-power': 'the curious ability of inanimate things to animate, to act, to produce effects dramatic and subtle'.[61]

As we saw earlier, environmental ethicists have long been aiming at unsettling the so-called 'hierarchy of being', which has human beings as the source and measure of all value. This is normally achieved by retaining the idea of human beings as the source and measure of value, and pointing out that some non-human beings possess the required value-relevant characteristic(s) too. This leads to what we have been calling—via Nancy Fraser—an affirmative approach to recognition. The transformative approach, on the other hand, calls for a 'deep restructuring of relations of recognition', and 'destabilizes group differentiation', and this is what Bennett seeks to achieve with her notion of vital materialism. Regarding human beings as vibrant matter rather than disembodied minds opens the door to what I want to call a strong affirmative (rather than a strictly transformative) recognition based less on human exceptionalism and subsequent surprise that some non-human beings are exceptional in the required way too,

---

[57] Bennett (2010), pp. 12–13; emphasis in the original.
[58] Bennett (2010), p. ix.   [59] Bennett (2010), p. xvi.
[60] Bennett (2010), p. xvi.   [61] Bennett (2010), p. 6.

and more on an ontological one-ness.[62] The 'surprise' here is a shared vibrancy, vitality across what is normally regarded as the ontological divide—even a shared capacity for independent action. As Bennett points out: '[N]o one really knows what human agency is, or what humans are doing when they are said to perform as agents. In the face of every analysis, human agency remains something of a mystery. If we do not know just how it is that human agency operates, how can we be so sure that the processes through which nonhumans make their mark are qualitatively different?'[63] This is not to say that Bennett regards humans and non-humans as ontologically identical: '[T]here are of course differences between the knife that impales and the man impaled, between the technician who dabs the sampler and the sampler, between the array of items in the gutter of Cold Spring Lane and me, the narrator of their vitality. But I agree with John Frow that these differences need "to be flattened, read horizontally as a juxtaposition rather than vertically as a hierarchy of being".'[64] This horizontality is important to Bennett, and she suggests that the key to unlocking recognition of it is a healthy dose of anthropomorphism: '[A] touch of anthropomorphism...can catalyze a sensibility that finds a world filled not with ontologically distinct categories of beings (subjects and objects) but with variously composed materialities that form confederations. In revealing similarities across categorical divides and lighting up structural parallels between material forms in "nature" and those in "culture", anthropomorphism can reveal isomorphisms.'[65]

In environmental ethics calls have often gone out for a 're-enchantment' of the natural world,[66] in an effort to inoculate it against charges of muteness, dumbness, worthlessness. Bennett looks to 'revitalize' rather than re-enchant, and in doing so she hopes to give back to the non-human world the voice it has lost. Christopher Manes locates the contemporary silence of nature in the demise of animism,[67] to the point where nature has shifted from an 'animistic to a symbolic presence, from a voluble subject to a mute object'.[68] For Manes, the silence of nature in contemporary culture contrasts with 'animistic cultures, those that see the natural world as inspirited, not

---

[62] Bennett (2010), p. xi.   [63] Bennett (2010), p. 34.
[64] Bennett (2010), pp. 9–10.   [65] Bennett (2010), p. 99.
[66] Morris Berman, *The Reenchantment of the World* (Ithaca: Cornell University Press, 1981).
[67] Manes (1996), p. 16.   [68] Manes (1996), p. 17.

just people, but also animals, plants, and even "inert" entities such as stones and rivers, are perceived as being articulate and at times intelligible subjects, able to communicate and interact with humans for good or ill. In addition to human language, there is also the language of the birds, the wind, earthworms, wolves and waterfalls—a world of autonomous speakers whose intents (especially for hunter-gatherer peoples) one ignores at one's peril.'[69] Bennett's point is not so much that the non-human world has a language (or languages), but that it has vitality, and that this vitality lends the non-human world a capacity for independent 'action'. The consequences of ignoring this vitality amount to a self-fulfilling prophecy in which the assumption that the non-human is dead, mute, simultaneously fuels an unsustainable attitude towards it and legitimates a sensory shutdown that forecloses the possibility of the discovery of non-human vitality: '[W]hy advocate the vitality of matter? Because my hunch is that the image of dead or thoroughly instrumentalized matter feeds human hubris and our earth-destroying fantasies of conquest and consumption. It does so by preventing us from detecting (seeing, hearing, smelling, tasting, feeling) a fuller range of the nonhuman powers circulating around and within human bodies.'[70]

COMPARING LATOUR AND BENNETT

There are striking similarities between Bennett and Latour. Both of them are aware that the non-human world does not 'act' in the purposive way that humans do (or are supposed to), so Latour creates a neologism—'actants'—to describe non-human actors. Bennett endorses the neologism,[71] and emphasizes how agentic capacity is spread 'differentially' across ontological types.[72] Picking up the strong affirmative theme we introduced earlier, the point is not so much that we should see the non-human world as sharing the capacity for purposive activity with human beings, but that human beings are 'actants' too. Actants make themselves known in the world, both for Latour and Bennett, by *surprising* us. Latour calls these potential provocations

---

[69] Manes (1996), p. 15.   [70] Bennett (2010), p. ix.
[71] Bennett (2010), p. ix.   [72] Bennett (2010), p. 9.

'propositions': 'I am going to say that a river, a troop of elephants, a climate, El Niño, a mayor, a town, a park, have to be taken as propositions to the collective.'[73] Bennett's point might be that if we had not gone into sensory shutdown, we might have heard the drip-drip of melting glaciers as a 'proposition' to be considered by the new collective Latour describes. 'Recognition of agency in nature therefore means that we should listen to signals emanating from the natural world with the same sort of respect we accord communication emanating from human subjects, and as requiring equally careful interpretation,'[74] says John Dryzek.

Bennett and Latour also share an interest in the idea of 'spokespersons'. We are very used to the idea of spokespersons in the human realm—particularly in the context of our representative democracies. Less so, perhaps, in the realm of science, but Latour claims that, '[W]e have to acknowledge that the notion of the spokesperson lends itself admirably to the definition of the work done by scientists in lab coats... the lab coats are the spokespersons of the nonhumans, and, as is the case with all spokespersons, *we have to entertain serious but not definitive doubts* about their capacity to speak in the name of those they represent.'[75] In this regard Latour is suggesting that listening to human claims and those of nature is not such a different exercise—they both involve interpretation. Even the human being's apparently unassailable retort to a supposedly inappropriate spokesperson—'you don't speak for me'—is open to contestation, since we all know that some of the time we may not be clear about our own best interests. As he says, '[W]ith the notion of the spokesperson, we are designating not the transparency of the speech in question, but the *entire gamut*, running from complete doubt (I may be a spokesperson, but I am speaking in my own name and not in the name of those I represent) to total confidence (when I speak, it is really those who I represent who speak through my mouth).'[76] In sum: '"Discussion", a key term of political philosophy that has been mistakenly understood as a well-formed notion, available off

---

[73] Latour (2004), p. 83.

[74] John Dryzek, *Deliberative Democracy and Beyond* (Oxford: Oxford University Press, 2000), p. 149. See also John Dryzek, *Foundations and Frontiers of Deliberative Governance* (Oxford: Oxford University Press, 2010), p. 34.

[75] Latour (2004), pp. 64–5; emphasis in the original.

[76] Latour (2004), p. 64.

the shelf, as it were, has now been quite profoundly modified: speech is no longer a specifically human property, or at least humans are no longer its sole masters.'[77]

Likewise, Bennett feels it is no obstacle that humans do the speaking: '[I]t will be objected that such communication is possible only through the intermediary of humans. But is this really an objection, given that even linguistic communication necessarily entails intermediaries? My speech, for example, depends on the graphite in my pencil, millions of persons, dead and alive, in my Indo-European language group, not to mention the electricity in my brain and my laptop. (The human brain, properly wired, can light up a fifteen-watt bulb.) Humans and nonhumans alike depend on a "fabulously complex" set of speech prostheses.'[78] The idea of 'prostheses' is picked up from Latour who concludes that is wrong to think that, '[H]umans and humans alone are the ones who speak, discuss, and argue.'[79] On the contrary, he says, 'lab coats [i.e. scientists] have invented *speech prostheses that allow nonhumans to participate in the discussions of humans, when humans become perplexed about the participation of new entities in political life*'.[80] Latour focuses particularly here on scientists as spokespersons for nature, but we need not be so restrictive. The prostheses can be created by anyone, and the key requirement is less expert knowledge and more a sensory openness and willingness to be surprised by Bennett's 'thing-power'. As Val Plumwood puts it in her notion of 'communicative interspecies ethics', 'most people have had some experience of communication with animals even if they do not call it by that name'.[81] According to her, no special skills are needed: 'all' that is required is a letting go of the 'arrogance and human-centredness of a culture that is convinced that other species are simpler and lesser, and only grudgingly to be admitted as communicative beings'.[82]

Of course this 'letting go' might itself be a skill, just as we discovered in Chapter 2 that 'listening' can be considered a skill (and there is more than a hint of the apophatic 'bracketing-off' in this too). We also saw then that listening might be more of a disposition associated with virtue, rather than a skill as such. Whether it is a skill or

---

[77] Latour (2004), p. 65.   [78] Bennett (2010), p. 36.
[79] Latour (2004), p. 66.   [80] Latour (2004), p. 67; emphasis in the original.
[81] Val Plumwood, *Environmental Culture: The Ecological Crisis of Reason* (London: Routledge, 2002), p. 189.
[82] Plumwood (2002), p. 189.

a disposition, we can learn from those who do it well, and we might find examples in unexpected places. Consider the case of Temple Grandin, the autistic who has made a name for herself with her capacity to interpret the moods and needs of animals—particularly domesticated cattle. Grandin claims that, '[A]utistic people can think the way animals think... Autism is a kind of way station on the road from animals to humans, which puts autistic people like me in a perfect position to translate "animal talk" into English. I can tell people why their animals are doing the things they do.'[83] Grandin's story, fascinating as it is in itself, is of broader significance in that even she, given the 'head start' of her autism, had to learn how to interpret the needs and wants of the animals with whom she came into contact. In her view we all suffer from a blind spot, an incapacity to know what to look for when we observe animal behaviour. She became interested in idiot savants, who can '*naturally* do things no normal human being can even be *taught* to do, no matter how hard he tries to learn or how much time he spends practicing.'[84] Her suggestion is that '[A]nimals are like autistic savants,'[85] meaning that, '[A]nimals have special talents normal people don't, the same way autistic people have special talents normal people don't.'[86] So, '[T]he reason we've managed to live with animals all these years without noticing many of their special talents is simple: we can't see those talents... Normal people can stare straight at an animal doing something brilliant and have no idea what they're seeing.'[87]

A key point for us is that, in Grandin's view, one does not have to be autistic to be able to understand animals better. 'I don't know if people will ever be able to talk to animals the way Doctor Doolittle could,' she writes, '[but] I do know people can learn to "talk" to animals, and to hear what animals have to say, better than they do now.'[88] The thought of 'listening schools' run by autistics is an intriguing one (not canvassed by Grandin herself though), and Grandin believes that better communication across the species boundary would make

---

[83] Temple Grandin, *Animals in Translation: Using the Mysteries of Autism to Decode Animal Behaviour* (London: Bloomsbury, 2005), pp. 6–7.
[84] Grandin (2005), p. 7.　　　　[85] Grandin (2005), p. 8.
[86] Grandin (2005), p. 8.　　　　[87] Grandin (2005), p. 8.
[88] Grandin (2005), p. 307.

not only animals happier, but humans too: 'I...know that a lot of times people who can talk to animals are happier than people who can't. People were animals, too, once, and when we turned into human beings we gave something up. Being close to animals brings some of it back.'[89]

THE POLITICAL

We have moved a long way in our discussion of recognition. At the beginning of the chapter we distinguished—with Nancy Fraser—between affirmative and transformative strategies for recognition. The former leaves categories unchanged, and asks 'simply' either for previously unrecognized categories to be regarded as possessing the required characteristics for recognition, or for their own specific characteristics to be revalued 'upwards'. Transformation, on the other hand, calls for relations of recognition to be restructured, and for the bases of group differentiation to be called into question. It seems to be assumed by Fraser and others that recognition is an intrahuman matter, but we saw David Schlosberg deploying the notion in the context of environmental justice. Schlosberg adopts a largely affirmative position, and points out (quite rightly) that some non-humans possess some of the characteristics that are sometimes predicated with regard to political considerability. The advantage of the affirmative approach adopted by Schlosberg is that, in the restricted 'crossover' range he identifies, claims for the *political* considerability of the beings he includes are relatively easy to make. This is because we are clear about

---

[89] Grandin (2005), p. 307. Counter-intuitively, perhaps, Grandin has used her talents for the benefit of the US meatpacking industry, designing restraining systems that ensure that cattle enter the abattoir in a contented frame of mind, thus improving the quality of the meat as well making the abattoir easier to manage. She writes, 'People always wonder how I can work in the meatpacking industry when I love animals so much. I've thought about this a lot...I remember looking out over the cattle yard at the hundreds and hundreds of animals milling around in their corrals. I was upset that I had just designed a really efficient slaughter plant...Now I'm writing this book because I wish animals could have more than just a low-stress life and a quick, painless death. I wish animals could have a *good* life, too, with something useful to do. I think we owe them that'; Grandin (2005), p. 307.

what characteristics count, and the difficulty lies more in establishing that some beings other than human beings possess those characteristics than in agreeing what the characteristics are.

In the transformative case the problem is reversed. We need to ask ourselves whether Latour's actants and propositions and Bennett's possessors of 'thing-power' can be regarded as political actors. It is all very well identifying vibrant materialities and recalcitrant objects, but is there anything in our understanding of what politics is that would enable us to mount an argument in favour of this reconstituted community being a *political* community? Bennett herself refers to,

> the hard question of the *political* capacity of actants. Even if a convincing case is made for worms as active members of, say, the ecosystem of a rainforest, can worms be considered members of a public? What is the difference between an ecosystem and a political system? Are they analogs? Two names for the same system at different scales? What is the difference between an actant and a political actor? Is there a clear difference? Does an action count as political by virtue of its having taken place 'in' a public? Are there nonhuman members of a public? What, in sum, are the implications of a (meta)physics of vibrant materiality for political theory?[90]

Bennett answers this question by drawing on the work of John Dewey, who we encountered in Chapter 2 in our exploration of listening. In his *The Public and its Problems* Dewey asks what constitutes a public, and how publics are formed.[91] For Dewey, publics are contingent and they form when a problem arises, around which people coalesce. As Dewey himself puts it: '[I]ndirect, extensive, enduring and serious consequences of conjoint and interacting behavior call a public into existence having a common interest in controlling these consequences.'[92] Dewey's own interest lies in determining why the Public has been replaced by a large number of publics, and what conditions might give rise to the rebirth of a broader Public. As he says, '[T]here is too much public, a public too diffused and scattered and too intricate in composition. And there are too many publics, for conjoint actions which have indirect, serious and enduring consequences are multitudinous beyond comparison, and each one of them crosses the others

---

[90] Bennett (2010), p. 94; emphasis in the original.
[91] John Dewey, *The Public and its Problems: An Essay in Political Enquiry* (Chicago: Gateway Books, 1946).
[92] Dewey (1946), p. 126.

and generates its own group of persons especially affected with little to hold these different publics together in an integrated whole.'[93]

Bennett's interest in Dewey lies less in the conditions for the creation of a metapublic and more in the formation of minipublics. Bennett notes that Deweyan publics form around a problem, and, although she does not say so herself, this should remind us of Latour's notion of the 'proposition', and the idea that, 'human and nonhuman actors appear first of all as troublemakers. The notion of *recalcitrance* offers the most appropriate path to defining their action.'[94] In Latour's analysis this recalcitrance, this troublemaking, is not—as he makes clear— restricted to the human realm. So if the 'political' public coalesces around a problem, and if this problem can arise in either the human or non-human realms, then the notion of the political 'smears' across the two realms. What makes an event political is not that it involves speaking humans, but that a public coalesces around it. Crucially, the event (the 'problem') might be prompted by non-humans. As Bennett writes, 'naming a *problem* (rather than an act of will) as the driving force behind the formation of a public, Dewey (almost) acknowledges that a *political* action need not originate in human bodies at all. For is it not the case that some of the initiatives that conjoin and cause harm started from (or later became conjoined with) the vibrant bodies of animals, plants, metals, or machines?'[95] Dewey's notion of a public as a product of conjoint action 'paves the way,' writes Bennett, 'for a theory of action that more explicitly accepts nonhuman bodies as members of a public, more explicitly attends to how they, too, participate in conjoint action, and more clearly discerns instances of harm to the (affective) bodies of animals, vegetables, minerals, and their ecocultures.'[96] In sum, '[T]heories of democracy that assume a world of active subjects and passive objects begin to appear as thin descriptions at a time when the interactions between human, viral, animal, and technological bodies are becoming more and more intense . . . it seems that the appropriate unit of analysis for democratic theory is neither the individual human nor an exclusively human collective but the (ontologically heterogeneous) "public" coalescing around a problem.'[97] This

---

[93] Dewey (1946), p. 137.   [94] Latour (2004), p. 81.
[95] Bennett (2010), p. 102.   [96] Bennett (2010), p. 103.
[97] Bennett (2010), p. 108. John Dryzek also enjoins us to think differently about what a political entity consists in, but what Bennett has in mind takes us beyond the idea that a 'discourse' might be such an entity; Dryzek (2010), p. 30.

brings powerfully to mind the burgeoning theory and practice of biosecurity as a *locus classicus* of the kind of politics to which Bennett refers.
Defined as 'the attempted management or control of unruly biological matter, ranging from microbes and viruses to invasive plants and
animals',[98] biosecurity quite precisely involves interactions between
constellations of the human and other-than-human. Moreover, our
experience of them is often characterized by the 'surprise' of which
Latour speaks, and publics do indeed coalesce around them—creating
a politics—in the way Dewey describes.

Despite her close reading and creative use of Dewey's notion of
the public and the conditions for its formation, Bennett leaves out an
essential part of his analysis—the key role of communication. Without
communication effective publics cannot be formed: '[I]nteractions,
transactions, occur *de facto* and the results of interdependence follow. But participation in activities and sharing in results are addi-
tive concerns. They demand *communication* as a prerequisite.'[99]
Further: '[W]ithout...communication the public will remain shad-
owy and formless, seeking spasmodically for itself, but seizing and
holding its shadow rather than its substance. Till the Great Society is
converted into a Great Community, the Public will remain in eclipse.
Communication can alone create a great community. Our Babel is not
one of tongues but of the signs and symbols without which shared
experience is impossible.'[100]

We know from Chapters 2 and 4 that Dewey entertained a dialogic
notion of communication in which receptivity—listening in the widest sense—played a crucial role. This suggests that the realization
of Nancy Fraser's transformative recognition in the kind of context
Latour and Bennett are sketching will crucially depend on successful
awareness of the 'signs and symbols'—not necessarily linguistic—of
which Dewey speaks. This is all of a piece with the argument made in
Chapter 4, where the redeeming of deliberative democracy's promise to be inclusive as well as deliberative was predicated on listening
hard for legitimate voices. That discussion took place in the context of
what we have defined in this chapter as 'affirmative' recognition: the
recognition of political subjects, given unchanged definitions of what

---

[98] Andrew Dobson, Kezia Barker, and Sarah Taylor (eds), *Biosecurity: The
Socio-politics of Invasive Species and Infectious Diseases* (London: Earthscan, 2013), p. 5.
[99] Dewey (1946), p. 152; emphasis in the original.
[100] Dewey (1946), p. 142.

political subjecthood might consist in. This would then simply be a question of, for example, listening out for the rational voice in women's speech. In the strong affirmative context, in contrast, the listening must be attuned to recognizing 'matters of concern'.

CONCLUSION

In this chapter I have deployed the conceptual tool of 'recognition' to help to analyse the question of what constitutes a political noise. A distinction was drawn between affirmative and transformative recognition, according to which affirmation leaves the criteria for recognition alone and demands that those seeking to be recognized meet those criteria, while transformation entertains the possibility of changing the criteria themselves. When it comes to political subjecthood, the Aristotelian criterion for recognition is the capacity for reasoned speech, so any entity or group that seeks recognition as a political subject will have to show itself capable of reasoned speech. This was the move that early feminists made, along the lines argued so persuasively by Mary Wollstonecraft. A transformative approach to political recognition would call into question the reasoned speech criterion for subjecthood. I then analysed the work of Bruno Latour and Jane Bennett and characterized them as occupying an intermediate position between affirmation and transformation. I classified this position as 'strong affirmation'. Latour and Bennett adopt the strong affirmative strategy of seeking similarities between those already granted political subjecthood and those potentially making a claim for it, but they draw attention to the surprise elicited at the realization that humans share the given characteristic with non-humans, rather than the other way round. For Latour this characteristic is speech impedimenta (we always knew non-humans had them, but it is a surprise to realize that humans have them too), and for Bennett the characteristic is vital materiality (we always knew non-humans were bundles of vital materiality but it is a surprise to realize that humans can be regarded in that way too).

On the face of it the affirmative approach to political subjecthood claims is sensible in that it indicates an identifiable conceptual lineage between already existing political subjects and entities that aspire to subjecthood. And the *strong* version enables the net to be cast wider than its weaker version allows because one is not bound so closely to the characteristics of the archetypal political subject as the model to follow. The temptation at this point is therefore to ask whether— on a strong affirmative account—Latour's actants and propositions, and Bennett's possessors of 'thing-power', can be regarded as political actors. And the even greater temptation is to try to answer this question along 'Factor X' lines—that is, is there enough Factor X-ness in actants and/or bundles of vital materiality for them to claim political subjecthood? My conclusion is that we should resist this temptation in favour of the Deweyan approach Bennett sketches, and which we discussed in the 'The political' section. The essence of this approach is that politics is created by *problems* rather than by *acts of will*. Publics coalesce around problems, and once they do then these problems become political problems. From this perspective any of the entities and phenomena referred to by Latour and Bennett—Latour's river, troop of elephants, a climate, El Niño, a mayor, a town, a park, and even Bennett's electricity grid—become political entities once they become a problem around which a public coalesces, or once they become a 'proposition to the collective', to use Latour's language.

Deborah Callister notes how Bobbie Sandoz sees beached whales as a 'form of "voice" that demands our attention'.[101] Once they attract our attention they become a politics, but, crucially, their 'becoming a politics' depends on 'the ways in which we (do not choose to) *listen* to natural voices'.[102] Her recommendation is for us to become deep listeners to the natural world.[103] 'What might we stand to gain,' she asks, 'if dominant practices valued the voices of nature... if we found ways to learn from those who *practice* listening to nature?'[104] There are two answers to this question. First, we would gain pragmatic forewarning of potential environmental danger, just as early coal miners were warned of dangerous gases by taking canaries down the mines. And

---

[101] Deborah Cox Callister, 'Beached whales: tracing the rhetorical force of extraordinary material articulations', in Emily Plec (ed.), *Perspectives on Human–Animal Communication: Internatural Communication* (Abingdon and New York: Routledge, 2013), p. 44.

[102] Callister (2013), p. 44 (emphasis in the original).

[103] As Anthony West says, the problem 'is not that the "beasts" are dumb, but that we are deaf'; Anthony Weston, *Toward Better Problems: New Perspectives on Abortion, Animal Rights, the Environment and Justice* (Philadelphia: Temple University Press, 1992), p. 74.

[104] Callister (2013), p. 50 (emphasis in the original).

there is plenty to listen to, according to natural sound expert Bernie Krause: 'explosive sounds occur when crevasses...form in the glacial span. The ice mass shatters as it is compressed...and in addition to the startling popping and groaning of the ice and the ever-present wind and frequent storms, calving glaciers release huge walls of frozen water...with a volatile, thunderous burst of sound.'[105] But, as Krause also warns, human noise is drowning out the sounds of the non-human natural world: 'to record one noise-free hour of material now takes more than two hundred times as long as it did when I first began more than four decades ago.'[106] The sting in the tail is that as the world fills with human noise, and as the sounds from the non-human natural world become ever fainter, the less likely we are to make the second gain: a new politics, characterized by publics coalescing around other-than-human materialities.

---

[105] Bernie Krause, *The Great Animal Orchestra* (London: Profile Books, 2012), p. 8.
[106] Krause (2012), p. 186.

6

Institutionalizing Listening

Consider this exchange between Councillor Mikulin and philosophy student Razumov in Joseph Conrad's *Under Western Eyes*:

> 'Listening is a great art,' observed Mikulin parenthetically. 'And getting people to talk is another,' mumbled Razumov. 'Well, no—that is not very difficult,' Mikulin said innocently.[1]

This brief conversation sums up the challenge that I try to meet in this final chapter. It is much easier to get people to talk than to listen, and this is as true of politics as it is of daily life. In what follows I take three typical political relationships and suggest ways in which listening might be improved in each of them. The first is the relationship an individual politician might have with her/his constituent. Not all political systems offer the same opportunities for contact between politicians and constituents. The UK system is well known for the potentially close links between members of parliament and their constituents. MPs famously 'return to their constituencies' on Fridays and they hold what are called 'surgeries' on Friday afternoons. Any constituent is free to make an appointment to see her or his MP at these surgeries, to make a complaint, to ask for help, or to pass a comment. This is therefore quite an intimate occasion, often conducted on a one-to-one basis. There may not be an exact equivalent in other political systems, but there is always the possibility of politicians and constituents coming together in relatively controlled conditions of potential dialogue, and this may be the archetypal relationship in a representative democracy: face-to-face contact between elected politicians and the people they represent.

---

[1] Joseph Conrad, *Under Western Eyes* (Oxford: Oxford University Press, 2008), p. 68.

The second relationship is that between politicians themselves. This contact can, of course, take many forms and occur in many places. I propose to confine myself here to the relatively formal occasions when politicians encounter each other in their parliamentary activities. This will include work 'behind the scenes' in committees, as well as the more public face of parliamentary work, in legislative debates. Politicians will claim that there is a difference between these activities, and their behaviour in them. They will say that the sometimes raucous, party discipline-driven behaviour on the floor of the legislative chamber is not mirrored in the more sedate and considered atmosphere of the committee rooms. This is probably true, in general, so any reflections on listening and how to improve it will have to take into account the difference between these two contexts.

The third relationship is that between the government and the people. What distinguishes this from the MP–constituent relationship is its scaled-up nature. This is not a face-to-face relationship of individuals, but an at-a-distance relationship of multitudes. We have had occasion throughout this book to comment on the difficulty of scaling-up good listening from the person-to-person context to the context in which governments claim to be listening to the people. In the Introduction we saw the difficulties in which governments get embroiled when they carry out listening exercises—criticized on the one hand for not listening hard enough, and on the other for weakness and vacillation if they change their minds after listening. Can anything be done to improve this situation? How should we judge good listening here? What advice can we give to governments keen to enhance their legitimacy (and that of the decisions they make) through listening better, without falling foul of either equivocation or vacillation?

As we consider these situations there are three issues we need to bear in mind, each of which draws on insights developed throughout this book. The first is the relationship between listening and power. We have learned that being listened to is experienced as power, particularly by those who are generally not listened to. We made the point that we cannot consider democracy's inclusionary work to be done once we claim simply to have allowed people to speak. Speech that is not heard is as good (or as bad) as no speech at all. This presents a problem for the listening version of what I referred to in Chapter 1 as 'sensory democracy'. In traditional terms speech is active and the senses (in this case the listening sense) are passive. The latter depend on the former in a way which is not true in reverse: the listening sense has nothing to 'work on' if there is no speech to hear. (Of course, this is only half the story. For speech to be even potentially meaningful it must be heard, as we pointed out in Chapter 1.) Thus, the difficulty with the listening version of sensory democracy is that it turns on the powerful doing something that they would rather not do. The challenge here, then, is to find ways in which this difficulty might be overcome.

The second issue to consider is whether listening can be learnt. In Chapter 2 we distinguished between thinking of listening as a skill and thinking of it as a virtue. This is important because if we believe that listening in the political context should be improved then we must be able to claim that it is improv*able*. In a general sense it makes no difference in this regard whether good listening is a skill or a virtue, since on both counts it can be enhanced, refined, and polished. But a virtue is usually regarded as more difficult to 'teach' than a skill. We talk about 'cultivating' a virtue and 'teaching' a skill. Skills can be broken down into their analytic components, and the eventual outcome is never really more than the sum of its parts. Virtues are cultivated holistically, and the outcome turns on a number of interconnected factors, any one of which can undermine the success of the end result. In what follows I do not take a stand on whether listening is a skill or a virtue, but since 'imparting skills' sounds prima facie more plausible than 'cultivating virtues', as far as politicians are concerned, I will focus on the former.

The third overarching issue we have grappled with in this book is how we distinguish between good and bad listening. In the face-to-face context this might seem obvious, and we learn to look for signs of good listening such as appropriate gestures, eye contact, the asking of confirmatory questions, allowing one's interlocutor to finish speaking, and so on. But even in this apparently simple context we learned that what is good and what is bad is not so clear. Definitions of good listening are bound up with the first of the issues I referred to briefly above, namely power. As we saw in Chapter 2 there is a cultural dimension to deciding what good listening is, so we need to take power and culture (and the relationship between them) into account when we are looking to improve political listening. One distinction we drew will be useful to us: that between process and outcome. In Chapter 3 I pointed out that most people instinctively judge good political listening in terms of outcomes. This is itself a function of a monological rather than a dialogical approach to politics, in which representation as an ongoing feature of the democratic process has broken down. The 'petitioner' will believe that s/he has one shot at getting her or his representative to listen and, because of the lack of opportunity for an ongoing dialogue with the representative, s/he will judge success by whether the representative has done what s/he wishes—rather than through any assessment of the procedure that has taken place. It would be going too far to claim that a procedural approach to determining good listening gets us off the horns of the power dilemma, but it has the great virtue of squaring with the way in which we judge the legitimacy of decisions in a democracy. Democratic legitimacy is dependent not on what the decision is, but how it is taken. If the decision-making procedure is regarded as democratic, then the decision that issues from it is democratic—regardless of what the decision is.[2] There is at least a symmetry here between the proceduralism of democratic legitimacy and a procedural approach to judging good democratic listening, and I will be using this as a guide in what follows.

The second useful distinction we drew was between cataphatic and apophatic listening. In the former case, the listening process is mediated by already existing categories and expectations, while the apophatic listener temporarily suspends these categories and expectations with a view (a) to listening to what is 'actually being said', and (b) to listening out for the unexpected and surprising. In this exploration of the political institutionalization of listening we will be taking apophatic listening as an ideal to which to aspire, and I will explain how and why in more detail in the next section.

FACE TO FACE

The simple yet potentially far-reaching idea here is that politicians should model their communicative relations at this level on what is regarded as good listening practice in whatever culture they are operating. But what does this mean, and how might it change politicians' face-to-face relations with their constituents? Recall how Sheila Shipley—in the nursing context—characterized the features of good listening in Chapter 2:

---

[2] One exception to this may be if the decision turns out to be one which is itself anti-democratic. Thus, the limiting case might be the election of a political party which is committed to ending democracy.

Listening is a planned and deliberate act in which the listener is fully present and actively engages the client in a nonjudgmental and accepting
manner. The purpose of listening is to fully understand and appreciate
the speaker's perceptions, experiences and messages. The act of listening
involves the use of empathy to understand the patient's lived experience.
The listener attends to verbal and nonverbal communication, and constantly strives to understand the spoken message as well as perceive the
underlying meanings and tones of the encounter. The listener utilises
reflection and feedback to clarify information and communicate that
the message has been heard and understood.[3]

This prospectus is pretty familiar to us by now. Shipley talks about the
aims of good listening in terms of understanding and appreciation of
the interlocutor's point of view. This is achieved by being non-judge-
mental and striving for empathy, by paying attention to verbal and
non-verbal cues, and by using questions to help establish the meaning
of what one's interlocutor is saying. This, as I say, is familiar, but we
should not let the familiarity blind us to the difference it would make
to the quality of communication between representatives and constituents if these practices were embedded in their encounters. Once
we recall that communication is central to this relationship, what is
striking is the fact that no professional attention is given to improving
its quality. This should sound as peculiar in the political context as it
would in the nursing context, but at present it does not. I will come
back to this shortly.

First, we need to emphasize an absolutely key part of Shipley's
description of good listening—a part which is likely to be overlooked
if we focus solely on the interactional aspects of face-to-face communication, important though these are. Iris Marion Young has claimed
that, '[N]o rules or formalities can ensure that people will treat others
in the political public with respect, and really listen to their claims.'[4]
Strictly speaking this is, of course, true, but we should not jump to
the conclusion that nothing at all can be done to increase the chances
of respectful treatment. Young herself spends some time discussing the rituals of 'non-Western and traditional' societies which seek
to do exactly that,[5] and the pay-off of isolating listening as the key

---

[3] Sheila Shipley, 'Listening: a concept analysis', *Nursing Forum: An Independent
Voice for Nursing* 45 (2010), no. 2, p. 133.

[4] Iris Marion Young, *Inclusion and Democracy* (Oxford: Oxford University Press,
2000), p. 57.

[5] Young (2000), p. 59.

component in achieving recognition and inclusion is that, as we know from Chapter 2, there are ways of improving listening. Here, the focus is precisely on the idea of 'rules and formalities' as I believe these offer the best chance for 'institutionalizing listening', as it were.

This is why Shipley's remark that listening is a 'planned and deliberate act' is vitally important. While this might seem counter-intuitive in the context of what we normally think of as 'conversation'—relaxed, flexible, spontaneous—it is essential to effective listening in the professional context. This suggests that we are talking about a situation that is 'more than conversation'. I began the book with a rhetorical question: why, if listening is so highly prized in daily conversation, is so little attention paid to it in that form of political conversation we call democracy? In the conclusion to Chapter 3 I suggested that 'conversation' is too imprecise a word to use in the political—and particularly the democratic—context. I recommended the use of 'dialogue' instead, and I pointed out that we can think of dialogue as a form of structured conversation.

'Structured' is what Shipley has in mind, I believe, when she refers to listening as a planned and deliberate act. As I remarked earlier in this chapter, the contrast between 'cataphatic' and 'apophatic' listening is important here. Cataphatic listening occurs when the listener brings her or his own categories to bear on what s/he is hearing, and interprets what is being said through these categories. The apophatic listener, in contrast, 'parks' these categories and strives, as far as possible, to allow the words s/he is hearing to speak for themselves. We can use these categories to analyse different 'moments' of politicians' activity. We need to strip away contingent factors, such as the degree to which individual politicians are good listeners, and focus on the structure of the encounter. At the end of Chapter 3 I distinguished between 'conversation' and 'dialogue' by referring to the latter as *structured disagreement underpinned by apophatic listening*. It is important to point out now that the 'structure' in question is not the scripted dialogue of the play or the set-piece political occasion. It is, rather, the structure that allows for apophatic listening to take place. Thus, Shipley's planning and the deliberateness are important because they are the means by which the imbalance of power between the constituent and the representative can shift, even if only temporarily. If these two interlocutors come together in a standard 'conversational' way, the power relations will remain in place, but if the encounter is planned and deliberate, and if the politician follows Shipley's advice, there is a chance that the constituent will experience *the power of being listened to*. This is a power we have had cause to refer to on a number of occasions in this book, and there is every reason why it could be experienced regularly by constituents if their representatives took listening seriously.

But how is this to happen? As Shipley says, one has to strive to listen well, and if we bear in mind that it is a skill that needs acquiring it is clearly not good enough simply to enjoin our political representatives to listen better—they need some guidance as to how to do so. There are a number of ways in which this might be achieved. Is it too far-fetched to imagine a professionalization of political representation, part of which would involve exposure to the skills of listening? Other professions have their training and qualifications, and while in the present climate of audits, inspections, and other infantilizing forms of accountability I hesitate to offer a new stick with which to beat public servants, there is a strong precedent for professional training where appropriate. This training could take the form of courses and classes, and while this is not the place to speculate on their content, they could draw on the experience of professions in which listening is already regarded as important, as well as on the insights of people for whom listening and silence have been long-standing features of their practices, such as the Quakers.[6]

Less ideally, there is also the possibility of a form of 'distance learning', trialled by academics at the University of Memphis, and aimed at prospective counsellors. The Memphis team developed a website 'with streaming video and advanced web technologies so that students can effectively practice the subtleties of active listening in an authentic counseling situation.'[7] As Jongpil Cheon and Michael Grant say, and as we had cause to note in Chapter 2, this method of teaching listening is less than ideal, since, 'In actuality, active listening skills are quite difficult to master because of the complex nature of communication: accurate comprehension often requires one to understand the nuances of non-verbal cues, recognize implicit emotions, and tease out personal

---

[6] The Quakers refer to 'creative listening', available at Quaker faith and practice: the book of Christian discipline of the Yearly Meeting of the Religious Society of Friends (Quakers) in Britain, <http://www.qfp.quakerweb.org.uk/qfp12-21.html> (accessed 15 March 2013).

[7] Jongpil Cheon and Michael Grant, 'Active listening: web-based assessment tool for communication and active listening skill development', *TechTrends* 53 (2009), no. 6, p. 24.

meaning.'[8] So while there is a limit to what one can do online because of the complex nature of the listening process, I include it here as an indication of the range of options open to any putative designer of a listening development programme for political representatives.

Mutatis mutandis, the discussion in the paragraph above applies to any formal face-to-face political encounters. In Chapter 4 I noted how little attention has been paid by political theorists to the practice of deliberation, for example—what actually happens (or does not happen) when people take part in deliberative democratic events.[9] This is odd, given the tremendous emphasis placed on deliberation by the theory, and the weight borne by it in the decision-making process. My analysis of the Bloomfield Track case suggested that listening played a more important role in the deliberative process than might appear at first sight—more important, perhaps, than deliberation itself. If this is the case, and if it is true even to some extent of other deliberative encounters, then listening deserves both independent theoretical and pragmatic attention. As far as the latter goes, it seems very likely that the quality of deliberation would be improved by participants being made explicitly aware of the need to listen well, and how to do so. We have also seen how the chance of deliberative democracy realizing its inclusionary intentions could be enhanced by a more systematic attention to listening. This is a matter of listening (out) for as well as listening to. Once again, listening out for previously unheard voices requires a particular sort of attention, rooted often in silence, and the structuration of this form of dialogue is so unlike ordinary conversation that it requires learning and practice. Deliberative democracy's promise of deciding policy according to the 'forceless force of the better argument' requires scrupulous attention to the range of arguments available, and it may imply organizing parts, moments, or aspects of the deliberative encounter in the manner of a truth and reconciliation committee where (as we have seen) the powerful are forced to listen to the powerless in a planned and structured fashion. In sum, the aim of these face-to-face encounters, whether it be between representatives and constituents or in deliberative forums, is to provide space where experience of the power of being listened to is the rule rather than the exception.

---

[8] Cheon and Grant (2009), p. 24.   [9] Pp. 109–10.

PEER-TO-PEER POLITICIANS

As I pointed out in the Introduction, politicians come into contact with one another in a variety of situations, some of which are more conducive to good listening than others. Elected members of legislatures are most often seen by the public on the floor of the legislature, usually at set-piece events when the chamber is full. In the UK at least, and when party discipline is being exerted, these occasions are archetypally cataphatic. The speeches and questions are usually pre-prepared, as are the replies. As we have seen, apophatic listening is the key to effective dialogue, and it is clear that the structure of the set-piece stand-off that characterizes the public face of legislative business is about as far from the appropriate apophatic structure as it is possible to be.

Not all encounters on the floor of the chamber are of this type, of course. Those who watch legislative debates on daytime television know that such debates can sometimes be poorly attended, and the paucity of members makes the high-octane, strident nature of the set-piece, full-chamber occasion much less likely. Yet the chances of apophatic listening taking place in these debates are still small, given the entrenched positions adopted by legislators. Then there are the 'free vote' debates, usually on what are called in the UK 'matters of conscience' (as if there are matters where conscience doesn't come into it). In free vote debates, one of the key cataphatic structures—party discipline—is removed, and so what I have called 'structured disagreement underpinned by apophatic listening' is more likely. This is also true, to a greater or lesser extent, in the committee work carried out by legislators, where party discipline plays a more muted role.

What we learn from these reflections is that one of the key structuring features of modern parliamentary democracies—party discipline—is precisely that which militates most powerfully against effective listening. This is a problem to which there is no easy solution. In the first place, there are many who would not regard it as a problem in the first place. Party discipline brings with it a number of benefits. The degree of predictability it affords helps parties as organizations to achieve their external goals; it benefits the operation of representative democracy by 'simplifying party choice'; it can enhance the quality of representatives by weeding-out wild-card candidates; it contributes to efficient decision-making in parliaments; and it can benefit party leaders in their negotiations with other parties, up to and including negotiations regarding possible coalitions.[10] But if we adopt a listening point of view then we see that, despite these benefits with regard to the efficient working of parliaments, the structuring effect of party discipline militates against dialogic democracy. Given that this is a structural problem, the most effective antidote is likely to be structural too. One area of obvious interest is the electoral system, since it is often claimed that some electoral systems tend to accentuate party discipline more than others. In this context one standard distinction drawn is that between 'candidate-centred' and 'party-centred' electoral systems.[11] In candidate-centred systems, electoral success depends on a close relationship between the candidate and her or his constituents, while in a party-centred system the candidate's political personality is determined more through party identity than through the characteristics of the individual candidate. The former seem more likely to encourage apophatic listening than the latter, not only between constituents and their representatives, but between the representatives themselves, and this is a function of the relative lack of party discipline in such systems.

But, of course, even if we argue that candidate-centred systems are a necessary condition for dialogue understood as structured disagreement underpinned by apophatic listening, they are by no means a sufficient condition. This is because even if politicians are not driven by party discipline, they are likely to be driven by ideology. Ideologies can be regarded as the unexamined frames through which most of us view the political world—essential aids to help us make sense of it and to help guide our actions, but inimical to a dialogic approach to democracy because of their necessarily cataphatic effect. The way in which political ideas, systems—and power itself—work, then, militates powerfully against institutionalizing listening in the 'intra-political' context.

[10] I am very grateful to my Keele colleague, Professor Richard Luther, for these points (personal communication, 12 April 2013).

[11] Royce Carroll and Monika Nalepa, 'Resources, enforcement and party discipline under candidate-centered PR', Academia.edu, 2012, available at <http://www.academia.edu/1829667/Resources_Enforcement_and_Party_Discipline_under_Candidate-Centered_PR> (accessed 24 March 2013).

Is there anything that can be done to turn this tide against effective political listening? In the first place, the structure of the encounters themselves needs to be examined. There is a huge array of attempts to organize multi-person debates in such a way as to maximize the possibilities for effective 'listening to' and 'listening out for'. The Occupy movement is just one recent example of this. The movement arose as a reaction to the economic crash of 2008, and while it struggled to articulate a coherent alternative to contemporary capitalist business as usual, it was marked by attempts to develop techniques of face-to-face participatory democracy on a large scale. Arguments as to the success of these techniques are polarized. On one side we find Craig Calhoun suggesting that inventions such as the 'human megaphone' enabled unusual levels of inclusion in noisy environments,[12] Douglas Rushkoff arguing that the complex rules for Occupy debates ensured that everyone had a chance to speak and everyone was heard,[13] and Manissa McCleave Maharawal suggesting that the 'progressive stack'—('the practice of prioritizing people on th[e speaking] list whose voices have been "traditionally marginalized"')—was a good way of promoting inclusion.[14] On the other side we see Todd Gitlin arguing that 'process-fetishism' is itself exclusionary,[15] Darcy Leach suggesting that the complexity that Rushkoff views as essential for effective inclusion actually works to exclude those 'not in the know',[16] and William Gamson and Micah Sifry intimating that the Occupy decision-making process

[12] Craig Calhoun, 'Occupy Wall Street in perspective', *British Journal of Sociology* 64 (2013), no. 1, p. 30.

[13] Douglas Rushkoff, 'Permanent revolution: occupying democracy', *The Sociological Quarterly* 54 (2013), p. 170.

[14] Manissa McCleave Maharawal, 'Occupy Wall Street and a radical politics of inclusion', *The Sociological Quarterly* 54 (2013), p. 179.

[15] Todd Gitlin, 'Postoccupied', *The Sociological Quarterly* 54 (2013), p. 228.

[16] 'Included in this system are at least three different kinds of meetings (GAs, SCs, and Working Groups) at which different kinds of business are conducted; several different kinds of participating groups, with different purposes and responsibilities (Working Groups, Operations Groups, Movement Groups, and Caucuses); four formal phases to the meeting (agenda items/proposals, working group report-backs, announcements, and soap box); eight hand signals; five facilitation roles (facilitator, stack-taker, stack-greeter, timekeeper, and minute-keeper); at least two ways of keeping the stack ("progressive stack", and "step-up, step-back"); as well as rules about how to make proposals (through a Working Group), how the consensus process works, and how many people it takes to make/block a decision'; Darcy K. Leach, 'Culture and the structure of tyrannylessness', *Sociological Quarterly* 54 (2013), p. 185.

might 'discourage participation by working-class people, minorities, and women'.[17]

Even if there were definitive lessons to draw from the Occupy experience, they would not be directly translatable to the peer-to-peer politician context we are discussing here, since they are designed for less structured and more inchoate occasions. Yet, at the very least, they amount to experiments in apophatic inclusionary listening from which we can learn. The rules of discursive engagement were intended to be dialogic, understood in the way I have described 'dialogue' here: 'To participate in any of the assemblies taking place throughout the United States and in many places around the globe means to stand or sit in a circle, with a handful of facilitators, and speak and listen in turn.'[18] Underpinning this was a recognition of the importance of listening; 'If one were to ask a participant about this process, which I have done countless times, they would most likely explain the need to listen to one another,'[19] reports Marina Sitrin. The testimonies we looked at in the previous paragraph, though, suggest that the techniques adopted and developed by the Occupy movement were aimed more at getting people to speak than encouraging them to listen—the overall intention is more declamatory than dialogic.

It is just possible that, by the time this book is being read, the UK will have a new prime minister. If so it is likely to be Ed Miliband, currently leader of the Labour Party. He is possibly the only politician who has had the experience of being a keynote listener—as opposed to a keynote speaker.[20] The role involved Miliband going table to table to hear what people were discussing, learning about the movement and what people wanted him to do in government to help.[21] Keynote listening is a transgressive act in a culture that prizes speaking—and,

---

[17] William Gamson and Micah Sifry, 'The Occupy movement: an introduction', *Sociological Quarterly* 54 (2013), p. 161.
[18] Marina Sitrin, 'Horizontalidad and territory in the Occupy movements', *Tikkun*, 8 March 2012, p. 32, available at <http://www.tikkun.org/nextgen/horizontalidad-and-territory-in-the-occupy-movements> (accessed 22 January 2013).
[19] Sitrin (2012), p. 32.
[20] Rob Hopkins, 'Ingredients of transition: engaging the movement', available at http://transitionnetwork.org/blogs/rob-hopkins/2010-11-29/ingredients-transition-engaging-council (29 November 2010) (accessed 8 April 2013).
[21] Hopkins (2010).

as we have learnt in this book, *political* culture is a speaking culture. The role of keynote speakers is well understood:

> Keynote *speakers* are invited to deliver a particularly important message, to inform and inspire a large audience, to focus a comforting sense of being a crowd, and to reinforce collective identity counter to the centrifugal forces of parallel streams, special interest groups and city tours. They are generally famous, and talk about achievements that have made them thus; and they generally have a polished presentation and a reassuring confidence. Intriguingly, apparently the keynote speakers have a significant impact on registrations—potential participants are persuaded to 'buy' if the headline acts are impressive. The audience at Keynote Speeches may take ideas and insights away for later use, but at the time they are supposed to be relatively passive.[22]

Keynote listeners, on the other hand, 'pick up the key notes arising from the conference, and...work them into on-going political and collective agendas'.[23] The International Leadership Association (ILA) conference from which these reflections are taken took place just before the Rio+20 UN Conference on Sustainable Development in October 2012, and the role of keynote listeners was thus 'to listen and respond to ideas arising from the gathering of leadership experts and scholars, to relate these to the emerging foci for the Rio+20 summit, and perhaps work these ideas into the "zero draft" documents'.[24] Keynote listeners have a much more understated role than their speaker counterparts (to such an extent that one ILA keynote listener turned down the invitation at the last moment—perhaps when she realized she was going to listen rather than speak[25]), but their role is vital in 'engaging people as listeners rather than speakers, and exemplifying an assumption that relevant knowledge is inherently diverse and found throughout a multiplicity of people'.[26] Is it too much to imagine parliamentary debates involving structured silences, systematic listening, and, in the UK parliament context anyway, a change of name for the House of Commons facilitator from 'Speaker' to 'Listener' to signal a reshaping of intent?

---

[22] Jonathan Gosling, Jackie Bagnall, Richard Bolden, and Anne Murphy, 'Keynote listening: turning the tables on the sage on the stage', *Business Leadership Review* 9 (2012), no. 1, p. 3.

[23] Gosling et al. (2012), p. 3.   [24] Gosling et al. (2012), p. 3.

[25] Gosling et al. (2012), p. 7.   [26] Gosling et al. (2012), p. 8.

GOVERNMENT LISTENING TO THE PEOPLE

On the face of it, little of what we have learned about good listening is applicable to the challenge of how the government might listen better to the people. This is because most of the good practice Sarah Shipley refers to, as we saw above, applies to the face-to-face context. We have had cause to refer often to the challenge of scaling-up good listening practices beyond face-to-faceness, and this has, of course, been a long-standing issue for democratic theory and practice in general. What used to be known as 'participatory democracy' struggled with the criticism that it was not feasible in large, complex societies where relations between people and politicians are remote rather than close at hand. Attempts to meet this criticism have taken a number of forms over the years, and recently there has been considerable interest in the potential for the new social media to narrow the gap between politicians and people.

The idea is that these media give instant voice to people who have not had a voice before, and allow them to offer opinions which are easily inserted into—and potentially taken up in—the public sphere. Stephen Coleman is surely right to say that, 'blogs lower the threshold of entry to the global debate for traditionally unheard or marginalised voices, particularly from poorer parts of the world which are too often represented by others, without being given a chance to present their own accounts.'[27] It is also true that people's blogs offer politicians a window on what their constituents are thinking,[28] and Coleman suggests that there is evidence that some blogs 'have attracted several top officials and politicians as their regular readers.'[29] So the new social media seem to constitute a novel vehicle for dialogue.

But while this is a seductive thought, if we adopt a listening perspective it may seem less attractive than at first sight. Coleman himself claims that, 'blogs are fast becoming sophisticated *listening* posts of modern democracy',[30] but then he rather undermines the claim by saying that, 'To blog is to declare your presence; to disclose to the world that you exist and what it's like to be you; to affirm that your

---

[27] Stephen Coleman, 'Blogs and the new politics of listening', *The Political Quarterly* 67 (2005), no. 2, p. 277. Though we should perhaps temper this with the knowledge that it is precisely poorer communities that lack access to the Internet.
[28] Coleman (2005), p. 275–6.   [29] Coleman (2005), p. 278.
[30] Coleman (2005), p. 274 (emphasis added).

thoughts are at least as worth hearing as anyone else's; to emerge from the spectating audience as a player and maker of meanings.'[31] This looks more like a characterization of blogs as stages from which to declaim, rather than posts at which to listen. So while it is true that we hear more voices then we did in the past and that we have easier access to them, the other side of the coin is that we spend so much time talking on social media that we do very little listening. It is hard to say for sure what effect this is having on our capacity for listening, but Gemma Fiumara, for one, thinks that, 'a culture that is almost saturated with the din of innumerable messages... [leads to]... the inhibition of our listening potential,'[32] and that, 'A knowledge, and therefore a culture, sustained by the indifference of a non-listening rationality is being massively produced.'[33] So while these new social media might be an answer to the question of how to get more voices into the public sphere, the price we pay could be an increasing incapacity to listen to what is being said. New technologies have 'broadened communication... [but]... they have also weakened the intimacy and directness of communication,'[34] and so it is an open question whether, 'blogs, wikis, social networks such as Facebook, Twitter, and MySpace... Flikr and Skype... will alleviate or accentuate barriers to transactional listening and community formation and depth'.[35] This situation has been more generally characterized as a debate that 'speaks without hearing,'[36] in which 'communicative abundance' has led to conditions where political debate is impoverished rather than enriched.

In this light we should perhaps be wary of claims that Twitter, for example, can repair relations of trust between politicians and the people.[37] Mark Margaretten and Ivor Gaber base this claim on the way

---

[31] Coleman (2005), p. 274.

[32] Gemma Corradi Fiumara, *The Other Side of Language: A Philosophy of Listening* (London and New York: Routledge, 1990), p. 82.

[33] Fiumara (1990), p. 112.

[34] Leonard Waks, 'John Dewey on listening and friendship in school and society', *Educational Theory* 61 (2011), no. 2, p. 201.

[35] Waks (2011), p. 204.

[36] Gavan Titley, 'Exclusion through openness? A tentative anatomy of the ritual of "migration debates"', *COLLeGIUM: Studies across Disciplines in the Humanities and Social Sciences* 11 (2012), p. 50, available at <http://hdl.handle.net/10138/32361> (accessed 5 April 2012).

[37] Mark Margaretten and Ivor Gaber, 'The crisis in public communication and the pursuit of authenticity: an analysis of the Twitter feeds of Scottish MPs 2008–2010', *Parliamentary Affairs* (2012), available at <http://pa.oxfordjournals.org/content/early/2012/08/07/pa.gss043.full.pdf+html> (accessed 12 March 2013).

that Twitter can be a conduit for 'authentic talk',[38] and while it might be true that Twitter gives politicians the opportunity to seem human and less remote, we have learnt (especially in Chapter 4) that trust is a function of dialogue rather than talk—however authentic the talk may be. Margaretten and Gaber do, however, recognize that not all politicians who use Twitter do so in the way they recognize as positive—tweets can also read like 'short press releases',[39] they say. It is also somewhat unfortunate that the Twitter hero of the article is MP Eric Joyce.[40] Besides wondering whether tweeting about a men's concealer pen and a High Heel Museum is quite the 'authenticity' we have in mind when building up political trust relationships,[41] we should also remember that self-promotion is a key aspect of his political persona. Twitter may well be a potential instrument for 'informal and two-way communication with constituents',[42] but it is also clearly a powerful tool for monological declamation.

The danger is that the sending of social media messages becomes an end in itself rather than part of a process of understanding. As Gavan Titley puts it: 'the intensive, incessant circulation of opinion, comment and information elides the conditions for political debate...by splintering political energy into continuous, compressed sequences of (minor) issues and events'.[43] What validates a message under these conditions is not the truth of its content, much less the degree to which it contributes to a meaningful dialogue, but its *circulation*. As Jodi Dean puts it, 'A contribution need not be understood; it need only be repeated, reproduced, forwarded' (or simply 'liked'?).[44] In this circumstance, the more that enunciation and circulation become the measure of success, the less listening and understanding are of importance. To the degree that the new social media contribute to this dynamic, they are less a contribution to democracy than a problem for it.

The debate over the role the Internet can play in (re)invigorating democracy will continue to rage. Its advocates will stress its

---

[38] Margaretten and Gaber (2012), p. 2.

[39] Margaretten and Gaber (2012), p. 18.

[40] This is the Falkirk MP who has once admitted to assault, and twice been arrested on suspicion of assault in the House of Commons bars.

[41] Margaretten and Gaber (2012), p. 18.

[42] Margaretten and Gaber (2012), p. 19.

[43] Titley (2012), p. 53.

[44] Jodi Dean, *Democracy and Other Neoliberal Fantasies: Communicative Capitalism and Left Politics* (Durham, NC, and London: Duke University Press, 2009), p. 27, quoted in Titley (2012), p. 53.

communicative potential, while its critics will point to the so-called 'digital divide', to the possibility of information overload, and to issues around agenda-setting. If there is a growing sense that 'there is not much room for excessive cyber-enthusiasm',[45] then our cautionary tale regarding listening might well add to it. On the one hand, British artist Gillian Wearing says that, 'media has changed us all... It has all created a bigger democracy, I would say. More people have a voice',[46] and, on the other, Eli Noam asks, 'if everybody speaks, who will be listened to?'[47]

So I believe we need to look elsewhere for models of good 'government–to-the-people' listening. Towards the beginning of the chapter I referred to three issues that need to be borne in mind as we consider this case. First, the relationship between listening and power; second, the question of whether listening can be learnt; and third, how to judge good listening. All three of these are pertinent here. We are looking for a mode of relationship between government and people that acts as a solvent of power; we are looking for signs of governments learning how to listen better, according to relevant criteria; and we will be basing these criteria on a procedural and apophatic understanding of good listening.[48]

Ortwin Renn, Thomas Webler, and Peter Wiedemann distinguish between three types of citizen participation involving deliberation, consultation, and referenda.[49] Nick F. Pidgeon, Wouter Poortinga,

---

[45] Maria Laura Sudilich, 'Can the Internet reinvent democracy?' *Irish Political Studies* 26 (2011), no. 4, p. 575.

[46] Gillian Wearing, 'I've always been a bit of a listener', *The Observer (The New Review)*, 4 March 2012, p. 9.

[47] Eli Noam, 'Why the Internet is bad for democracy', *Communications of the ACM* 48 (2005), no. 10, p. 58. And there may be a vicious circle at work here, since '... as the Internet leads to more information clutter, it will become necessary for any message to get louder. Much of the political information, therefore, will become distorted, shrill, simplistic'; Noam (2005) p. 60.

[48] All of these are conspicuously not present in set-piece party conferences. 'The conference [Conservative Party conference of 2010], for me, is not a place where we go to be listened to,' said one delegate, Nadia Cenci. 'What would make me go again is if I had someone's ear, rather than them having mine.' Quoted in John Harris, 'Party faithful soak up gripes about bins—but is anyone at the top listening?' *The Guardian*, 7 July 2012, p. 13.

[49] Ortwin Renn, Thomas Webler, and Peter Wiedemann (eds), *Fairness and Competence in Citizen Participation: Evaluating Models for Environmental Discourse* (Dordrecht: Kluwer Publishers, 1995). See also Michel Callon, Pierre Lascoumes, and Yannick Barthe, *Acting in an Uncertain World: An Essay on Technical Democracy* (Cambridge, MA, and London: The MIT Press, 2009).

Gene Rowe, Tom Horlick-Jones, John Walls, and Tim O'Riordan sum up the differences between these forms of citizen participation as follows: '*deliberative methods*...allow for fair and competent debate and discussion between all parties, such as consensus conferences, citizen juries, and planning cells; traditional *consultation methods*, including public meetings, surveys, focus groups, and mediation, where there is little or no extended debate; and finally, *referenda* in which people do have democratic power, but that are not generally deliberative in nature.'[50] From the listening point of view, the second and third of these options fall some way short of what we are looking for. Referenda fall seriously foul of our requirement that good listening be regarded in a procedural way, since practically the entire focus is on the outcome (the decision) rather than on the process. The lack of deliberation in referenda both compounds and reflects this problem. As Pidgeon and his colleagues point out, consultations are not typically deliberative in nature either. The standard tools of consultation—surveys, for example—are directed at citizens who make their views known in isolation from one another, and without any expectation that the government is aiming to promote a dialogue either between citizens, or with the government itself. While some forms of consultation might provide spaces within which deliberation could take place—focus groups, for example—this is not at all their principal objective. Likewise, the messages that go out from focus groups are listened to by government monologically at best—there is no expectation that they are there to initiate an ongoing dialogue over an extended period of time.

In principle, the first of the forms of citizen participation outlined—deliberative methods—looks to be the most likely candidate of the three as far as institutionalizing listening is concerned. But, even here, whatever listening is taking place (and we saw in Chapters 3 and 4 that relatively little attention is paid to the dialogic mechanics of deliberative encounters) is confined to the participants. No doubt the 'results' of the consensus conferences, the citizens' juries, and so on will be passed upwards, yet we could regard this process as just a beefed-up form of consultation without any dialogic component. But there is promise here, both in the sense that there is a focus on procedure,

---

[50] Nick F. Pidgeon, Wouter Poortinga, Gene Rowe, Tom-Horlick Jones, John Walls, and Tim O'Riordan, 'Using surveys in public participation processes for risk decision making: the case of the 2003 British GM nation? Public debate', *Risk Analysis* 25 (2005), no. 2, p. 468 (emphasis in the original).

and that there is the potential for *surprise*—any properly deliberative procedure is unpredictable in terms of outcomes. Thus, any government which sponsors a deliberative form of participation is, in effect, exposing itself to the possibility of a decision it might not favour. This amounts to a ceding of power, which is of a piece with our sense that being listened to can amount to an experience of power as well as a turning of its tables. But there is room for improvement, and I propose to spend a little time analysing one high-profile example of this form of citizen participation, which took place in the UK in the summer of 2003—the so-called GMNation?[51] debate—with a view to sketching the form of an ideal type listening relationship between the government and the people.

The background to GMNation? is comprehensively described in Gene Rowe, Tom Horlick-Jones, John Walls, and Nick Pidgeon's article on the debate.[52] During the late 1990s, in Europe in general and the UK in particular, the debate around GM crops was heavily polarized, and farm-scale experiments were the subject of direct action attempts—often successful—to destroy the crops. This was also a period in which policy makers were trying to come to terms with the fallout from the so-called 'mad cow' crisis, and levels of confidence in the capacity of politicians and the science community to make sound decisions were low. Interestingly for us, given what we have said elsewhere in this book about trust and legitimacy and the way in which governments tend to play the 'listening card' when decisions and the processes that lead to them are questioned, the House of Lords Science and Technology Committee recognized a 'crisis of trust' in UK science policy-making.[53] Their recommendation was to introduce 'greater openness and transparency' into the policy process, and the GMNation? debate was a direct result of a subsequent recommendation to government by the newly formed Agriculture and Environment Biotechnology Commission (AEBC).[54] Significantly, again, the AEBC said it was important that GM policy 'expose, respect and embrace the differences of view which exist, rather than bury

---

[51] GMNation? is always written with a question mark.

[52] Gene Rowe, Tom Horlick-Jones, John Walls, and Nick Pidgeon, 'Difficulties in evaluating public engagement initiatives: reflections on an evaluation of the UK GMNation? Public debate about transgenic crops', *Public Understanding of Science* 14 (2005), no. 4, pp. 331–52.

[53] Rowe et al. (2005), p. 333.   [54] Rowe et al. (2005), p. 333.

them.[55] This should remind us of the distinction drawn elsewhere in this book between listening *to* and listening *out for*—this is a clear case of the latter. The upshot of all this was a letter from the then Secretary of State for Environment, Food and Rural Affairs, Margaret Beckett, to the AEBC, confirming that there would be a public debate on the commercialization of GM crops. The government, she said significantly, was committed to a 'genuine, balanced discussion, and also to *listening to what people say*'.[56] The process would involve two strands, looking at the economics and the science of the commercialization of three types of GM crop, in addition to the public debate, with the overall intention being to 'create *a dialogue* between all strands of opinion on GM issues'.[57]

So, unbidden, three of the key themes in this book—listening, trust, and dialogue—turn up in the discussions leading to the UK GMNation? debate of the summer of 2003. This is circumstantial evidence enough to suggest that it is worthwhile taking a more detailed look at the process itself to see how far it meets our requirements for a robust procedure through which the government might be said to be listening to the people.

Rowe, Horlick-Jones, Walls, and Pidgeon offer a comprehensive description of the process.[58] It began with nine 'Foundation Discussion Workshops', eight of which comprised 16–20 members of the lay public with no previous interest in GM issues, while the ninth was made up of people who were already engaged with transgenic crop controversies. These workshops were absolutely key, and might be regarded as a remarkable innovation. For their aim was *to use their outcomes to frame the subsequent discussion of GM crops*. As Rowe and his colleagues put it, this would '*make it possible to design the debate process in such a way that lay perspectives could shape the terms of the engagement*'.[59] This is a dramatic departure from the 'information deficit' model of policy-making, according to which any disagreement between policy makers and the public is put down to the latter's lack of

---

[55] Quoted in Rowe et al. (2005), p. 334.

[56] Quoted in Rowe et al. (2005), p. 334 (emphasis added).

[57] Quoted in Rowe et al. (2005), p. 334 (emphasis added). For a very different approach to the GM question see Richard Hindmarsh and Anne Parkinson, 'The public enquiry as a contested political technology: GM crop moratorium reviews in Australia', *Environmental Politics* 22 (2013), pp. 293–311.

[58] Rowe et al. (2005), pp. 334–5.

[59] Rowe et al. (2005), p. 335 (emphasis added).

understanding of the facts. Bear in mind, again, the distinction between 'cataphatic' and 'apophatic' listening. In the policy-making context, the cataphatic equivalent is where experts decide the terms of debate and interpret each and every contribution to it in those terms. This was the pre-GMNation? situation to which the House of Lords Science and Technology Committee was responding, and which eventually led to the AEBC's recommendation to government to hold a national debate. On the face of it, the Foundation Discussion Workshops and the role they played in the whole process look like a determined attempt to put apophatic principles into effect in the policy-making context. One criterion offered by Michel Callon, Pierre Lascoumes, and Yannick Barthe for judging the degree to which a dialogic process is in place is 'how *early* laypersons are involved in research',[60] and another is the extent to which this involvement is carried through the process.[61] On the first count the GMNation? debate scores rather well, but perhaps less well on the second. As far as the first criterion is concerned it is hard to overestimate the difference between shaping the terms of debate on the one hand, and operating within the constraints determined by someone else, on the other. Andrea Cornwall and Mamoru Fujita capture this perfectly with their striking notion of 'ventriloquising the poor'.[62] They develop this idea in connection with their analysis of the World Bank's 'Consultations with the Poor' exercise, carried out at the end of the last millennium. The idea was to capture the views of actual poor people around the world, and, to this end, work was done with 20,000 people from 23 countries.[63] Cornwall and Fujita's conclusion speaks for itself:

> The voices of the poor are presented...as if they arose unmediated from open-ended, participatory research. Closer inspection of the Methodology Guide, however, scotches any notion that this was an inductive, iterative process of listening and learning. Rather, the guide is peppered with pre-framed categories and circumscribed questions...[There are] 'tips' on how to start the discussion, how to use the prescribed tools, the format to be adopted, and sometimes precise questions to seek an answer to during focus group discussions.[64]

---

[60] Callon, Lascoumes, and Barthe (2009), p. 158 (emphasis in the original).

[61] Callon, Lascoumes, and Barthe (2009), p. 160.

[62] Andrea Cornwall and Mamoru Fujita, 'Ventriloquising "the poor"? Of voices, choices and the politics of "participatory" knowledge production', *Third World Quarterly* 33 (2012), no. 9, pp. 1751–65.

[63] Cornwall and Fujita (2012), p. 1752.

[64] Cornwall and Fujita (2012), pp. 1754–5.

These 'pre-framed categories' are a symbol and an instance of cataphatic listening, and they can only result in ventriloquism rather than authentic witness. The result in this particular case, according to Cornwall and Fujita, is as follows:

> The voices [of the poor] are editorialised so as to tune out any discordant sounds and present an overarching narrative that is in perfect harmony with the World Bank's own policies…In the discussions…we hear one side of the story: that the state is failing to provide decently and equitably to people who are poor. What we do not hear is the voices who express their desire for a state that would see them as citizens, a state that would be their safety net, that would nurture and support them.[65]

So, if government is bold enough to take the risk of allowing the public to write the rules for debate, it can truly claim to be listening at possibly the most crucial moment of the policy-making process. This strategy of 'early involvement' may be one way of dealing with the problem of listening at the big-N scale. As Jim Macnamara points out, 'When thousands or millions of citizens speak publicly, listening needs to overcome cacophony and deal with competition for attention and diversity.'[66] More prosaically, while New Labour's master-strategist, Philip Gould, might have argued that, 'it wasn't enough for politicians to lecture from on high; they had to listen to what people wanted and then see how they could deliver it',[67] all this did was create a headache for his boss, ex-Prime Minister Tony Blair, who said that was a fine idea, but that 'unfortunately the people were all saying different things'.[68] Part of the answer to his conundrum lies in doing the hard listening at the beginning when the terms of reference are being developed, since that way there is less likelihood of hard-to-accommodate discord further down the line.

Once the work of the GMNation? Foundation Discussion Workshops was complete, three mechanisms for public participation were put in place in the summer of 2003. First, there was a series of open public meetings arranged in three 'tiers'. The first tier was at national level, widely advertised and professionally facilitated. The

---

[65] Cornwall and Fujita (2012), p. 1761.

[66] Jim Macnamara, 'Beyond voice: audience-making and the work and architecture of listening as new media literacies', *Continuum: Journal of Media and Cultural Studies* 27 (2013), no. 1, p, 171.

[67] Simon Hattenstone, 'If you accept death, fear disappears', *The Guardian (G2)*, 21 September 2011, p. 7.

[68] Tony Blair, 'This much I know', *The Observer Magazine*, 12 June 2011, p. 6.

second-tier meetings took place at local level, and were hosted by local authorities or major organizations, and the third tier—'highly variable in terms of their character and formality'[69]—were organized by local voluntary organizations. Then there was an interactive website, and finally a series of ten closed discussion groups (which met twice each) conceived as 'narrow-but-deep' events, involving 77 members of the general public. Significantly, Rowe, Horlick-Jones, Walls, and Pidgeon report that, 'the Foundation Discussion Workshops and Tier 1 events were enjoyable for participants, and generally perceived to be fairly and competently run by the organizers.[70] I surmise that the reason why these events were especially enjoyable is that participants knew they were being listened to. This is obviously true of the Foundation Discussion Workshops for the reasons I discussed above, and the very fact that the tier 1 debates were carefully organized and widely pro-moted by the GMNation? sponsors would have been internalized by participants as evidence that what was said in them would be taken seriously. Evidence from elsewhere in this book suggests that power consists (in part) in being listened to, and that is what happened in the discussion workshops and the tier 1 debates. While I have seen no evidence to suggest that tiers 2 and 3 were unproductive, the fact that they weren't picked out as being as enjoyable as the workshops and tier 1 debates is perhaps due to their being self-organized events in which people were, effectively, just talking amongst themselves. While this might have value in itself, it is much less productive as a source of 'power through being listened to'—precisely because participants could not be confident that anyone in a position of power actually *was* listening.

What can we learn about good government-to-the-people listen-ing from this brief discussion of the GMNation? debate? Earlier in this section I said that there were three issues to bear in mind: a mode of relationship between government and people that acts as a solvent of power, signs of governments learning how to listen better, and a particular understanding of good listening. With regard to the first of these, the crucial ingredients are that the government adopt, as far as possible, an apophatic approach to listening, and that it be seen to be doing so. The GMNation? Foundation Discussion Workshops are a good example of how this might work in practice in that the workshops set the terms of the subsequent debate. This amounts to suspending

---

[69] Rowe et al. (2005), p. 335.   [70] Rowe et al. (2005), p. 338.

pre-conceived categories in favour of the apophatic strategy of allowing them to emerge. This is very different to merely responding to, and
working within, parameters set by someone else. Moreover, the government is seen to be listening in this arrangement precisely because
the workshops are setting the terms of debate—without the workshops
there would be no terms and therefore no debate. These workshops
are, therefore, a good example of apophatic listening, transferred to
the realm of scaled-up policy-making.

The third issue (I will come back to the second) is whether we find a
procedural understanding of good listening in the GMNation? debate.
This raises the question of the criteria against which the debate's sponsors judged the event's success. Rowe, Horlick-Jones, Walls, and
Pidgeon comment that, 'The sponsor perspective on what would make
the exercise a "success" was not initially very clear, beyond the general
aim of somehow involving the public in debate on the GM issue.'[71]
When pressed, though, the Steering Board produced a list that is strik-
ingly procedure-orientated: 'to allow the public to frame the issues',
'to focus on getting people at the grass roots level whose voice has not
yet been heard to participate in the programme', 'to create new and
effective opportunities for the deliberative debate about the issues.'[72]
Interestingly, these apophatic and inclusionary intentions became less
marked the more the Steering Group was pressed by Rowe and his
colleagues to produce indicators for success. Then they seemed to fall
back on more standard 'consultation' type criteria, such as the extent
of public awareness of the programme, and a more or less explicit
resiling from the apophatic criterion in favour of 'the extent to which
"informed commentators" felt the exercise had been credible.'[73] Rowe
and his colleagues themselves drew up a list of nine criteria for success,[74] none of which captures the potentially radical apophatic and
inclusionary intentions of the Steering Group's first attempt at developing criteria for judgement. Given that these nine criteria are 'dis-
tilled from a review of the relevant literature',[75] there seems to be a case
for revisiting that literature and subjecting it to the kind of critique
suggested by this enquiry into listening. At the heart of this critique
will lie the demand that criteria be procedural, and that processes
must be apophatic and inclusionary. These processes correspond in

[71] Rowe et al. (2005), p. 336.   [72] Quoted in Rowe et al. (2005), p. 336.
[73] Rowe et al. (2005), p. 336.   [74] Rowe et al. (2005), p. 337.
[75] Rowe et al. (2005), p. 337.

a radical way to the twin aims of listening to and listening out for, respectively. In sum, they are likely to lead to an abandonment of the traditional 'clear-cut choice' model of decision-making,[76] in favour of an 'iterative model that may be described as a series of rendezvous'.[77]

The second issue relates to learning to listen, and here the evidence of the GMNation? debate is less promising. Just as we would hope that individual politicians could learn to listen better, so our expectation should be that governments will understand the difference between deliberation, consultation, and referenda and, if they are serious about listening beyond the occasional act of 'listening exercise' legitimation, will analyse the effectiveness of participation events such as GMNation? against relevant criteria, and seek improvements. Significantly, though, the GMNation? debate fund 'was insufficient to allow the Steering Board to find its own systematic evaluation'.[78] Given that evaluation is a *sine qua non* for learning, arrangements for learning from this particular national debate fell at the very first hurdle. With hindsight it is probably accurate to say, indeed, that GMNation?, with all its faults, was the high-water mark of attempts by the UK government to 'listen to the people'. With the notable exception of the Committee on Radioactive Waste Management (CoRWM),[79] which developed recommendations for government on the safe disposal of higher activity radioactive waste between 2003 and 2006, based on rigorously inclusive principles, nothing like GMNation? has been seen since.

At the time of writing, the latest controversial technology to hit the headlines is hydraulic fracturing ('fracking'), designed to release natural gas through fracturing shale rock. There is little doubt that this is an issue of public interest that is likely to be with us for some time. Moreover, it is polarizing opinion in exactly the same way that GM crops did (and still does). Yet there is no sign that the UK government will set up a process for listening to, and out for, public opinion(s). To date there has been one brief science-based enquiry into the seismic implications of fracking, as a result of a number of earthquakes in the north-west of England in April and May 2011. Studies confirm that these earthquakes were caused by operations carried out by Cuadrilla Resources,

---

[76] Callon, Lascoumes, and Barthes (2009), p. 223.
[77] Callon, Lascoumes, and Barthes (2009), p. 223.
[78] Rowe et al. (2005), p. 336.
[79] See <http://corwm.decc.gov.uk/en/crwm/cms/about_us/our_history/our_history.aspx> (accessed 21 March 2013).

and a report was commissioned by the Department of Energy and Climate Change (DECC) with a view to recommending methods of mitigating the likelihood of seismic activity.[80] The present signs are that the government is going to press ahead with this technology without any dialogue with the public, and in this regard the political class shows no signs of wanting to learn how to listen better, let alone put in place a programme that might help it to do so. The public engagement strategy adopted by the UK government in relation to fracking is diametrically opposed to that followed in the GMNation? debate we analysed in this section. The key moment there was the round of Foundation Discussion Workshops, at which, in principle at least, the very terms of debate were established. I suggested that this amounted to putting apophatic listening into practice in the policy-making context. In the fracking controversy, by contrast, the government is monologically establishing the terms of debate (and very narrowly, too, in that, thus far, only the seismicity issue has been examined). This is policy-making by cataphasis which, as we have learned, is virtually guaranteed to lead to incomprehension and mistrust.

CONCLUSION

In essence, the refusal to listen is an act of what Matthew Flinders calls 'depoliticization'.[81] According to Flinders this takes three forms: institutional, procedural, and ideological. Institutional depoliticization occurs when decision-making is out-sourced to what he calls 'arm's-length' organizations; the procedural form is when new rules have the effect of prescribing or proscribing given outcomes, thus removing political discretion; and ideological depoliticization is the result of framing political choices in such a way as to exclude wholesale alternatives. Each of these has the effect of reducing the number of decisions taken in the public sphere—in other words, reducing the

---

[80] Christopher Green, Peter Styles, and Brian Baptie, 'Preese Hall shale gas fracturing: review and recommendations for induced seismic mitigation', *Induced Seismicity Mitigation Report*, April 2012, available at <https://www.gov.uk/government/uploads/system/uploads/attachment_data/file/48330/5055-preese-hall-shale-gas-frac-turing-review-and-recomm.pdf> (accessed 22 March 2013).

[81] Matthew Flinders, *Defending Politics: Why Democracy Matters in the Twenty-first Century* (Oxford: Oxford University Press, 2012), pp. 102–5.

amount of *politics*. In this context, listening is an act of re-politicization, and the demand to be listened to is a political demand. Listening in any walk of life is a gesture of vulnerability and of a willingness to take risks, and the outcome is uncertain. Good political listening thus undermines the conditions for each of Flinders' forms of depoliticization, all of which are designed to shield democratically elected politicians from engagement with people. Depoliticization is an act (or a succession of acts) of closure, and everything we have learned about listening in this book suggests that it is the performance of opening out and opening up. As a political demand, listening discredits the outsourcing of decision-making for its determination to narrow down the range of legitimate dialogue—indeed, for undermining the need for dialogue (and hence for listening) at all. Proceduralism that proscribes certain outcomes and guarantees others has the same effect, as does the ideological approach that rules out alternative ways of looking at and acting in the world. Thus, any programme for re-politicizing the body politic—indeed, for re-establishing the body politic as a site of democratic contestation—must have listening, as a normative demand, at its heart.

In *Just Gaming*, Jean-François Lyotard writes that, 'For us, a language is first and foremost someone talking. But there are language games in which the important thing is to listen, in which the rule deals with audition. Such a game is the game of the just. And in this game, one speaks only inasmuch as one listens; that is, one speaks as a listener, and not as an author.'[82] At the beginning of the book I drew a parallel between good manners in daily conversation and the definitional (dialogic) demands of democratic politics. Lyotard suggests that there is more at stake even than this: it is not just quotidian conversation or democratic debate that demand good listening, but politics itself. To think that politics begins and ends with talk is to misunderstand its nature and undermine its potential. The shadow of Aristotle's equating the political being with the speaking being looms large over our theory and our practice. In this book I have tried to re-imagine politics from the point of view of listening—to replace Aristotle with Epictetus, so to speak: 'Nature hath given men one tongue but two ears, that we may hear from others twice as much as we speak.'

---

[82] Jean-François Lyotard, *Just Gaming* (Minneapolis: University of Minnesota Press, 1975), pp. 71–2.

Bibliography

Andersen, Daniel Bryan, 'From Deliberation to Dialogue: the Role of the I–Thou in Democratic Experience' (PhD thesis, University of Oregon, 2012).

Aristotle, The Politics (Harmondsworth: Penguin, 1962).

Baiocchi, Gianpaolo, Einar Braathen, and Ana Claudia Teixeira, 'Transformation institutionalized? Making sense of participatory democracy in the Lulu era', 11 June 2012, available at <http://gianpaolobaiocchi.wordpress.com/2012/04/16/transformation-institutionalized-new-essay-on-the-lula-era/> (accessed 6 December 2012).

Beall, Melissa, Jennifer Gill-Rosier, Jeanine Tate, and Amy Matten, 'State of the context: listening in education', International Journal of Listening 22 (2008), no. 2, pp. 123–32.

Beatty, Joseph, 'Good listening', Educational Theory 49 (1999), no. 3, pp. 281–98.

Benhabib, Seyla, 'Toward a deliberative model of democratic legitimacy', in Benhabib (ed.), Democracy and Difference: Contesting the Boundaries of the Political (Princeton: Princeton University Press, 1996).

Bennett, Jane, Vibrant Matter (Durham, NC, and London: Duke University Press, 2010).

Bentham, Jeremy, The Principles of Morals and Legislation (Darien, CT: Hafner Publishing, 1970).

Berman, Morris, The Reenchantment of the World (Ithaca: Cornell University Press, 1981).

Bickford, Susan, The Dissonance of Democracy: Listening, Conflict, and Citizenship (Ithaca and London: Cornell University Press, 1996).

Bickmore, Kathy and Serihy Kovalchuk, 'Diverse ways of creating classroom communities for constructive discussions of conflict: cases from Canadian secondary schools', in Peter Cunningham and Nathan Fretwell (eds), Creating Communities: Local, National and Global (London: CiCe, 2012).

Bizzari, Kim and Mariano Iossa, 'From hearing to listening: improving the dialogue between DG Trade and civil society', ActionAid, 2007, available at <http://trade.ec.europa.eu/doclib/docs/2007/may/tradoc_134642.pdf> (accessed 6 December 2012).

Black, Laura, 'How people communicate during deliberative events', in Tina Nabatchi, John Gastil, G. Michael Weiksner, and Matt Leighninger (eds), Democracy in Motion: Evaluating the Practice and Impact of Deliberative Civic Engagement (Oxford: Oxford University Press, 2012).

Blair, Tony, 'This much I know', The Observer Magazine, 12 June 2011, p. 6.

Bolitho, Jane J., 'Restorative justice: the ideals and realities of conferencing for young people', *Critical Criminology* 20 (2012), no. 1, pp. 61–78.

Bovenkerk, Bernice, *The Biotechnology Debate: Democracy in the Face of Intractable Disagreement* (Heidelberg, London, and New York: Springer, 2012).

Boyd, William, *Waiting for Sunrise* (London, New Delhi, New York, and Sydney: Bloomsbury Publishing, 2012).

Braithwaite, John, 'Setting standards for restorative justice', *British Journal of Criminology* 42 (2002), no. 3, pp. 563–77.

Brontë, Charlotte, *Villette* (1853), available at <http://www.literature.org/authors/bronte-charlotte/villette/chapter-29.html> (accessed 21 August 2012).

Bruneau, Emile and Rebecca Saxe, 'The power of being heard: the benefits of "perspective-giving" in the context of inter-group conflict', *Journal of Experimental Social Psychology* 48 (2012), no. 4, pp. 855–66.

Buchan, Bruce, 'Listening for noise in political thought', *Cultural Studies Review* 18 (2012), no. 3, pp. 36–66.

Burbules, Nicholas, *Dialogue in Teaching: Theory and Practice* (New York and London: Teachers College, Columbia University, 1993).

Burke, Edmund, 'Speech to the Electors of Bristol', 3 November 1774, available at <http://press-pubs.uchicago.edu/founders/documents/v1ch13s7.html> (accessed 18 August 2012).

Bussie, Jacqueline Aileen, 'Reconciled diversity: reflections on our calling to embrace our religious neighbours', *Intersections* 33 (2011), pp. 30–5.

Calder, Gideon, 'Democracy and listening', in Mary-Ann Crumplin (ed.), *Problems of Democracy: Language and Speaking* (Oxford: Inter-Disciplinary Press, 2011).

Calhoun, Craig, 'Occupy Wall Street in perspective', *British Journal of Sociology* 64 (2013), no. 1, pp. 26–38.

Callister, Deborah Cox, 'Beached whales: tracing the rhetorical force of extraordinary material articulations', in Emily Plec (ed.), *Perspectives on Human–Animal Communication: Internatural Communication* (Abingdon and New York: Routledge, 2013).

Callon, Michel, Pierre Lascoumes, and Yannick Barthe, *Acting in an Uncertain World: An Essay on Technical Democracy* (Cambridge, MA, and London: The MIT Press, 2009).

Caluwaerts, Didier and Min Reuchamps, 'The G1000: facts, figures and some lessons from an experience of deliberative democracy in Belgium', available at <http://www.rethinkingbelgium.eu/rebel-initiative-files/events/seventh-public-event-g1000-european-citizens-initiative-malaise-democracy/G1000-Background-Paper.pdf> (accessed 27 January 2013).

Caron, Bruce, 'Community, Democracy and Performance: The Urban Practice of Kyoto's Higashi-Kujo Madang. Santa Barbara: The New Media

Studio', 2003, available at <http://junana.com/CDP/corpus/index.html> (accessed 24 April 2012).

Carroll, Royce and Monika Nalepa, 'Resources, enforcement and party discipline under candidate-centered PR', 2012, Academia.edu, available at <http://www.academia.edu/1829667/Resources_Enforcement_and_Party_Discipline_under_Candidate-Centered_PR> (accessed 24 March 2013).

Carson, Rachel, *The Sense of Wonder* (New York: HarperCollins, 1998).

Cheon, Jongpil and Michael Grant, 'Active listening: web-based assessment tool for communication and active listening skill development', *TechTrends* 53 (2009), no. 6, pp. 24–32.

Chun, Wendy Hui Kyong, 'Unbearable witness: towards a politics of listening', *Differences: A Journal of Feminist Cultural Studies* 11 (1999), no. 1, pp. 112–49.

Coleman, Stephen, 'Whose conversation? Engaging the public in authentic polylogue', *The Political Quarterly* 75 (2004), no. 2, pp. 112–20.

Coleman, Stephen, 'Blogs and the new politics of listening', *The Political Quarterly* 67 (2005), no. 2, pp. 272–80.

Conrad, Joseph, *Under Western Eyes* (Oxford: Oxford University Press, 2008).

Cornwall, Andrew and Mamoru Fujita, 'Ventriloquising "the poor"? Of voices, choices and the politics of "participatory" knowledge production', *Third World Quarterly* 33 (2012), no. 9, pp. 1751–65.

Couldry, Nick, *Listening Beyond the Echoes* (Colorado: Paradigm Publishers, 2006).

Crouch, Colin, *Post-Democracy* (Cambridge: Polity Press, 2004).

Cruikshank, Julie, *Do Glaciers Listen? Local Knowledge, Colonial Encounters, and Social Imagination* (Vancouver and Toronto: UBC Press, 2005).

Cusick, Carolyn, '*Speaking, Listening and Communicative Justice: Educating Epistemic Trust and Responsibility*' (PhD thesis, Vanderbilt University, 2012).

Dean, Jodi, *Democracy and Other Neoliberal Fantasies: Communicative Capitalism and Left Politics* (Durham, NC, and London: Duke University Press, 2009).

Dewey, John, *Democracy and Education* (New York: Macmillan, 1916).

Dewey, John, *The Public and its Problems: An Essay in Political Enquiry* (Chicago: Gateway Books, 1946).

Dhawan, Nikita, 'Hegemonic listening and subversive silences: ethical–political imperatives', *Critical Studies* 36 (2012), pp. 47–60.

Dobson, Andrew, Kezia Barker, and Sarah Taylor (eds), *Biosecurity: The Socio-politics of Invasive Species and Infectious Diseases* (London: Earthscan, 2013).

Doorey, David, 'The medium and the "anti-union" message: "forced listening" and captive audience meetings in Canadian labor law', *Comparative Labor Law and Policy Journal* 29 (2007), no. 2, pp. 79–188.

Downing, John, 'Grassroots media: establishing priorities for the years ahead', *Global Media Journal (Australia Edition)* 1 (2007), no. 1, pp. 1–16, available at <http://www.commarts.uws.edu.au/gmjau/iss1_2007/pdf/HC_FINAL_John%20Downing.pdf> (accessed 10 April 2012).

Dreher, Tanja, 'Media, multiculturalism and the politics of listening', in E. Tilley (ed.), *Power and Place: Refereed Proceedings of the Australian and New Zealand Communication Association Conference 2008* (Palmerston North, NZ: Massey University, 2008), pp. 1–14.

Dreher, Tanja, 'Speaking up or being heard? Community media interventions and the politics of listening', *Media, Culture and Society* 32 (2010), no. 1, pp. 85–104.

Drollinger, Tanya, Lucette Comer, and Patricia Warrington, 'Development and validation of the active empathetic listening scale', *Psychology and Marketing* 23 (2006), no. 2, pp. 161–80.

Dryzek, John, *Deliberative Democracy and Beyond* (Oxford: Oxford University Press, 2000).

Dryzek, John, *Deliberative Global Politics: Discourse and Democracy in a Divided World* (Cambridge: Polity Press, 2006).

Dryzek, John, *Foundations and Frontiers of Deliberative Governance* (Oxford: Oxford University Press, 2010).

Duranti, Alessandro (ed.), *Linguistic Anthropology: A Reader* (2nd edn, Malden, MA, Oxford, and Chichester: Wiley-Blackwell, 2009).

Eckersley, Robyn, 'Foreword', in Bernice Bovenkerk, *The Biotechnology Debate: Democracy in the Face of Intractable Disagreement* (Heidelberg, London, and New York: Springer, 2012).

Elster, Jon (ed.), *Deliberative Democracy* (Cambridge: Cambridge University Press, 1998).

Elstub, Stephen, 'The third generation of deliberative democracy', *Political Studies Review* 8 (2010), pp. 291–307.

Ende, Michael, *Momo* (London: Penguin, 1984).

Fishkin, James, *When People Speak: Deliberative Democracy and Public Consultation* (Oxford: Oxford University Press, 2009).

Fiumara, Gemma Corradi, *The Other Side of Language: A Philosophy of Listening* (London and New York: Routledge, 1990).

Flinders, Matthew, *Defending Politics: Why Democracy Matters in the Twenty-first Century* (Oxford: Oxford University Press, 2012).

Forrester, John, *Planning in the Face of Power* (Berkeley, Los Angeles, and London: University of California Press, 1989).

Fraser, Nancy, *Justice Interruptus: Critical Reflections on the 'Postsocialist' Condition* (New York and London: Routledge, 1997).

Fredriksson, Lennart, 'Modes of relating in a caring conversation: a research synthesis on presence, touch and listening', *Journal of Advanced Nursing* 30 (1999), no. 5, pp. 1167–76.

Freire, Paulo, *Pedagogy of the Oppressed* (30th anniversary edn, New York: Continuum Academic Publishing, 2007).

Gambetta, Diego, ' "Claro!": an essay on discursive machismo', in Jon Elster (ed.), *Deliberative Democracy* (Cambridge: Cambridge University Press, 1998).

Gamson, William and Micah Sifry, 'The Occupy movement: an introduction', *The Sociological Quarterly* 54 (2013), pp. 159–63.

Garrison, Jim, 'A Deweyan theory of democratic listening', *Educational Theory* 46 (1996), no. 4, pp. 429–52.

Garrison, Jim, 'Compassionate, spiritual, and creative listening in teaching and learning', *Teachers College Record* 112 (2010), no. 11, pp. 2763–76.

Gastil, John, Katie Knobloch, and Meghan Kelly, 'Evaluating deliberative public events and projects', in Tina Nabatchi, John Gastil, G. Michael Weiksner, and Matt Leighninger (eds), *Democracy in Motion: Evaluating the Practice and Impact of Deliberative Civic Engagement* (Oxford: Oxford University Press, 2012).

Geiser, Urs, 'Reading political contestation in Pakistan's Swat Valley—from deliberation to "the political" and beyond', *Geoforum* 43 (2012), no. 4, pp. 707–15.

Giddens, Antony, *Beyond Left and Right: The Future of Radical Politics* (Cambridge: Polity Press, 1994).

Gitlin, Todd, 'Postoccupied', *The Sociological Quarterly* 54 (2013), pp. 226–28.

Glotfelty, Cheryll and Harold Fromm (eds), *The Ecocriticism Reader: Landmarks in Literary Ecology* (Athens, GA, and London: University of Georgia Press, 1996).

Goodin, Robert, *Innovating Democracy: Democratic Theory and Practice after the Deliberative Turn* (Oxford: Oxford University Press, 2008).

Goodin, Robert, 'How can deliberative democracy get a grip?' *Political Quarterly* 83 (2012), no. 4, pp. 806–11.

Gordon, Mordechai, 'Listening as embracing the other: Martin Buber's philosophy of dialogue', *Educational Theory* 61 (2011), no. 2, pp. 207–19.

Górniak-Kocikowska, Krystyna, 'The factor of listening in Karl Jaspers' philosophy of communication', in Helmut Wautischer, Alan M. Olsen, and Gregory J. Walters (eds), *Philosophical Faith and the Future of Humanity* (Heidelberg, London, and New York: Springer, 2012).

Gosling, Jonathan, Jackie Bagnall, Richard Bolden, and Anne Murphy, 'Keynote listening: turning the tables on the sage on the stage', *Business Leadership Review* 9 (2012), no. 1, pp. 1–9.

Grandin, Temple, *Animals in Translation: Using the Mysteries of Autism to Decode Animal Behaviour* (London: Bloomsbury, 2005).

Gray, Sean, 'Silent citizenship in democratic theory and practice: the problems and power of silence in democracy', unpublished paper delivered at the 2012 American Political Science Association Conference, New Orleans, 2012.

Graybar, Steven and Leah Leonard, 'In defense of listening', *American Journal of Psychotherapy* 59 (2005), no. 1, pp. 1–18.

Great Ape Project, available at <http://www.greatapeproject.org/en-US/oprojetogap/Missao> (accessed 4 October 2012).

Green, Christopher, Peter Styles, and Brian Baptie, 'Preese Hall shale gas fracturing: review and recommendations for induced seismic mitigation', *Induced Seismicity Mitigation Report*, April 2012, available at <https://www.gov.uk/government/uploads/system/uploads/attachment_data/file/48330/5055-preese-hall-shale-gas-fracturing-review-and-recomm.pdf> (accessed 22 March 2013).

Green, Jeffrey Edward, *The Eyes of the People: Democracy in an Age of Spectatorship* (Oxford and New York: Oxford University Press, 2010).

Habermas, Jürgen, *Communication and the Evolution of Society* (Boston: Beacon Press, 1979).

Habermas, Jürgen, *The Theory of Communicative Action Volume 1* (Cambridge: Polity Press, 1991).

Habermas, Jürgen, *Justification and Application: Remarks on Discourse Ethics* (Cambridge: Polity Press, 1993).

Habermas, Jürgen, *Between Facts and Norms: Contributions to a Discourse Theory of Law and Democracy* (Cambridge, MA: The MIT Press, 1996).

Hansen, David, 'Horizons of listening', in *Philosophy of Education 2003* (Urbana, IL: Philosophy of Education Society), pp. 22–5.

Hardin, Russell, 'Deliberation: method, not theory', in Stephen Macedo (ed.), *Deliberative Politics: Essays on Democracy and Disagreement* (New York and Oxford: Oxford University Press, 1999).

Harnden, Toby, 'Republican debate: Rick Perry forgets key part of policy in major gaffe', *The Telegraph*, 10 November 2011, available at <http://www.telegraph.co.uk/news/worldnews/republicans/8880467/Republican-debate-Rick-Perry-forgets-key-part-of-policy-in-major-gaffe.html#> (accessed 25 June 2012).

Haroutunian-Gordon, Sophie and Megan Laverty, 'Listening: an exploration of philosophical traditions', *Educational Theory* 61 (2011), no. 2, pp. 117–24.

Harris, John, 'Party faithful soak up gripes about bins—but is anyone at the top listening?' *The Guardian*, 7 July 2012, pp. 12–13.

Hattenstone, Simon, 'If you accept death, fear disappears', *The Guardian (G2)*, 21 September 2011, p. 7.

Hindmarsh, Richard and Anne Parkinson, 'The public enquiry as a contested political technology: GM crop moratorium reviews in Australia', *Environmental Politics* 22 (2013), pp. 293–311.

Hislop, Ian (ed.), *Private Eye Annual 2008* (London: Private Eye Productions, 2008).

Hobbes, Thomas, *Leviathan* (Oxford: Basil Blackwell, 1946).

Hoggart, Simon, 'The unfamiliar sound of Labour cheers', *The Guardian*, 16 June 2011, p. 4.

Honneth, Axel, 'Redistribution as recognition: a response to Nancy Fraser', in Nancy Fraser and Axel Honneth, *Redistribution or Recognition? A Political–Philosophical Exchange* (London and New York: Verso, 2003).

Hopkins, Rob, 'Ingredients of transition: engaging the movement', available at <http://transitionnetwork.org/blogs/rob-hopkins/2010-11-29/ingredients-transition-engaging-council> (29 November 2010) (accessed 8 April 2013).

Husband, Charles, 'Media and the public sphere in multi-ethnic societies', in S. Cottle (ed.), *Ethnic Minorities and the Media* (Buckingham and Philadelphia: Open University Press, 2000).

Jaramillo, Nathalia, 'Dialogic action for critical democracy', *Journal for Critical Education Policy Studies* 9 (2011), no. 1, pp. 72–95.

Jonas-Simpson, Christine, Gail Mitchell, Anne Fisher, Grazia Jones, and Jan Linscott, 'The experience of being listened to: a qualitative study of older adults in long-term care settings', *Journal of Gerontological Nursing* 32 (2006), no. 1, pp. 46–54.

Jungkunz, Victor, 'The promise of democratic silences', *New Political Science* 34 (2012), no. 2, pp. 127–50.

Kafka, Franz, 'A report for an academy' (1917), available at <http://records.viu.ca/~johnstoi/kafka/reportforacademy.htm> (accessed 12 September 2012).

Kelly, Catriona and Barbara Fraser, 'Listening between the lines: social assumptions around foreign accents', *Australian Review of Applied Linguistics* 35 (2012), no. 1, pp. 74–93, available at <http://www.nla.gov.au/openpublish/index.php/aral/article/viewFile/2359/2827> (accessed 11 April 2012).

Key, V. O., *Public Opinion and American Democracy* (New York: Knopf, 1961).

Kompridis, Nikolas, 'Receptivity, possibility, and democratic politics', *Ethics and Global Politics* 4 (2011), no. 4, pp. 1–16.

Krause, Bernie, *The Great Animal Orchestra* (London: Profile Books, 2012).

Lam, Mei Seung, 'The gentle art of listening: skills for developing family–administrator relationships in early childhood', *Early Childhood Education Journal* 47 (2000), no. 4, pp. 267–74.

Latour, Bruno, *The Politics of Nature: How to Bring the Sciences into Democracy* (Cambridge, MA, and London: Harvard University Press, 2004).

Laverty, Megan, 'Dialogue as philosophical inquiry in the teaching of tolerance and sympathy', *Learning Inquiry* 1 (2007), pp. 125–32.

Laverty, Megan, 'Can you hear me now? Jean-Jacques Rousseau on listening education', *Educational Theory* 61 (2011), no. 2, pp. 155–69.

Leach, Darcy K., 'Culture and the structure of tyrannylessness', *The Sociological Quarterly* 54 (2013), pp. 181–91.

Lees-Marshment, Jennifer, 'Political marketing and opinion leadership: comparative perspectives and findings', in Ludger Helms (ed.), *Comparative Political Leadership* (New York and Basingstoke: Palgrave Macmillan, 2012).

Levin, David Michael, *The Listening Self: Personal Growth, Social Change and the Closure of Metaphysics* (London and New York: Routledge, 1989).

Lyotard, Jean-François, *Just Gaming* (Minneapolis: University of Minnesota Press, 1975).

McCleave Maharawal, Manissa, 'Occupy Wall Street and a radical politics of inclusion', *The Sociological Quarterly* 54 (2013), pp. 177–81.

Macedo, Stephen (ed.), *Deliberative Politics: Essays on Democracy and Disagreement* (New York and Oxford: Oxford University Press, 1999).

Machiavelli, Niccolò, *The Prince* (Harmondsworth: Penguin, 1961).

Macnamara, Jim, 'Beyond voice: audience-making and the work and architecture of listening as new media literacies', *Continuum: Journal of Media and Cultural Studies* 27 (2013), no. 1, pp. 160–75.

Maitland, Sara, *A Book of Silence* (London: Granta, 2008).

Manes, Christopher, 'Nature and silence', in Cheryll Glotfelty and Harold Fromm (eds), *The Ecocriticism Reader: Landmarks in Literary Ecology* (Athens, GA, and London: University of Georgia Press, 1996).

Margaretten, Mark and Ivor Gaber, 'The crisis in public communication and the pursuit of authenticity: an analysis of the Twitter feeds of Scottish MPs 2008–2010', *Parliamentary Affairs* (2012), available at <http://pa.oxfordjournals.org/content/early/2012/08/07/pa.gss043.full.pdf+html> (accessed 12 March 2013).

Marsh, Sue, 'The government said it was listening to us: it was a sham', *The Guardian*, 9 January 2012, p. 22.

Martin, James, 'The rhetorical citizen', *The CSD Bulletin* (London: University of Westminster, 2009).

Michel, Alexandra and Stanton Wortham, 'Listen beyond the self: how organisations create direct involvement', *Learning Inquiry* 1 (2007), pp. 89–97.

Miles, David, 'Love thy enemy', *Huffington Post*, 4 June 2012, available at <http://www.huffingtonpost.com/david-miles/love-thy-enemy_1_b_1568445.html> (accessed 22 August 2012).

Mill, John Stuart, *Utilitarianism, On Liberty, and Considerations on Representative Government* (London: J. M. Dent & Sons Ltd, 1972).

Miller, Joshua, 'Caring to disagree: democratic disagreement as civic care', *Polity* 44 (2012), no. 3, pp. 400–25.

Mineyama, Sachiko, Akizumi Tsutsumi, Soshi Takao, Kyoko Nishiuchi, and Norito Kawakami, 'Supervisors' attitudes and skills for active listening with regard to working conditions and psychological stress reactions among subordinate workers', *Journal of Occupational Health* 49 (2007), pp. 81–7.

Mondada, Lorenza, 'Embodied and spatial resources for turn-making in institutional multi-party interactions: participatory democracy debates', *Journal of Pragmatics* 32 (2012), no. 10, pp. 39–68.

Mouffe, Chantal, 'Deliberative democracy or agonistic pluralism', *Political Science Series* 72 (2000), pp. 1–17, available at <http://www.ihs.ac.at/publications/pol/pw_72.pdf> (accessed 31 January 2013).

Murakami, Haruki, *1Q84 (Book Three)* (London: Vintage, 2012).

Nabatchi, Tina, John Gastil, G. Michael Weiksner, and Matt Leighninger (eds), *Democracy in Motion: Evaluating the Practice and Impact of Deliberative Civic Engagement* (Oxford: Oxford University Press, 2012).

Noam, Eli, 'Why the Internet is bad for democracy', *Communications of the ACM* 48 (2005), no. 10, pp. 57–60.

Noddings, Nel, 'Why should we listen?' in *Philosophy of Education, ed. Kal Aston* (Urbana, IL: Philosophy of Education Society, 2003), pp. 19–21.

Oakeshott, Michael, 'The voice of poetry in the conversation of mankind', in *Rationalism in Politics and Other Essays* (London: Methuen, 1962).

Obama, Barak, 'Obama speech to Arizona Gifford's memorial', War on Terror News, 14 January 2011, available at <http://waronterrornews.typepad.com/home/2011/01/obama-speech-to-arizona-giffords-memorial.html> (accessed 14 June 2011).

Orr, Deborah, 'Listening is fantastically powerful and soothing—we need more of it', *The Guardian*, 31 March 2012, p. 47.

Outhwaite, William (ed.), *The Habermas Reader* (Cambridge: Polity Press, 2000).

Parker, Walter, 'Listening to strangers: classroom discussion in democratic education', *Teachers College Record* 112 (2010), no. 11, pp. 2815–32.

Parkinson, John, *Democracy and Public Space: The Physical Sites of Democratic Performance* (Oxford and New York: Oxford University Press, 2012).

Peake, Bryce, 'Listening, language, and colonialism on Main Street, Gibraltar', *Communication and Critical/Cultural Studies* 9 (2012), no. 2, pp. 171–90.

Pearce, Jenny, 'Power and the activist', *Development* 55 (2012), no. 2, pp. 198–200.

Penman, Robyn and Sue Turnbull, 'From listening…to the dialogic realities of participatory democracy', *Continuum: Journal of Media and Cultural Studies* 26 (2012), no. 1, pp. 61–72.

Peters, John Durham, 'Media as conversation, conversation as media', in James Curran and David Morley (eds), *Media and Cultural Theory* (Abingdon and New York: Routledge, 2006).

Pidgeon, Nick F., Wouter Poortinga, Gene Rowe, Tom-Horlick Jones, John Walls, and Tim O'Riordan, 'Using surveys in public participation processes for risk decision making: the case of the 2003 British GM Nation? public debate', *Risk Analysis* 25 (2005), no. 2, pp. 467–79.

Plec, Emily (ed.), *Perspectives on Human–Animal Communication: Internatural Communication* (Abingdon and New York: Routledge, 2013).

Plotica, Luke Philip, 'Deliberation or conversation: Michael Oakeshott on the ethos and conduct of democracy', *Polity* 44 (2012), no. 2, pp. 286–307.

Plumwood, Val, *Environmental Culture: The Ecological Crisis of Reason* (London: Routledge, 2002).

Putnam, Robert, *Making Democracy Work: Civic Traditions in Modern Italy* (Princeton: Princeton University Press, 1993).

Raelin, Joseph, 'Dialogue and deliberation as expressions of democratic leadership in participatory organizational change', *Journal of Organizational Change Management* 25 (2012), no. 1, pp. 7–23.

Rancière, Jacques, *Disagreement: Politics and Philosophy* (Minneapolis and London: University of Minnesota Press, 1999).

Renn, Ortwin, Thomas Webler, and Peter Wiedemann (eds), *Fairness and Competence in Citizen Participation: Evaluating Models for Environmental Discourse* (Dordrecht: Kluwer Publishers, 1995).

Rice, Suzanne, 'Moral perception, situatedness and learning to listen', *Learning Inquiry* 1 (2007), pp. 107–13.

Rice, Suzanne, 'Toward an Aristotelian conception of good listening', *Educational Theory* 61 (2011), no. 2, pp. 141–53.

Rice, Suzanne and Nicholas Burbules, 'Listening: a virtue account', *Teachers College Record* 112 (2010), no. 11, pp. 2728–42.

Rosanvallon, Pierre, *Counter-Democracy: Politics in an Age of Distrust* (Cambridge: Cambridge University Press, 2008).

Rosencrantz, Lawrence, *America Adrift: Restoring the Promise of our Democracy* (ebook ISBN 978-1-61916-174-0, 2011).

Rousseau, Jean-Jacques, *The Social Contract* (Harmondsworth: Penguin, 1968).

Rowe, Gene, Tom Horlick-Jones, John Walls, and Nick Pidgeon, 'Difficulties in evaluating public engagement initiatives: reflections on an evaluation of the UK GMNation? public debate about transgenic crops', *Public Understanding of Science* 14 (2005), no. 4, pp. 331–52.

Roy, Arundhati, *Listening to Grasshoppers: Field Notes on Democracy* (London: Penguin, 2009).

Rushkoff, Douglas, 'Permanent revolution: occupying democracy', *The Sociological Quarterly* 54 (2013), pp. 164–73.

Saikia, Yasmin, 'Insaniyat for peace: survivors' narrative of the 1971 war of Bangladesh', *Journal of Genocide Research* 13 (2011), no. 4, pp. 475–501.

Saward, Michael, *The Representative Claim* (Oxford: Oxford University Press, 2010).

Schlosberg, David, *Defining Environmental Justice: Theories, Movements and Nature* (Oxford: Oxford University Press, 2007).

Schultz, Katharine, *Listening: A Framework for Teaching across Difference* (New York and London: Columbia University Press, 2003).

Schultz, Katherine, 'After the blackbird whistles: listening to silence in classrooms', *Teachers College Record* 112 (2010), no. 11, pp. 2833–49.

Sennett, Richard, *Together: The Rituals, Pleasures, and Politics of Cooperation* (Yale: Yale University Press, 2012).

Shipley, Sheila, 'Listening: a concept analysis', *Nursing Forum: An Independent Voice for Nursing* 45 (2010), no. 2, pp. 125–34.

Sifianou, Maria, 'Disagreements, face and politeness', *Journal of Pragmatics* 44 (2012), no. 12, pp. 1554–64.

Siisiäinen, Lauri, *Foucault and the Politics of Hearing* (London and New York: Routledge, 2013).

Sim, Stuart, *Manifesto for Silence* (Edinburgh: Edinburgh University Press, 2007).

Sitrin, Marina, 'Horizontalidad and territory in the Occupy movements', *Tikkun*, 8 March 2012, available at <http://www.tikkun.org/nextgen/horizontalidad-and-territory-in-the-occupy-movements> (accessed 22 January 2013).

Smith, Graham, *Deliberative Democracy and the Environment* (London and New York: Routledge, 2003).

Spivak, Gayatri Chakravorty, 'Can the subaltern speak?', in Gary Nelson and Lawrence Grossberg (eds), *Marxism and the Interpretation of Culture* (Urbana, IL: Illinois University Press, 1988).

Squires, Mike, 'Final diagnosis of Lansley's health plans', *The Guardian*, 16 June 2011, p. 37.

Stickley, Theodore and Dawn Freshwater, 'The art of listening in the therapeutic relationship', *Mental Health Practice* 9 (2006), no. 5, pp. 12–18.

Stone, Christopher, 'Should trees have standing? Towards legal rights for natural objects', *Southern California Law Review* 45 (1972), pp. 450–501.

Stringfellow, William, 'Protestantism's rejection of the Bible', in Bill Wylie Kellermann (ed.), *A Keeper of the Word: Selected Writings of William Stringfellow* (Michigan: Wm. B. Eerdmans Publishing Co., 1994).

Sudilich, Maria Laura, 'Can the Internet reinvent democracy?' *Irish Political Studies* 26 (2011), no. 4, pp. 563–77.

Tan, Qian Hui, 'Smell in the city: smoking and olfactory politics', *Urban Studies* 50 (2013), no. 1, pp. 55–71.

Thill, Cate, 'Courageous listening, responsibility for the other and the Northern Territory Intervention', *Continuum: Journal of Media and Cultural Studies* 23 (2009), no. 4, pp. 537–48.

Tilly, Charles, *Trust and Rule* (Cambridge: Cambridge University Press, 2005).

Titley, Gavan, 'Exclusion through openness? A tentative anatomy of the ritual of "migration debates"', *COLLeGIUM: Studies across Disciplines in the*

Humanities and Social Sciences 11 (2012), p. 50, available at <http://hdl. handle.net/10138/32361> (accessed 5 April 2012).

Todd, Sharon, *Learning from the Other: Levinas, Psychoanalysis, and Ethical Possibilities in Education* (New York: SUNY Press, 2003).

Uhr, John, 'Auditory democracy: separation of powers and the location of listening', in Benedetto Fontana, Cary J. Nederman, and Gary Remer (eds), *Talking Democracy: Historical Perspectives on Rhetoric and Democracy* (University Park, PA: Pennsylvania State University Press, 2004).

Vice, Susan, 'How do I live in this strange place?' *Journal of Social Philosophy* 41 (2010), no. 3, pp. 323–42.

Waks, Leonard, 'Listening and questioning: the apophatic/cataphatic distinction revisited', *Learning Inquiry* 1 (2007), no. 2, pp. 153–61.

Waks, Leonard, 'Two types of interpersonal listening', *Teachers College Record* 112 (2010), no. 11, pp. 2743–62.

Waks, Leonard, 'John Dewey on listening and friendship in school and society', *Educational Theory* 61 (2011), no. 2, pp. 191–205.

Wearing, Gillian, 'I've always been a bit of a listener', *The Observer (The New Review)*, 4 March 2012, p. 9.

Weston, Anthony, *Toward Better Problems: New Perspectives on Abortion, Animal Rights, the Environment and Justice* (Philadelphia: Temple University Press, 1992).

Whitehead, Kevin and Brett Bowman, 'The professional consequences of political silence', *Journal of Social Philosophy* 43 (2012), no. 4, pp. 426–35.

Wilde, Oscar, 'The remarkable rocket', in *The Happy Prince and Other Tales* (1888), available at <http://www.online-literature.com/poe/179/> (accessed 17 March 2013).

Wintour, Patrick and Polly Curtis, 'Gordon Brown "penitent" after bigot gaffe torpedoes election campaign', *The Guardian*, 28 April 2010, available at <http://www.guardian.co.uk/politics/2010/apr/28/gordon-br own-penitent-bigot-gaffe-campaign> (accessed 25 June 2012).

Wolvin, Andrew and Carolyn Gwynn Oakley, *Listening* (5th edn, Madison, WI: Brown & Benchmark Publishers, 1996).

Wortham, Stanton, 'Listening for identity beyond the speech event', *Teachers College Record* 112 (2010), no. 11, pp. 2850–73.

Young, Iris Marion, 'Polity and group difference: a critique of the idea of universal citizenship', *Ethics* 99 (1989), no. 2, pp. 250–74.

Young, Iris Marion, 'Communication and the other: beyond deliberative democracy', in Seyla Benhabib (ed.), *Democracy and Difference: Contesting the Boundaries of the Political* (Princeton: Princeton University Press, 1996).

Young, Iris Marion, *Inclusion and Democracy* (Oxford: Oxford University Press, 2000).

Zaki, Jamil, 'The curious perils of seeing the other side', *Scientific American Mind* 23 (July/August 2012), no. 3, pp. 20–1.

Zion, Deborah, Linda Briskman, and Bebe Loff, 'Psychiatric ethics and a politics of compassion: the case of detained asylum seekers in Australia', *Journal of Bioethical Enquiry* 9 (2012), no. 1, pp. 65–75.

Zúñiga, Ximena, Jane Mildred, Rani Varghese, Keri DeJong, and Molly Keehn, 'Engaged listening in race/ethnicity and gender intergroup dialogue courses', *Equity and Excellence in Education* 45 (2012), no. 1, pp. 80–99.

Index